A FISTFUL OF RUBBERS

Book Two of The Sid Tillsley Chronicles
by
M. J. Jackman

ISBN: 978-0-9905655-4-3
Paperback Version – 2nd edition

Published by LL-Publications 2009, 2014
www.ll-publications.com

Edited by Zetta Brown
Proofreading by Janet S.
Book layout and typesetting by jimandzetta.com
Cover art and design ©2014 by Patrick JP Currier,
(www.patrickjpcdesign.com)

Printed in the UK and USA

D1351244

Other Books by M. J. Jackman

The Sid Tillsley Chronicles
The Great Right Hope
A Fistful of Rubbers
Acracknophobia

All are available from Amazon, BN.com,
and other online retailers!

Great praise for

The Great Right Hope
Book One of The Sid Tillsley Chronicles

"*The Great Right Hope* is one of the best vampire stories I have read since *Buffy the Vampire Slayer*. *The Great Right Hope* was keenly devised with wittiness and excitement in a way that the reader can appreciatively observe the pleasure that Jackman has displayed while creating his awe-inspiring world."

—Amy Ramsey
Ramsey's Reviews

"I never thought I could say I would be a fan of a character who is such a train wreck, but Sid is hilarious, entertaining and, strangely enough, charming. Maybe charming is too strong a word..."

—Bitten by Books
www.bittenbybooks.com

"Sid's alcohol and tobacco consumption should have killed him along with his frustration at gays, women and humour, yet his OTT persona seems endearing and believable because we've met parts of him in our own lives...Why should such a misogynistic, homophobic moron be lovable too? That's writerly skill for you. It is certainly the most unusual vampire book I've read and the most hilarious. Read it at your peril."

—Geoff Nelder
www.compulsivereader.com

A Few More Reviews for

A FISTFUL OF RUBBERS

Book Two of The Sid Tillsley Chronicles

"When blood thirsty vampires are a threat and are not your main concern, you know you have problems...Intriguing and offbeat, *A Fistful of Rubbers* is a strong recommendation."

—*John Taylor*
Taylor's Bookshelf/Midwest Book Review

"The action of Sid's right fist, supported by his Middlesbrough pals, and fuelled by Bolton Bitter beer, drives the story on its drunken, bruising and hilarious journey."

—*Geoff Nelder*
www.compulsivereader.com

"What I really liked about *A Fistful of Rubbers* is the interaction between Sid and the boys and the well-crafted dialogue. I really have not read anything quite like it. It is so refreshing to read a quirky and original vampire story that does not regurgitate the same old plotlines and characters that are so common in this genre. What we get instead is a fresh perspective and characters who are seared into your brain, whether you want them there or not."

—*Bitten by Books*
www.bittenbybooks.com

And finally, it ends with

ACRACKNOPHOBIA

"It's a mystery, a wonderment, how Jackman kept track of the twists and body count. Not even the most teeth-sharpened vampire aficionado will be able to guess how this one ends. I commend this book to all readers of both humour and vampire genres. Enjoy."

—Geoff Nelder
Cafe Doom

Acknowledgements

Thanks to everyone who enjoyed *The Great Right Hope* enough to purchase the sequel (sickos!), and thanks to those who've simply bought it out of pity, blood ties, or voodoo.

Thanks to my publisher Jim Brown who gave Sid Tillsley a chance of life in the literary world. Thank you to his better half Zetta Brown for editing The Sid Tillsley Chronicles series and kicking my arse on regular occasions because I can't use commas, Also thanks to Ian Holman for some help with *The Great Right Hope* right at the start.

To my mum, whom I really hope doesn't read this, and to my dad, who doesn't read and would prefer me to paint my garage door than mess around with such nonsense, or as he'd put it, "bollocks."

A big hello to all members of The League of Extraordinary Gentlemen whose formation was inspiration for one of the later scenes of this book.

Finally, thank you to Peelo, the love of my life, who occasionally makes me cups of tea.

This book is dedicated to Jason Knott's shitty little beard.

Previously, on
the Sid Tillsley Chronicles...

THE WORLD HAS CHANGED. For nearly three hundred years, the Agreement allowing vampires and humans to live together has set the foundations of a symbiotic relationship. Six months ago, this relationship was pushed to the limit when the Firmamentum brought chaos. The Firmamentum: the birth of a human and a vampire unlike their own kind. Two monsters born to fight each other, unstoppable by any other living soul, or so it was once thought...until Sid Tillsley came along.

Sid accidentally killed Sparle's human nemesis—the Bellator—by running him over in a Montego Estate and then killed the vampire beast Sparle with a big right hook. Suddenly, the vampires had a hunter to fear.

The Vampire-Human Coalition established to uphold the Agreement plunged into disarray after the death of Michael Vitrago, the vampire dictator who kept order between the species with an iron fist. His ego was his bane, and Sparle ripped him to shreds in hand-to-hand combat. With Vitrago gone, so was the might of the Agreement. The first act without the warlord was to disband the Lamian Consilium, the vampire council, and mankind's sister group, the Hominum Order, to create a single Coalition.

Solidarity was key to the survival of the Agreement, and the Coalition sought to bind the vampire species as well as they could, which is why Ricard, wisest of the vampire race, was sentenced to death for harbouring his son Sparle and unwittingly unleashing him upon the world. The vampire nation called for Ricard's death, and the Coalition pandered to its will.

GREAT BRITAIN has always been a stronghold of the lamian nation, and the most powerful vampires reside on its shores. However, the green and pleasant lands are no longer protected by a dragon, and with Vitrago gone, the country is vulnerable to vampires who care not for the Agreement or mankind's rights.

The Coalition's greatest threat is Gunnar Ivansey, who grows stronger by the day, festering in a pit of his own hatred. He has declared war on the Agreement and has a personal vendetta against Sid Tillsley. The Agreement took away Gunnar's freedom, choking him with the Coalition's human-pampering ways—but he's angrier with Sid Tillsley for punching his knob off.

And last, but by no means least, there's Sid: ex-benefit-fraudster, dogger, homophobe, alcoholic, and now hunter of the undead. Reece Chambers, a masterful and prolific vampire hunter, has nestled Sid firmly under his wing. Years earlier, Gunnar had slaughtered Reece's father in front of him, but with Sid by his side, Reece finally has a chance of vengeance. Both he and Sid have death warrants on their heads, but Sid doesn't care. He gets a pack of cigarettes every time he knocks a vampire out.

Sid lives for the best Bolton Bitter in the land, and that magical nectar is served in The Miner's Arms. However, not all is rosy in the life of the vampire hunter. Those vampire-council bastards launched an attack of pure evil and used their powers to shut down The Miner's Arms! Sid is distraught. He can't find a pint better than The Miner's in all of Middlesbrough, and now, he only cares about one thing—getting his pub back.

...Oh, and he desperately needs a shag too.

1

DUST SWIRLED THROUGH THE COLD WINTER NIGHT making ever changing, hypnotic patterns in the yellow light of the streetlamps above. Yet, the intricacies of the shapes were nothing compared to the complexity of the dust's former state.

Wolfgang Fortzgard had walked the earth for a millennium. He'd influenced many artists during the Renaissance. He'd ensured the apparent suicide of Adolf Hitler and helped bring down the Berlin Wall. On the other hand, he'd taken thousands of lives and caused misery to all that fell to his fang. This, however, was not the reason for his quick but, nonetheless, violent death.

Twenty Embassy Number Ones were the reason for Wolfgang Fortzgard's death, the number of premium-brand cigarettes that Reece Chambers agreed to give Sid Tillsley for every vampire killed on this particular hunt in Leeds.

Sid lit up a John Players Special, a brand he'd earned for a previous excursion, and stained his gnashers a darker shade of yellow.

"Sid, have you made contact?" Reece buzzed through the radio.

Sid started zipping and unzipping the fly of his skin-tight jeans in an attempt to access the radio microphone, which was, in fact, hidden in the zip of his leather jacket. He still hadn't come to grips with the advanced technological systems Reece had bestowed upon him. As was often the case, Sid hadn't listened to Reece's detailed instructions at all.

A scream filled the night air as a local partygoer left a nightclub to see a middle-aged, obese skinhead flashing his penis at her.

"Sorry, love!" yelled the accidental flasher. "But if you fancy it, I'll meet you in the Kebabateria in half an hour!" He was never a man to turn down an opportunity. She didn't hear him. She was too busy running.

"Sid, have you made contact?" Reece buzzed through once more. "It's your top button on your jacket you..." he tailed off with abuse.

Sid found the microphone. "Reet. Got it. Aye, I twatted one of the bastards. You want me to go in?"

"Do you think you can handle it?"

"As long as you get the beers in for last orders, I can."

"Kick ass."

Sid shook his head. Reece was grating on Sid's nerves more and more, acting like a high-ranking American general. Reece had been panicking about this night for weeks, their biggest "mission" so far. Sid knocked three times on the door of the secret nightclub, and the security shutter on the door slid open.

"Who are you? Where's Wolfgang?" said a deep, gruff voice, which could only come from a fellow brick shithouse.

"Who? Woolbag? Ya must mean the tall fella," said Sid, looking back at the pile of ash on the pavement, dispersing in the wind. Sid returned his attention towards getting inside the club. "Erm...He said...erm...you were a wanker and told me to tell you that you're a twat!"

Sid had forgotten to turn off his microphone, and Reece heard everything. Sid had ignored all the lines Reece had given him, ruining weeks of planning! Reece punched the side of the van in which he was sitting. He'd gone through considerable toil to obtain the information about the shipment of human sacrifices.

But Reece, however, was a little naïve about the situation. He'd forgotten they were in the North of England, Leeds, where it was easier to start a fight than it was in Harlem dressed as a Black and White Minstrel.

"Who you calling a twat, you twat!" replied the man behind the door. Sid had finally met his intellectual match.

The door opened and out came a bearded and tattooed giant who dwarfed Sid in both width and height, but all the muscles in the world can't protect the chin. Sid flashed the right, sending the giant's jaw in the same direction. The man-mountain hit the deck like all the rest.

Sid opened his trousers a couple of times and announced, "I'm in. He was a normal fella. He didn't explode or 'owt. Hang on, better make sure." A run-up followed by a powerful kick to the unconscious man's crotch confirmed his suspicions. "Aye, a normal fella."

Reece winced. Sid had been kicking far too many people in the groin of late. He could tell if they were a vampire or not by the way they reacted to his left foot. If they woke up, they were a vampire who got their just deserts. If they were a man...

"Reet, I'm going in." Sid pushed open the door and was greeted with a wall of sound.

"BASS IN THE PLACE, LONDON!"

The music was deafening. Hundreds of partygoers danced manically to the hard beat of the music.

Sid looked around and was surprised at how swanky the place was, considering it looked derelict from the outside. These vampires were classy, even if most of them were a little bit too much like *them lot*. Sid lit up another tab en route to the dance floor and no one noticed him, too caught up in their hedonistic revelry. He stood admiring the dancers giving it their all. Sid had never been a good mover and was the first to admit it. It would take several pints to get him on the floor and that would only be at The Miner's on ladies' night, but now, the pub was shut...He tried to let the pain go.

These were *real* dancers, though, and too much for him to cope with even with a few beers inside him. Reece didn't like him drinking when he was on a job, and he'd only had six or seven before tonight. Nope, he'd have to be well and truly plastered to show these girls his moves on the floor. Maybe if the lasses hung around after he'd smacked everyone, he'd have a few beers and show them his abstract, yet fun-filled interpretation of the Time Warp.

Sid unzipped his jacket as the sights were making him uncomfortably hot. He'd never seen so many women in a club, and there was more flesh on show than clothing. It was a ratio Sid approved of. How could any red-blooded man not become a little aroused by it all?

And that's when Sid got noticed.

Thinking that the zipper on his trousers was the microphone was a costly mistake. Little Sid popped through to say hello to the large group of vampires who instantly stopped dancing.

"Ah, fook!" said Sid, struggling to get Little Sid back into his tight jeans.

No one likes it when some twat gets his cock out on the dance floor, and vampires were no exception. However, when the most dangerous vampire hunter in history turns up with his cock in his hand...

Panic is the best way to describe what happened next. Not all in the crowd were vampires, and a lot of the girls were locals. They were mostly prostitutes, addicts, waifs, and strays who wouldn't be missed but had been encouraged to attend tonight's party with the promise of free drugs and alcohol. They looked around, bewildered. Half of the crowd fled for the exits while the other half prepared for a fight.

"It's Tillsley! Tillsley is here!"

"Let's finish him! We outnumber him!"

Many voices piped up, but Sid managed to put his old man away and was ready for battle before they could take advantage of his unfortunate predicament. Twenty vampires, male and female, circled their nemesis, closing in, ready to kill.

"Reet, you bastards are in for it." Sid took the fight to the vampires. Wading in, he windmilled haymakers with every step. He'd discovered that it was the best course of action when taking on a crowd. His research was mostly carried out when the 'boro were at home to Newcastle and Geordies spilled out to some of his local haunts.

Jab-cross-hook. Every punch he threw brought with it the satisfaction of a dead vampire and twenty premium-brand fags. Once more, dust filled the air as vampires fell to the right hand of Sid Tillsley, Vampire Hunter. Fear of the man was already legendary.

"Get out of here!" screamed one of the vampires, watching the human demolition derby in mid-flight. Many of the vampires, realising the futility of their efforts, turned and fled. But like all demolition derbies, sooner or later they ran out of petrol. Sid's assault slowed and the dust dissipated. As it cleared, he stood wheezing with his hands on his knees.

The remaining vampires regrouped. There were about ten left. Tears streaked some cheeks, while some howled in anguish at the loss of their brethren. Seeing their opportunity, they attacked as one. Sid took a deep breath as the mob approached. He was too tired to throw any punches, so he played rope-a-dope.

A barrage of kicks and punches rained down upon him. It wasn't the best of ideas, to take a few punches from ten immortals in order to get your breath back, but then, Sid wasn't like the other boys.

"Use the weapon, Sid!" Reece screamed through the radio into Sid's ear. They'd gone through this a hundred times since Sid's last rope-a-dope. Sid insisted he could take it, but it was a ridiculous strategy. Therefore, Reece had developed a UV lamp capable of burning vampires while allowing Sid to fend them off and catch his breath before smacking them again.

Sid ignored the veteran vampire hunter, whom he considered a "Southern fanny" who didn't know how to brawl properly. The vampires continued their onslaught, but it was to no avail; Sid assumed they were Southern fannies too. The vampires needed something more deadly. The glint of a blade told Sid it was time to use the secret weapon. He unleashed the UV torch from his coat.

Sid Tillsley was the most powerful and successful vampire hunter in the history of the world.

Sid Tillsley was armed with vampire-killing weaponry.

Sid Tillsley was, unfortunately, a buffoon.

Sid didn't understand the purpose of the lamp since he hadn't listened when Reece had explained it to him, so he used it as a bludgeon, clubbing the vampires in the head with the UV lamp in his left hand and the power of seven pints of ale in his right. Sid dealt out justice to the vampire race, his right hand finishing off the ones groggy from the pummelling they'd taken from twenty pounds of stainless steel.

Soon, there was nothing left but ash and a mashed-up lamp. After a minute, Sid regained enough breath to light up another cig.

"Sid, where are you?" Reece called desperately through the intercom. "I'm coming in!"

"E-e-easy, m-m-mon," Sid managed between breaths and puffs. "I'm reet. All the ones that wanted a scrap are dead. Loads legged it with the prossies. They could've fookin' left me one. I'm gonna get meself a beer."

Reece charged in, admired Sid's handiwork, and smiled. The nightclub looked like a used barbeque pit. "How many did you kill?"

"I dunno, more than last time, like," he said, pouring himself a beer from behind the bar. "I needed a bigger half-time rest. Took some good'n's from some of the bigger bastards." He rubbed his ribs.

"Are you OK? Do you want me to have a look?" said Reece, reaching over to remove Sid's jacket.

"Get away, lad." Sid shooed. "I don't want any fussin' over. I only took a few. Nothing that a few nights off with a few ales won't fix." He lit up another cigarette in order to start the healing process.

"We don't have much time. I must gather everything I can." Reece ran through the nightclub, looking for an office, anywhere a computer or papers could be found to give him more information on the vampires' movements. "Help me, Sid."

"Fook off! I've done me bit. I'm gonna enjoy this beer until you're done." Sid supped the beer between some tabs. It was pissy lager, but it was free pissy lager. He watched Reece rushing around like a mad man in his black camouflage gear with his grey ponytail bouncing around. Sid shook his head. "You look like a shit ninja."

Reece ignored him and gathered into a briefcase anything that might be of use. He looked at his watch. "We have to go! Come on, I'll buy you a beer."

Sid followed him, picking up as many bottles of spirits as he could carry.

Reece shook his head wearily. The important thing was getting Sid away from the booze. He sprinted ahead of Sid who ambled without officially breaking into a run. It was only the offer of free beer that made him hurry at all. Reece knew the drill. He ran to his car and then came back to get Sid, who got in the passenger side. They raced away through the night, back to the relative safety of Middlesbrough.

2

BRIAN GARFORTH'S "SWORDY-SENSE" WAS SPOT ON AGAIN, and he couldn't believe his luck. This lass was as classy as they come. She had the lot: great tits and a great arse.

Yeah, the lot.

She also had her full quota of limbs and didn't have any scars or noticable tics. Brian Garforth was about to bag himself a red-hot stunner.

He never expected to see a lass like this in the snooker hall where he was giving Peter Rathbone a few frames. Rathbone, the lying arsehole, reckoned he'd once made a break of seventy-two. Now, Brian was a fair player, ten times better than Rathbone, but his highest break was only forty-nine. Not bad, considering snooker was bloody hard, possibly the hardest of all sports. And it was a sport. Brian had put the nut on the last idiot who had dared call it a "game." Nothing as hard and psychologically destructive could be referred to as a "game." Them professionals thought they were something special with their mineral waters, their deep screw, and intentional positioning.

Bastards.

Even though Brian had drunk enough to take him past the "confidence" phase and into the "pissed" phase, he still managed to rack up a forty-three break and had a length of the table black in front of him. It would've been a special moment by itself, having the opportunity to reach this most illustrious sporting achievement, but when the stunner from his dreams walked into Merlin's Snooker Hall, the night got better, much better.

She was obviously a snooker slag, the sort that got fired up by a man with straighter-than-straight cueing. He'd banged everything in the centre of the pockets, and that was a sure way to get the ladies drooling. On top of that, he was wearing his new suit, which Sid and that wanker Rich had bought him for helping Sid give that big, angry vampire bastard a pasting a few months back.

His new red wool suit was pretty special. It was like the last one except the crotch wasn't withered, and it wasn't wearing thin at the knees due to all the late-night action. He was looking dapper and sinking pot after pot. Still, this lass wasn't the normal standard of clientele for a snooker hall. Normally, it was just scag heads, prostitutes, and low-end snooker slags content with watching swordsmen smash in long blacks. This lass was high end. Only a half century would drop her drawers.

He pretended not to notice as she walked nearer the table, admiring how all the colours were on the spots, even though many, many reds were lying deep in their cushiony graves. She couldn't keep her eyes off him, and Brian knew she wanted it. She returned to the bar and looked over, watching him chalk his cue and line up the long bomber that tested him. Maybe she was here for the snooker, maybe she wasn't...either way, she was gonna get nailed.

TH-CLUNK!

The black slammed into the back of the pocket with the white ball ricocheting off five cushions before coming to rest in perfect position on a loose red.

"Fifty," spat Rathbone.

Brian held the cue between his legs and stroked the weapon of the master, the giant cock of a snooker god.

"Howay, petal," he said, dropping the blonde beauty a seductive wink. "I just reached me half century. Get us an ale in and I'll wrap this frame up."

Brian approved of her longing gaze, urging him to leave the snooker table and take her aggressively over the one-armed-bandit. That wasn't going to happen. He'd left himself perfect on the loose red. As a bona fide snooker slag, she'd know with this sort of positional play, he meant business. He slammed the red home with an aggressive thrust of the right hip. It was his patented power thrust that enabled him to generate tremendous cue speed and also hump like a hummingbird on ecstasy.

By the time she returned, Brian had racked up an impressive sixty-two and left himself a red that had been carelessly left at balk. She brought with her the most expensive champagne the club had to offer—well, the label called it champagne, the contents, on the other hand...

Brian was the Smithson Estate's most educated scholar and the only male of the Northern subspecies to ever indulge in a glass of vino, but that was saved for private times when he was getting down and dirty...extremely dirty. In a snooker hall like this, a man could get beaten to death if he was seen drinking tart-fuel.

"Do ya think I'm some kinda woofter or summat?" he cried. "Get me a pint of ale, woman!" he reprimanded, turning his back on her.

The red at balk and the yellow for position left Brian with another red-black opportunity. This would take him to seventy-three, beating Rathbone's fictitious highest break. The red went in dead centre, the black was on the spot, and he had a great angle.

He lined himself up, but out of the corner of his eye, he noticed the snooker slag was buying him lager, the Southerner's drink.

"Bitter! For the love of god, woman, bitter!" He may be risking a shag, but he wasn't drinking any of that fizzy shite.

He lined up the pot again, and, using his newly-found anger, drove the black with extra venom, jawing it. "FOOK!" he screamed.

"Sixty-six," called out a smug Rathbone.

Brian threw his cue down, unable to hide his annoyance.

"Hard luck, Brian. You nearly reached my best break," gloated Rathbone. He spoke louder than normal so the stunner could hear.

"Fook off, ya horrible little twat!" said Brian on impulse.

Rathbone mumbled something inaudible and went off to the fruit machine to punt some more of his hard-earned benefit money.

The beauty gave Brian his pint of ale before resting against the table. Her beautiful, blonde hair spilled down over her low-cut top exposing the ample cleavage of two heavenly twins. Her legs didn't seem to end as they meandered their way to a non-existing skirt. Brian decided to forgive her for her earlier faux pas.

"Eh'up, lass," said Brian. "Shall we take a seat?"

She nodded before making her way to Merlin's shitheap of a bar. Brian watched her hips as she walked, and he felt a stirring. No blue pill would be required on this adventure. They both propped themselves on barstools. She was about six inches taller than him, but he didn't care. He'd nailed bigger lasses before, including one who was technically a giant.

"Did you like me snooker? You won't find much straighter cueing in all of the 'boro," he boasted.

"It was impressive. You use your hips very well."

The compliment had an Eastern-European tinge to it—Brian wasn't renknowned as a scholar for nothing. She was too gorgeous for a snooker slag. Putting two and two together, Brian came to the conclusion that she must be either a hooker or one of them lasses trying to marry to get into the country. Either way, she was gonna get a damn good shaggin'.

"You into your snooker then, pet?"

"Not really, no. However, I can appreciate any man who is skilled in sport. They say a man's sporting prowess is linked to his ability to make love to a woman...I have high hopes for you."

Brian offered his hand. "Brian, Brian Garforth, and you're right. By the way, I'm also shit-hot at badminton."

The beauty called over to the barman to refill Brian's glass. Hookers never bought you drinks, and he doubted whether Russian brides would either, as they were poor as 'owt until they took half your house. Who the hell was she then? He looked down her top again. He decided he didn't care who she was.

"You are a beautiful man, Brian Garforth," she said.

"I've been told that more times than you can possibly imagine, petal. I think it's time that you got to see a little bit more of this beautiful body back at your place...after I get back from the pissers."

He jumped off the barstool and went to shake the snake.

HELENA ICHVAMOVICH WATCHED THE HIDEOUS CREATURE walk away to the toilets, the thought of which made her nauseous. She was one of the most beautiful vampires of her generation. Since she'd come of age, she'd seduced some of the most powerful politicians and leaders of the world, human and vampire alike. Even the great Michael Vitrago had fallen for her charms.

But the world had changed. With the death of Sparle and the emergence of Sid Tillsley, everything had been turned on its head. Now, she'd been sent here to sleep with Brian Garforth.

She'd emptied her stomach for days when she first received the details of her assignment. She tried to contact him a week ago, but the sight of him in the flesh had caused her to weep. He was disgusting. Vile. From ten feet away, she could smell the venereal diseases festering in and around his genitals and was amazed they hadn't killed him. How could the Coalition ask her to allow that thing near her...*in* her?

Helena swallowed down some vomit. She had to do this. It was for the good of the vampire race. She needed to get to Tillsley, and that wasn't possible with Reece Chambers hanging around. Brian Garforth was her way in.

He returned from the toilets. Everything about him was horrible: his pitted, pale skin, the wispy thin moustache, the goatee beard. She couldn't imagine kissing those cracked lips or running her fingers through his greasy, gelled-back hair. Dying it black did not make him look younger.

"Back to your place, then?" he asked. A visible urine stain spread across his red woollen suit. "Hang about. I'll just tell Rathbone."

The little man playing the fruit machine was somehow more horrible than Garforth. He was so greasy, there was more grease than man, and his dirty clothes looked like they were pulled from a deep fat fryer. His hair stuck to his head and was the definition of "lank." If she had to sleep with him too...

"Rathbone," Brian yelled, "I'm off shaggin'!"

God help me, Helena thought.

"FOOK ME! THIS IS SWANKY, DARLIN'," said Brian, looking around the lavish hotel suite. "What did you say you did again?"

"I'm a lawyer working out of London, Brian," said the snooker slag. "I'm here on business for a couple of weeks. I have meetings with clients all day, every day, but will be free most nights."

Brian, who wasn't really into conversing with women, investigated the contents of the mini-bar. "Aye, yep, that's great, petal. You like cats, you say? Fantastic."

"I hope to see you a lot more over the next two weeks," she said. "I hope we can get to know each other intimately."

He knew there were sexual undertones, but he knew what she really meant. Ladies from all across the 'boro knew what Brian Garforth was all about. They all knew that a long-term prospect with one of the Northeast's finest swordsmen was as unlikely as them not visiting the clap clinic after the steamy encounter. "Just don't get in the way of me drinking time with the lads. If you start getting all clingy, I ain't having it."

Brian read the flabbergasted look on her face and rolled his eyes. "That's the problem with you pretty sort; you're all so far up your own arses, you can't understand that sometimes a bloke wants to get pissed up with his mates."

HELENA COULDN'T BELIEVE HER EARS. This piece of excrement, this disgusting little man wouldn't give up drinking with his friends in scummy, rundown pubs to spend time with the most beautiful female in the world?

Helena prayed to the Creator that she would be allowed to kill this creature after this terrible event in vampire history was brushed under the carpet. He opened up a beer and swigged at it nonchalantly, not questioning why she had taken an interest in him. Why would someone like her even contemplate *spitting* on something like him? He hadn't even asked her name.

They'd walked past numerous people in the streets on the way back to the hotel. Everyone knew this horrid, little man and all had shouted lewd comments about what he was going to get up to. Each comment had been a hammer to her skull, a permanent stain on her soul. It was the most degrading experience, but she had a job to do. It was her duty.

"That's not a problem with me," she said. "I'm busy too. Your friends though, will I be able to meet them?"

"Less talk, gorgeous, less talk." He drunkenly stumbled over to where she stood, frozen with fury. He grabbed her by the shoulders and looked deep into her eyes. "Tonight was made for something beautiful." Helena turned away. His breath burnt her nostrils. "Something beautiful between two, oh-so-beautiful people."

God help me.

BRIAN FELT HER PULL BACK. *Shy one here, Brian,* he thought. *Will have to take it easy at first before getting freaky.* He stayed close to her as she slowly backed away from him. The wall prevented her escape.

Slowly, he ran his hands down her shoulders and round her back to take hold of her tiny top. He pulled it down slowly to reveal the most magnificently pert breasts he'd ever seen, both in real life and in magazines. They weren't just pert, they were massive as well.

"Howay the lads!"

He yelled the battle cry before driving his head as deep into the cleavage as he could manage and proceeded to wiggle his head around, blowing raspberries while bloody well enjoying himself.

TRAPPED AGAINST THE WALL, Helena considered two options: kill him or fulfil her mission. Only her love for her people allowed him to pull down her top without her ripping his throat out.

Without warning, he rammed his greasy little head in between her breasts. She looked down in horror at his little bald spot and the sickness returned. Oil slicked on her skin as he squirmed manically from side to side, but worst of all...he wouldn't stop.

God help me.

BRIAN STOOD UP, confident that this woman would now be suitably primed. But first, it was his turn to enjoy a little personal pleasure.

He ripped down his trousers and pants in one mighty flourish, rose to his full height, and placed his hands on his hips. There was no mistaking what he wanted. As he suspected, no little blue pill was required. He looked down at his old fella which had reached an angle of almost ninety degrees, a feat not accomplished in the last couple of years, and quickly wiped a little yellow splodge off the end, hoping that she didn't notice. The snooker slag had a vacant look on her face. Obviously an inexperienced lass. She was going to learn quickly tonight. He pushed down on her shoulders, and, without any force at all, she dropped to her knees.

"Champion."

HELENA LOOKED THE DEVIL IN THE EYE and fought the gag reflex with all her might. She couldn't look at his penis. It was horrible. She dropped her gaze and was forced again to fight the gag reflex when she caught a glimpse of his stained Y-fronts. She truly was a heroine of the vampire race.

In her mind she saw the mountains of her homeland in the distance as she ran like lightning through the streams of the valley. The musical notes of the water brought joy to her heart as did the lone eagle that soared above, calling to a future mate. She ran with all her speed. She hadn't seen her beloved in over a decade.

BRIAN WAS COCK-ON-LEGS, THE PENIS WHO WALKS. He was Middlesbrough's Finest Swordsman. He put his hands behind his head and smiled as he admired the act being carried out on his person, even if the lass was a bit shite. The lasses of the 'boro were normally all over his old fella like a dog was all over a week-old donner kebab. This lass couldn't melt a Cornetto.

HELENA ROSE TO HER FEET AND WISHED FOR DEATH. Numbly, she let Brian lead her to the bed and lay her down. She was aware things were being done to her, but in this state of detachment from her body, time stood still. This was truly Hell. However, she remained in another place in her head. It was the only way she could get through this night and through the rest of eternity.

BRIAN REMOVED HIS HAND from an intimate place of his stationary lover and was enraged at what he found. Bone dry!

"Fook me, lass, aren't ya ready yet? Looks like Plan B is in order."

He rubbed his hands over his greasy hair before rubbing it across his member. A few applications later, and he was greasier than a used-car salesman.

Foreplay complete.

"Howay the lads!"

HELENA SWAM THROUGH THE WARM CURRENTS of the ocean, and the water soothed her body. The distant call of a gull echoed softly against the towering cliffs next to her. It was so tranquil, floating on the Indian Ocean with her beloved Gawain. It wasn't often she'd experienced such utter peace...

And then her world was flipped upside down.

"REET, LASS, I'M ALMOST DONE, LIKE," said Brian, who had built up a mighty sweat in a remarkably short amount of time. "Just gonna turn you around for me final flurry, if ya don't mind?"

Brian turned her over and onto all fours.

THE BIRDS SANG AND THE WIND BLEW through the trees of the coastline. Helena and Gawain circumnavigated the cliffs until they reached glorious, golden sands, which burnt their feet as they emerged from the waves. Suddenly, pain engulfed the world. Fire ripped across the shore and devoured everything with the heat of the sun.

"OOOOOOHHHHHHHHHH...YA BASTARDS!" Brian's knees trembled until he almost fell to the floor.

"Eh? What the fook?"

Opening his eyes, he saw something completely unexpected: a big pile of ash on the bed with a little pile balancing precariously on the end of his throbbing, yet waning, member.

"Shit."

PETER RATHBONE STAGGERED DOWN THE ROAD back to his scummy abode. It was a good night, all in all. Garforth had cued well but hadn't managed to beat his seventy-two break. He'd pulled an absolute stunner, though, gorgeous she was. The dirty bastard would be running her through at this very moment. Rathbone was glad that the snooker slag knew Garforth hadn't beaten his biggest break. He loved outdoing Garforth. He loved outdoing everyone.

Rathbone had ended up drunk as a lord after coming up trumps on the bandit, nine quid up! Derek, the owner of the snooker hall, sold off his homebrew at eighty pence a pint, and it was probably the methanol in the brew that had taken away his vision after three or four pints—but he'd regained it after the seventh.

He walked past The Miner's Arms, which was boarded up. He missed it a lot more than he thought he would. Aye, it was expensive, but the beer could not be beat. Shame. Rathbone still had four quid left and could've murdered a couple of pints of Bolton Bitter. The motor oil in the snooker hall homebrew had made him thirsty.

He carried on home. He had a bit of work coming his way over the next couple of days. He was going to change the brake pads on Garforth's Capri and fit some heated seats into Sid's recently purchased Nissan Bluebird. Apparently, the cold leather wasn't doing Sid's piles any favours. Leather seats, though, were proper posh. Rich had been throwing his money at Sid like there was no tomorrow.

"Got a light, pal?"

Rathbone hadn't noticed the youth who now stood in front of him. Big lad, wearing one of them hoodies that all the 'boro locals were wearing these days. "Go get fook—"

The lad leapt, bundling Rathbone into an alley. He fell onto his back with the youth on top of him, pinning his arms to the ground.

"You little twat. You canna be from around here. Don't you know my mate is Sid Tillsley?" said Rathbone, name-dropping.

"Of course I do. Why do you think you're in this predicament?"

Shit. This weren't a kidda, this was one of them vampire bastards! He had those pointy teeth going on.

"Where is Tillsley hiding?" growled the vampire.

"The fat bastard couldn't hide if he tried."

"Then tell me, human! Don't make matters worse for yourself."

The vampire's head darted forwards. The headbutt was like a thunderclap in Rathbone's head. He came to, but struggled to talk as blood poured down his throat. "Ya...ya...wanker!"

Rathbone knew he was in trouble, but it was just past kicking-out time. There were lots of people about. If one of the lads turned up, they might be able to give this twat a pasting.

"You're lucky, human. You're not the reason I stalk the night. Your death will be quick."

Rathbone felt a sharp but brief pain in his neck. He wasn't tired a minute ago, but now, all he wanted to do was sleep. Darkness fell. Funny...he'd normally only fall asleep after a late-night wank to Babestation.

3

GUNNAR IVANSEY HATED THE FREAK THAT GLARED BACK at him in the mirror. His reflection was a perversion of what was once a god. He wanted to die, to end it all, but he wasn't strong enough for that. Fear of death kept him alive. He couldn't rid himself of the survival instinct still running strong through his bloodstream. Pride hung on, but only by the fingernails.

His bright blue eyes stared back with the same intensity they always had, even more so, but they were all he recognised. Before, his face and his head were clean shaven, but now, a thick, black beard covered his jawline, and straight black hair fell over his face. He no longer cared for his appearance. He looked at his naked body, sculpted out of rock, striated muscles clinging to his dense skeleton. And then, he looked between his legs to his two lonely testicles. They sat unaccompanied, with no penis to call their own.

Gunnar had suffered some strange side effects ever since Sid Tillsley punched his cock off. Gunnar's body had adapted so that he could excrete urine, but it hadn't adapted so he could lose excess semen.

A vampire produced sperm like a human, albeit at a slower rate. Through the months, the gradual build up had swelled his testicles until they'd become red and painful beyond the boundaries of vampire physiology. He hoped that somehow his body would adapt, but hope was all he had.

The testosterone build up affected his moods, and he found it difficult to control his rage. Once the flow started, it was unstoppable. Gunnar thrived on violence, but he wanted to wield it, not expel it subconsciously.

Sid Tillsley had taken away Gabriel, his kindred spirit. He'd taken away his dignity, his life—and then his pecker. Sid Tillsley was going to pay for everything he'd done, but first, there were other matters to attend to.

The Lamian Consilium had disbanded, leaving behind a travesty in its wake. All that remained was the Coalition where vampires dealt with humans as equals. Since Michael Vitrago's death, the Coalition had no real power. There was no heart or strength in any of the vampires who sat around that cursed table. They held the Agreement for their own pockets and played games with monkeys in suits.

Now, a member of the Coalition was pulling his strings.

Gunnar spat on the floor. This was his final task. The price for his work: the name of a man who offered the chance of peace.

"CAN YOU PASS ME A PIPETTE, PLEASE, HAAS?"

"Certainly, Smythe." The scientist left his bench to pass his colleague the pipette. There were only two scientists in the vast lab populated by cutting-edge equipment. The investors in this research had deep pockets. "How is the synthesis progressing?" Haas asked.

"Better than expected. I will have a sample on a multi-gram scale within the week. Purity looks good, while the toxicological effects are, obviously, of no concern," said Smythe with a smile.

"But of course. How long until we can manufacture on a tonne scale?"

"A month at the latest. If the next trial is successful, we've a lot to look forward to."

"Some will want our heads for this," warned Haas.

"That's something I'm not worried about. Take a look in the microscope."

Haas looked in the microscope and quickly retracted his glance. "My god, Smythe. It has slowed the process a hundred-fold. How have you managed it so quickly?"

"I'm not just here for my good—" Smythe was interrupted by the head-splitting scream of a siren. "That's no fire alarm. Quickly, Haas, back up your data and gather your most valuable samples." Smythe began to collect his most important lab work.

"What is it?"

"An intruder."

Haas looked confused. "Security will deal with them, surely."

"What sort of intruder would warrant the alarm?"

"They'll never break through. We're too well protected. Who would dare attack us here?"

"Exactly." Smythe pressed a button on the intercom. "Security? Security? Is anyone there? Speak to me, damn it!" There was no reply. "Hurry, Haas. They must have breached the front gate."

GUNNAR ROARED. The incessant, ringing alarms made it impossible to think. "Turn it off!" he screamed.

There was only one security guard left alive. The front gates to the chemical plant were well guarded, but no one could've planned for this. All the soldiers who'd tried to hold the gate were dead, massacred, except for one. The remaining guard stood covered from head to toe in blood, unscathed, but in shock. However, Gunnar always found a way to grab someone's attention.

"Turn it off!" he shouted over the din.

The guard didn't react quickly enough. Gunnar lifted him from the ground and pressed his ear next to the siren. The guard screamed as his eardrum burst under the intense sound. Gunnar rammed the guard's head through the siren before giving the guard one more chance to turn the alarm off. This time, his orders were understood. The guard tapped in the code to shut down the alarm before collapsing.

Gunnar savoured the beautiful silence, but it didn't last long. He could hear vans approaching, which meant new friends to play with. He stamped down hard on the guard's stomach who instantly coughed up a large slug of blood.

Gunnar cocked an ear. "Playtime."

There was no warning. Bullets tore through the guardhouse and through Gunnar. He charged through the door at the mercenaries lined up outside. He relished every slug of metal that burnt through his body. A high-powered rifle took him clean off his feet. He hit the ground hard and laughed. His testosterone was raw power. He was unstoppable. He nipped up onto his feet and disappeared into the shadows of the chemical plant. The soldiers spread out, not willing to follow into the darkness where death waited.

"Hold your fire!" shouted the captain of the guard. "Some of the liquids in the pipes are flammable! The whole thing could go up!"

"Scared of the dark?" called Gunnar from the safety of the valves and pipes that meandered through the works. Safety wasn't what he was looking for.

"What is that thing?" screamed one of the soldiers.

"How did it get up after that?" asked another, as fearful as his colleague.

"Form ranks, soldiers. It doesn't matter what it is, just kill it," said the captain with a nerve of iron.

Gunnar smiled. He looked forward to breaking that will. He flanked them and stood theatrically in the moonlight away from the plant.

"There he is! Open fire!"

With arms outstretched, Gunnar welcomed every bullet that ravaged his flesh. Since losing his penis, all pain was a relief. It masked the eternal suffering from his throbbing gonads. The heat of the metal tearing his muscles in half and shattering his bones was pure ecstasy. Suddenly, he felt something different: intense agony followed by gratifying relief. His testicles had been blown clean off. All pain, all suffering...gone. Freedom at last. He collapsed.

"Cease fire!"

Gunnar lay prostrate on the floor. He closed his eyes and found peace. He could smell the gunpowder and the cooking of his own flesh, and he savoured every second. Every beautiful second.

Until the healing began.

Gunnar's eyes snapped open. "No..."

He'd always been a fast healer, but since his testosterone levels had skyrocketed, so had his ability to regenerate. Muscle knitted back together, bones reformed, bullets ejected from his body, and then...his testicles...How? Hate turned his blood to acid. He sat up.

"Open fire!"

The bullets didn't even slow him. No theatrics. No games. No torture. In a minute, the carnage was over and Gunnar's bloodlust finally waned. He saw nothing until he wiped blood and gore from his eyes. He couldn't even recall the slaughter.

He was covered from top to toe in his enemies' entrails. Enemies? They were just victims, prey. A pack of rabid wolves couldn't have made more mess.

HAAS DESPERATELY SCOOPED ARMFULS OF SAMPLES INTO a coolbox as the sirens screamed danger. "Do you think they'll deal with the intruder?" he shouted over the din.

Smythe, who was backing up data on the computer called back, "We are still getting out of here regardless." Suddenly, the sirens ceased. The resulting peace did not change Smythe's reasoning. "If someone's breaking in here, then it's going to be for this, isn't it? If a vampire knows of this, what will they do to us? I'm not taking a chance."

Realisation dawned on Dr. Haas and he quickened his pace.

The door into the lab emitted a bleep and a hulking guard followed. The doctors heaved a sigh of relief.

"Sirs, we need to leave, ASAP."

"What's going on out there?" asked Smythe.

"We think it's Gunnar Ivansey."

A huge explosion shook the room. Microscopes smashed onto the floor along with hundreds of samples.

"Haas, have you got everything you need?" asked Smythe.

"Almost."

"Then hurry the fuck up!" yelled the guard.

GUNNAR LAUGHED UNCONTROLLABLY as flames engulfed him. A foolish guard had succumbed to fear as Gunnar had approached, and his carelessly aimed bullet blew away half of the plant in an explosion that would be seen for miles around. Gunnar was making the impact he intended. He would obtain the name of his saviour from his mystery contact in the Coalition as sure as this whole place would be razed to the ground before sunrise.

Reinforcements were stationed in the main plant building from where all the pipework originated from. As flames took ownership of his clothes, he became a burning torch. He ran into the building and towards the control room, bringing fear to everyone who witnessed him. As soon as he was inside, bullets hit him from every possible angle, but there was still time for fun.

He ran directly at a guard standing transfixed by Gunnar's flames. The guard lifted his pistol and desperately emptied it before Gunnar wrapped himself around the petrified human.

The guard screamed as he burnt alive. Gunnar held tight, staring into his victim's eyes so that he could feel all of the man's pain. He basked in it. The guard's blood boiled inside him, coursing through his organs. Gunnar didn't notice the bullets penetrating him, but when one ended the agony of his burning toy, rage consumed him once more.

Gunnar snapped back into consciousness. Again, he'd lost memory of the destruction he'd caused. Why he held a decapitated human head in his hands was a mystery to him. He tossed it aside as one would a piece of rubbish. Something else had caught his eye: a white coat in a lab.

He climbed a stairwell to the adjacent laboratory and propped himself against the door as two scientists desperately gathered up samples while a guard hurried them up, like a parent ushering their children to school.

He took a calming breath. "Why the great hurry, gentlemen?"

Both scientists dropped their samples onto the floor when they saw Gunnar, still smouldering, stood casually at the door. The guard, however, wasn't as easily scared.

"He's here in the lab! Come quick!" he barked into his walkie-talkie.

Gunnar examined his nails. "Were you expecting me to try and stop you? Call who you want. Don't mind me."

"They're on their way, vampire. Do with me as you please," said the guard defiantly.

"Of course I will," said Gunnar, but before he could have his fun, two figures appeared behind the scientists.

"Maybe next time." The guard laughed and disappeared out of the lab with the two scientists. The back-up, two vampires, advanced towards Gunnar.

He continued to pick at his nails. "I was wondering if this facility was going to be better guarded. The armed cattle were a pleasant distraction, but I was hoping this place was more important. If you're the only lamia here, this whole research centre must be worthless. What could they make here that could warrant guards—defenders—such as yourselves? Vampire haemorrhoid cream?"

"Hold your tongue," one of them said. "The Coalition has put a great reward on your head."

"And what do you intend to do about it?" Tired of talking, Gunnar flew at the two vampires.

THE SCIENTISTS, FOLLOWED BY THEIR GUARD, only made it to the bottom of the lab stairs and into an adjoining warehouse before Gunnar was back on their trail. He'd executed the vampire guards without breaking into a sweat. They were old and powerful, but no match for him. With Michael and Gabriel gone, he was the ultimate predator. He caught up with the scientists as they were about to reach the exit.

He reached the guard first and drove his fist through his back, obliterating his spine and driving his heart out of his chest cavity. With a yank, he freed it. It was a maneuoveur that'd taken many years of practise to perfect but was well worth the effort. The scientists were too busy trying to escape to notice the horror. One desperately tried to type the security code into the exit control panel.

Gunnar walked behind them. "What's in the bag?" he asked calmly. The nearest scientist screamed and turned, clutching the bag to his chest like a mother might hold a child. The scientist's eyes focused on the guard's heart, which Gunnar tossed up nonchantly like a bleeding cricket ball.

"What's in the bag?" asked Gunnar again.

"Say nothing, Haas!" screamed his partner.

"Oh, please..." Gunnar darted across and forced the guard's heart into the other scientist's mouth. Gunnar expected a look of terror, not one of satisfaction.

"A vampire?" he said surprised. "You're barely bigger than a normal man."

The scientist licked his lips before baring his fangs, a last stand.

Gunnar burst out laughing. "Playing with chemicals? Pathetic! Why waste your time with the games of humans?" Gunnar didn't want an answer. He took the bag from the one named Haas and rummaged through its contents. "Bag-snatching is not normally my sort of thing." He took out a test tube. "Is this some sort of weapon? What would happen if I made you ingest this rubbish?"

"It's non-toxic," said Haas.

"Really?" said Gunnar. "Open wide."

Haas instantly obeyed. He was a vampire too, but he may as well have been an eighty-year-old human for all the good it would do him. Gunnar placed the test tube in Haas's mouth. "Does that hurt?"

Haas shook his head around the test tube.

"Not even a little bit?" Gunnar smiled and unleashed a punch that shattered the test tube in the doctor's mouth. Glass lacerated his tongue, gums, and throat. Haas collapsed to the floor coughing up blood and tearing at his throat.

The other scientist fell to the floor and picked up a hard drive that had fell out of the bag. "Take it! Take all of it!"

"Why would I want it?" asked Gunnar.

"You don't know what we do here, do you?" the scientist said in disbelief.

"I don't even care."

"Our research can change everything. Whoever owns this formula controls the Coalition. You could rule the world."

A wicked glint crossed Gunnar's eyes. "I don't want to rule the world, Doctor." His hand darted out and grabbed the helpless vampire's throat, slowly squeezing, his nails entering the flesh. "I want to end it."

4

SANDERSON WAS BORED. He'd listened to these losers discuss bureaucratic bullshit for two solid hours. They hadn't even discussed the thing threatening to bring about their downfall: Gunnar Ivansey. They pretended to be so cool, so controlled. Why put on an act? All that mattered in situations like these was the truth, and the truth was they were screwed.

This cavern was where the first-ever Coalition meeting was held nearly three hundred years ago. Michael Vitrago was the glue that held the Coalition, the country, and possibly the world, together. He was a killing machine, a monster, but in hindsight, Sanderson realised Vitrago was what the only thing that could make the Coalition work.

It'd been decided that tradition would dictate and the Coalition meetings would continue to be held in this great cavern, a mile beneath central London. The idiots believed this stronghold was a symbol of their unity. Why did they bother? Sanderson could see it on their faces: they held no hope in their hearts. Sanderson, himself, had sat on the Coalition for years, much to the chagrin of most of the arseholes here. He was a soldier, not a politician, and his job was covering up the atrocities caused by the vampire race. It made him sick, but he did it for the greater good.

Sanderson surveyed the group: eleven vampires and eleven humans, but most council members took backseats, letting the big dogs argue it out. There was once twelve of each until six months ago when Vitrago ripped Ben Edric's throat out for divulging classified information. And then, there was the mysterious disappearance of Lucia just after Tillsley killed Sparle. When it came to bloodsuckers, Lucia was unusual. She was of sound mind. She'd be missed, that was for sure, especially if her father came looking for answers as to her whereabouts.

In the Coalition's infinite wisdom, they'd decided on a new direction, and, as a result, the Hominum Order and the Lamian Consilium were abolished. Bwogi, a vampire elder, hoped to convince the vampire world a new age of collaboration was afoot. As a result, younger vampires had replaced some of the old.

Bwogi was trying to fill Vitrago's shoes and it made Sanderson cringe. Africa was a hard place, and it was hard to believe this bureaucrat was raised there. Bwogi looked soft and he was soft. But it had stunned everyone when he'd signed his friend Ricard's death warrant for harbouring Sparle. Still, Bwogi didn't have the nerves to watch when they'd tied the old timer to a tree, leaving him for the dawn. Maybe if the vampires supporting the Agreement were stronger, Bwogi's idealist ways would hold sway. However, the vampires were waning and they needed an iron fist, or at least the pretence of one, and Bwogi was neither. The British Army was the best chance the Coalition had, unless they were willing to invest in one right hand from Middlesbrough.

"...Which brings us to the matter of Gunnar Ivansey."

Sanderson's ears pricked up. At last, there was something interesting to discuss. Charles had brought up the topic, and Sanderson was amazed the fat accountant hadn't lost a few pounds from all the stress he was under. Charles still burst out of his designer clothes and still stared over those annoying half-moon specs. Sanderson hated him more than the vampires. Charles was here because of his connections and brought nothing to the table except worthless discussion.

Augustus pounced on the subject. "Ivansey is threatening the Agreement on the same scale Ricard did when he let Sparle loose. Ivansey knew exactly what he was doing when he attacked the chemical plant in Seal Sands, Teesside. He wanted anarchy and he got it. Since Ricard's execution, he has continuously attacked Coalition resources, and we haven't come close to stopping him."

Sanderson laughed on the inside. Augustus and Ivansey were as thick as thieves during the World Wars. Something damn good must have happened for Augustus to turn against Ivansey, and Augustus was most likely on the receiving end of something real nasty. It hadn't affected his looks, though...there was no justice in the world. Sanderson looked at his own hands: scarred, knuckles missing, arthritis in a couple of fingers. It'd been a hard life. His face was in a much worse state and grey hair was overtaking at a depressing rate.

"Ivansey is growing in confidence. The attack on the chemical works was unbelievably brash, even for him," said Caroline.

Sanderson could get nothing from her face of stone. She and Bwogi were running the Coalition, but she was the true political might. Her dark, pretty face and soft features were as good a camouflage as the vampire's. She was power-dressing in a sharp navy blue suit, not that she needed to. Sanderson wondered whether it was something from her past that had turned this middle-aged woman into such a hard-nosed bitch. Even Vitrago had listened to Caroline.

"The entire attack was caught on CCTV."

Jeremy Pervis! Sanderson shuddered at the sound of the man's voice and despaired that the coward still sat within this group. He didn't trust him as far as he could throw him, although he could probably throw the skinny little bastard a fair way. If a vampire ever got hold of Pervis, he would sell out his mother. Fear controlled his every action.

"It was a horrific display," Pervis struggled with his words. He was petrified of Ivansey. "He ran through wave after wave of bullets. You can see on his face that he...he...loved every minute."

Sanderson grimaced. There was no way Pervis slept at night. He needed taking out before he did something stupid. Vitrago would've acted in a second, just like he did with Ben Edric. Bwogi would prescribe counselling.

"What did he take from the plant?" asked Caroline.

"Nothing...we think...we hope," said Pervis. "We believe he was making a statement. Showing us he no longer cares."

Sanderson took in a deep breath. It was time for him to get involved. "He never cared. The animal proved that six months ago when he tortured Rickson Flatley."

Pervis sank into his seat. Flatley and Pervis had been partners assigned to track down Tillsley, and Flatley, a damn good soldier, had faced a grizzly end. Sanderson scowled, thinking, *Why couldn't Ivansey have killed you instead, you ginger, skinny prick!*

"That was a different beast to the one we face now," said Augustus. "He's now in a completely different league. The explosions from the chemical site were seen for miles around. The devastation was on par with what Sparle caused. Ivansey knew it was ours."

"Why attack that plant?" asked Caroline.

"The plant was due to make the first trial batch of Haemo next week," said Garendon, a newly recruited vampire who specialised in scientific research and development. Sanderson hadn't made his mind up on him yet. He wasn't a prolific feeder, that was for sure. He was smart, but he was quiet, too quiet. His thick black hair was unkempt, and he didn't bother with the fashions as did the rest of his race. In fact, he looked like he'd just run out of the lab. "Our progress had been excellent. The attack couldn't have come at a worse time."

"How could he've known about Haemo?" asked Bwogi.

That's what I want to know, Sanderson thought, looking from face to face. He had his suspicions.

"What happened to Doctors Haas and Smythe?" asked Caroline.

"I don't need to divulge how, but they died at the scene," said Garendon. "They were brilliant and won't be easily replaced. It was Smythe who discovered penicillin—not Alexander Fleming, as is popularly believed. A fine legacy for anyone to leave behind."

Sanderson nodded his head. He hated vampires, but he wasn't blind to their positive impact on the world.

"Has this set back the Haemo project?" asked Bwogi, the million-dollar question Sanderson couldn't wait to hear the answer to.

"All the data was recovered from the plant," explained Garendon. "Backups of the files were found by the scattered remains of the scientists. Still, our large-scale facilities and the loss of personnel have set us back well over a year. The Haemo formula is sound, but dosing it to the vampire population isn't possible anymore. Making a suitable formulation was difficult, and the plant Gunnar destroyed was the only one of its kind. There's no quick fix. We need to plough millions back into the project as quickly as we can."

"That's being taken care of," said Caroline. "Anything you need, it's yours. The Prime Minister won't object if we tap into taxpayer's money for such a thing." She shook her head at the predicament. "There's no way Ivansey could've known the plant was making Haemo."

"If he knew what Haemo was, we'd know about it by now," said Charles.

"He hates the Coalition and everything we stand for," said Augustus. "Haemo is a drug that will supress a vampire's thirst and need to kill. Ivansey would wage war on the very idea. But, I believe his attack on the plant is a coincidence. Murder and hatred are the only things that drive him. He's attacked so many of our installations, for him, this is just another one, I'm sure of it. Haemo is beyond Top Secret. He couldn't have known about the development...unless there's a leak."

Sanderson scanned the room in a flash and wasn't surprised to find every other councillor doing the same. Everyone had suspected a leak somewhere in the Coalition, but this was the first anyone had mentioned it. No one was giving away anything, which made Sanderson sneer in disgust. He hated politicians and these were the best of them, or, as he saw it, the worst.

"If the confidentiality of the Haemo project is breached, the consequences will be dire," said Bwogi, nervously biting on his knuckle. "With the knowledge of Haemo's power, the vampires of the old world will flock to Ivansey."

"No," said Augustus. "Ivansey was never a leader; he was a totem. But that was a different time. Now, he's a dinosaur, an echo from a violent, brutal age. Ivansey's always been psychotic, but he's turning into an abomination. He won't align with anyone or anything. He wants nothing but pain for every living thing, and he's no better than the monster Sparle. If his actions are kept within the confines of this room, he will not become an icon, or, once we act, a martyr."

"So we have two tasks on our hands," said Caroline. "To stop Gunnar, and then—who knows? Who knows what other monsters will wash up on our shores."

"Yes," said Augustus, "but if we can put an end to Ivansey, we can send a message to the others. We have to deal with him first."

"He must be destroyed!" Pervis cried out like a scared child, nearly sending Sanderson into fits of laughter.

Caroline pretended he wasn't there. "Which leads to the question of how can we kill Ivansey?"

The lack of ideas became apparent to everyone but Sanderson. "We can take him, but there'll be a price."

"No, Sanderson. No more risks to the Agreement," said Caroline, pointing a finger at him.

"Tillsley can kill him," Sanderson argued. "Tillsley can make all this go away."

No one objected straight away. That was a good sign. Before the Firmamentum, if he'd even hinted at such a thing, Vitrago would've torn him in two. Now, things were on a knife edge and they were willing to consider anything.

"This Coalition was established to uphold the Agreement, but we are also here to allow both species to live in peace," said the vampire Sebastian. Another new face on the Coalition, and one Sanderson trusted least of all.

"Peace? Who did you murder last night?"

"Sanderson, Sanderson." Sebastian shook his head mockingly. He was the youngest vampire here and was commissioned to modernise both the Coalition and the Agreement. When Sanderson was in charge of cleaning up vampire activity, he always had a long night when this sick freak was involved. "We've been here as long as you. We're all animals, but you just happen to be below me in the food chain." The vampire's mocking tone didn't sit well with the veteran soldier.

"Is that a threat?" asked Sanderson. What were the idiots thinking giving this animal power? If Sanderson was to put money on a leak, it would be on Sebastian. He even looked evil. His green eyes reminded Sanderson of a snake's, and he was paler than the rest of the bloodsuckers, the pitch-black hair contributed to the effect. But Sebastian wasn't as beautiful as his brethren. At least there was some justice.

Sebastian laughed. "I'm sure you'll take it that way. We're here to talk business. Tillsley has killed many lamia over the past six months. How can we condone that?"

"We can't do anything of the sort," said Charles. "The Coalition stands for unity between the races."

Sanderson shook his head. "We send Tillsley to kill Ivansey, and then, we make Tillsley disappear. It'll be easy enough. He isn't exactly hard to find. Why haven't you killed him already?"

"That's a good question," said Caroline. "Officially, there's a bounty on his head. Vampires have tried to capitalise on the hefty reward, but Reece Chambers is watching him like a hawk. As the assassination attempts failed, Tillsley's legend grew. He attacked a nightclub in Leeds earlier this week and twenty were killed. He's obliterating the morale of the younger generations while Chambers uses him like a puppet."

Sanderson did his best not to smile.

Caroline continued. "At first, we kept him alive in case we needed him. If it wasn't for him, we'd still be chasing Sparle around the country. Now, he's just a nuisance, and I'd commit more resources to his disappearance if it wasn't for Ivansey's wave of destruction in the North. We have Helena

Ichvamovich infiltrating Tillsley's circles. I believe one of her subordinates killed one of Tillsley's drinking companions, which is unfortunate. If we press too much, Chambers will hide him."

"What are you suggesting, Caroline?" asked Bwogi.

Sanderson groaned on the inside. If Bwogi was a human, he would be a vegan, anti-fur, anti-animal testing, tree-hugging hippy.

"It would be idiotic to cut down our options at this moment in time," she said.

Sanderson nodded inwardly, pleased that not everyone was detached from reality.

"We cannot use Tillsley," pleaded Bwogi. "He's a hunter. The Coalition's job is to destroy all who hunt the lamia. He's no different."

"How naïve are you?" asked Sanderson. He knew he would be in trouble, but he didn't care. "Tillsley can end Ivansey's reign of terror with one punch. With their history, Ivansey will be gunning for Tillsley."

"These are delicate times, Sanderson," said Bwogi. "Your hotheadedness could end everything. The Coalition cannot be seen supporting a vampire hunter. It only takes a few lamia to turn against us, and there is no Michael Vitrago to fear anymore. Luckily, no one is challenging us—yet. Any vampire faction could use Ivansey's personal war to springboard their own campaign for power and an end to peace."

Sanderson laughed. "Peace? Are you joking? And for all your words, Bwogi, you still haven't come up with another way of stopping him, have you?"

"I...I...no." Bwogi averted his gaze. "No, I haven't."

"Well I have. We get Tillsley to turn that piece of shit into dust."

"We cannot do that, not yet, anyway," said Caroline. "We will double our efforts tracking Ivansey. We're fire fighting, but we've no choice. Ivansey comes first, and then the rest...whoever they are."

Sanderson couldn't let it lie. "If you're not going to use Tillsley, then you better get that Haemo plant back up to full production, because all you fuckers are gonna need it when the shit hits the fan."

"It won't come to that," said Sebastian. "We will deal with Ivansey."

"We?" questioned Sanderson.

"No, you, actually," interrupted Charles. "You will deal with Ivansey. Rempstone, a young man from the armed services, will be joining us shortly. He will pick up your current duties, and you will move on to more pressing matters."

"Who hired him?" asked Sanderson. It was the first he'd heard of it, which annoyed him, but he was pleased he wouldn't have to attend these pointless meetings anymore.

"I did," said Charles.

Sanderson suppressed another groan. He knew exactly what they were getting: an office jockey. Were these idiots trying to distance themselves from the military completely or just get rid of him? They'd already lost

Viralli, Vitrago's right-hand man. He'd jumped ship after Sparle was killed. He'd disappeared from the face of the earth along with Lucia. With Viralli going rogue, Sanderson would need eyes in the back of his head from now on.

"Have we come any closer to tracking down Lucia?" asked Pervis. Obviously missing his crush. He didn't have the confidence to look at her when she was at these meetings.

"No," said Bwogi. "We know she's alive, otherwise we would've heard from her father before now."

"Why would she just disappear like that? It doesn't make any sense," said Pervis.

Probably scared you're going to put a webcam in the toilets, thought Sanderson.

"We have our best trackers on it. There isn't much more we can do," said Caroline.

"I just hope she's OK," said Bwogi with genuine concern. "I'd have put more vampires on her trail if it wasn't for the approaching celebration of the Occursus."

"Yes," said Charles, "I was hoping we'd get to that." He rooted through some papers in front of him before finding the object of his foraging. He peered over his half-moon lenses. "We are over budget. This figure is quite farcical."

Bwogi nodded. "I understand your concerns, but if ever the vampire nation needed a positive boost, it would be the Occursus."

"But still—"

Augustus interrupted. "Perhaps, Charles, you do not understand the significance. The Occursus represents the first meeting of two vampires from separate families. The first time each family realised they weren't alone on the planet."

This did not satisfy Charles. "We are millions—"

"Which is insignificant in the grand scale of things." Augustus sat forward in his seat, staring pointedly at Charles. "It's only held once a decade, and we're going to throw a party of such magnitude, the vampire race will forget there are any troubles in the world. We'll make them believe the Agreement is as strong as when Vitrago ruled."

Charles said nothing and went back to shuffling through his papers irritably.

Sanderson smirked. *What a pussy.*

Bwogi nodded. "We must pray that Ivansey does not turn his attention our way again soon. If he bypasses the Occursus security..." Bwogi shivered. "The Occursus must be nothing but a complete success."

AFTER THE MEETING, Sanderson strode through the underground chambers of the Coalition headquarters. He was a lot happier now his responsibilities were passed to a younger recruit. Now, Sanderson could spend his time planning for the inevitability of war. He was a good leader and a better soldier who wasn't afraid to get his hands dirty. War, he was good at. Ivansey was turning into a distraction, and it was time to finish him.

"Sanderson."

Aw, fuck! The soft voice made him cringe. He turned on his heel, hoping the encounter would be as brief as possible. "Bwogi."

Bwogi looked haggard. His hair was a mess, and his eyes did not shine like they should. At times like these, pillars of strength were needed.

"How are the security arrangements for the Occursus?"

"Security will be sufficient."

"Sufficient isn't good enough, Sanderson."

"Surely, by definition, it is?" Sanderson enjoyed watching Bwogi squirm.

"There can be no breaches of security. The Occursus must be perfect; otherwise, we'll be one step closer to war."

"Look, I've organised army patrols and even a navy cruiser off the coast. What more can I do? My replacement—what's he called?—Rempstone, is the man on the job. Now, let me get on with hunting Ivansey, and you get back to doing whatever the fuck you're actually meant to do, because all you've done so far is land us in a world of shit."

Sanderson turned his back on Bwogi and strode down the corridor. He knew he was getting away with some shocking displays of behaviour, and he enjoyed it immensely. He'd done his job securing the big vampire event, the Occursus, but nothing was airtight.

Nothing.

5

LUCIA VOMITED VIOLENTLY INTO THE TOILET. Morning sickness was something that shouldn't plague a vampire. Having to get up in the daylight hours to be sick wasn't a useful characteristic and evolution had taken care of it a long time ago. This, however, was no normal pregnancy.

Lucia was having Arthur Peasley's baby.

She'd been impregnated by a human. The first mixed conception between lamia and human in history. Lucia emptied her stomach again before flushing the toilet. The gestation period of a vampire was two years, but she felt ready to drop, and she'd only been pregnant for six months.

"Make me a cup of coffee while you're up, darlin'," he called through.

She walked into the cramped kitchen and put the kettle on. She couldn't say no to Arthur. She looked back through his small flat to where he lay on the double bed watching Middlesbrough's American football team on the television. He lay back with his head in his hands, naked to the world. Lucia smiled. How was he human? His muscular symmetry was perfect. His thick black hair, not a strand out of place, shone, giving the impression of a halo.

Never had she imagined loving anyone as much as that man. Never before had she taken a human into her bed; never before had she fallen in love. He came into her life and changed everything.

"Is that coffee coming or what?"

"Yes—" she was interrupted by Arthur breaking wind, "...my love."

"Good. Put some more cream in this time. The last lot you made was nasty shit, baby."

"Of course, darling." She obliged and took it through.

"No cookie?" he said, disappointed.

"Sorry, darling. Oh, I'm going to be sic—" She rushed through to the bathroom and only just made it.

"Shut the door! I'm trying to watch the football!"

Lucia managed to shut the door with her foot before thowing up again. Things certainly weren't quite as wonderful as they once were. It had been magical at first. Arthur was so pleased he was going to become a father. But, as her pregnancy developed, the romance died.

She pulled the chain after she was certain she wasn't going to be sick again, for fifteen minutes at least. The chain didn't work. She pulled harder but didn't manage to flush it until the fourth attempt.

She washed her hands in the sink and despaired at the lack of hot water. She wasn't convinced Arthur was a particularly good plumber. She tried not to catch her own reflection in the mirror, but the brief glance was enough to plunge her further into depression. She'd gained weight with the pregnancy, and her cheekbones, which once would've stopped any man in their tracks, were hidden under a layer of blubber. Her long dark hair hung limp where it had once been glossy, thick, and the envy of every woman. Even her bright emerald green eyes had lost their fire. Still, she'd gladly sacrifice all for the love of her man and her unborn child.

"Will you please get round to fixing that toilet, Arthur?" she asked nicely as she came back into the room.

"Awww man!" groaned Arthur. "I'm up to my elbows in other peoples' shit all day long. The last thing I wanna do when I get home is to put my hand in more shit."

"You're a plumber. It'll only take you a couple of minutes."

"Baby, please don't nag me!"

"I'm not nagging," she protested. "I just want a bathroom that actually works. I'm carrying your child, you know?" she said, clutching her bump protectively.

"Awww, , don't guilt trip me."

"What are you talking about? I just want you to fix the toilet. Is that too much to ask? We can move to my place. It's ten times bigger than this apartment."

Arthur threw his hands in the air. "I'm never good enough for you, am I? You have to rub it in that you have millions of dollars and I'm a lowly plumber."

"No, it isn't that at all," she said, reaching for his shoulder. "I just want you to know that we have other options."

He shrugged her off. "I'm the man in this relationship, woman. I'm the bread winner and this is my castle and I am the king."

"I know, darling, but—"

"Middlesbrough is my home. These people took me as one of their own even though my heritage lies on distant shores. They let me into their world and they'll do the same for you. Will your friends do the same for me?"

"I haven't even met any of your friends, apart from when Sid Tillsley ogled my breasts in front of the elders of the Lamian Consilium."

"Well, you shouldn't have dressed like a slut!" he yelled.

"How can you say that to me?" she said, wiping away a tear. "I never even get the chance to dress up! You never take me anywhere!"

Arthur closed his eyes. "And the nagging starts again! You're like a broken record, woman, and not a good one like 'All Shook Up.' I've had enough. I'm going down the pub where people actually appreciate me for who I am. People who don't wanna change me!" He pulled some clothes on in a matter of seconds and still managed to look immaculate. Maybe it was the sequins.

"You've changed, Arthur! You used to respect me. You said you loved me!" she called after him as he stormed out into the hallway.

"I do love you, but I can't take much more of this!" he yelled back, grabbing his coat from the hook.

"I'm pregnant with your child, Arthur! *Your* child! You should be looking after our future rather than drinking in shitholes with your loser friends!" shouted Lucia desperately as the beautiful man slammed the door of his flat. She fell to her knees in tears, but hoped filled her heart when the door opened once more.

"I need to take a dump. Don't think I'll make it to the pub."

Lucia broke down into tears, again, as the toilet door slammed shut and horrible noises echoed down the hallway. Ten minutes later, Arthur stormed out leaving a vapour trail. "That beef pie you made last night was like passing an anvil."

And with that, Arthur Peasley left the building.

6

"How do, Brian," said Sid, while supping a pint of Bolton Bitter. He took a mighty draught, but his sneered-up nose said it wasn't quite hitting the spot.

"Alreet, our Sid," said Brian, walking into The Badger from the cool winter evening. "How's the ale?"

"It ain't bad, mon, but I can't half miss The Miner's. I can't believe them vampire bastards shut it down. This ale ain't exactly piss, but it just ain't the same. It ain't kept reet. It doesn't get you dying for another pint."

"You want another one?"

"Aye, dying for one," said Sid, owner of an empty pint glass.

Brian smiled to himself as he made his way to the bar. "Eh'up, Jimmy. Two pints of Bolton, please."

The young barman wrung his hands together, awkwardly. "There are plenty of other pubs you can drink in, Brian," he said, avoiding eye contact. "The beer is much better in The Pig and Whistle. Why don't you try drinking in there? They get more women in there too."

Brian cocked an eyebrow. "What are you trying to say, Jim?"

The young barman went from wringing his hands to nervously pulling at his brown curly locks. "This ain't The Miner's, Brian."

"I know it ain't The Miner's, Jimmy. If The Miner's was open, I wouldn't be in this shithole."

"You're...you're scaring away the other customers."

"What're you talking about? I wouldn't say boo to a goose, me."

"Last week, you didn't have to hit Tony. He was one of me best customers."

Brian held up his hands. "That was self-defence."

"You shagged his gran!"

"Aye, but she's a carefree, single woman. It has nowt to do with Tony."

"It was at his granddad's funeral!"

"People grieve in different ways, Jimmy," said Brian, knowledgably. "I was the victim of an attempted assault."

Jimmy knew he was on to a loser. He cast a tear-filled eye on the empty chairs and tables. "No one drinks here anymore. Even *he* can't drink enough beer to cover my losses." He nodded towards the big, bald behemoth but kept his eyes fixed on the floor.

"That's unfair on our Sid. He's a big puppy dog at heart."

Jimmy's eyes shot up for a second to take in Sid lighting up a fag. The barman's shoulders somehow slumped further. "He can't smoke in here. You know it's illegal, Brian. Please, tell him."

"It's your pub, Jimmy, you tell him," said Brian with a wry grin.

With metaphorical cap in hand, Jimmy walked around the bar and approached the scariest thing in Middlesbrough. "Please, erm, sir, can you, please, extinguish your cigarette?...Please?"

Sid looked up from his seat at the haggard barman. "What's up, lad?"

"Can you...can you p-p-please put out your cigarette?"

"Why, mon?" asked Sid innocently.

"It's against the law."

"No coppers around, lad. You've got nowt to worry about." Sid lit up for the fifty-eighth time that day. He was on Silk Cut and had obtained two hundred for landing an uppercut on Eduard Fabrico, a sick and twisted vampire who would never make the mistake of using the last sheet of toilet paper in the gents ever again.

Sid did have a good point. There were no coppers anywhere near The Badger. Agreed, The Badger was definitely not The Miner's Arms, but then The Miner's was rougher than the Mos Eisley Cantina. The Badger wasn't the place to take your mum for her birthday, and it was still a no-go area for the Cleveland Police Force. And even if a local bobby did see Sid smoking, they wouldn't say anything anyway.

"Smoking puts off the other patrons, Sid."

"There ain't any other fooker in 'ere! Pour the beers and stop playing silly buggers."

That was the cue for poor Jimmy to shut up. He'd come to realise that "silly buggers" normally ended up with concussions. Jimmy muttered under his breath and went back to the bar to pull the pints, making sure they weren't a millilitre under the mark. There were some laws these scoundrels *did* live by.

"Good lad, Jim," said Brian taking the beers over to Sid. Both lads took a draught and both gave a little sigh of disappointment.

"How's Kev, then?" asked Sid.

"He ain't in a good way, apparently."

"Poor bastard. He's worked in that pub his entire life. I could murder a pint of well-kept Bolton too."

"Aye, same here. Kev's missus is proper worried about him, I was told. He ain't talking. He ain't eating as much. He ain't even drinking. He spends all his time up his allotment."

"Fooking 'ell, it must be bad. You been to see Kev?"

Brian screwed up his face."What would I wanna go and do that for?"

The Northern man doesn't do compassion.

"Fair play. Where're the other lads?"

"Good point, Sid. I dunno. Both of 'em said that they'd be down for a session."

Speaking of the devil, a greasy, little, horrible bastard devil, Peter

Rathbone made his filthy presence known. He went straight to the bar without asking anyone else if they wanted a drink and ordered a beer, Redcar Best Bitter. He couldn't drink the Bolton in here, as it reminded him of what he missed in The Miner's. Jimmy the barman shuddered as he served the greasy, horrible, little bastard. Rathbone took his beer over to his sort-of friends, said nothing, and sat down.

Brian tried not to look at Rathbone much, as it wasn't an enjoyable experience. However, right now, he couldn't keep his eyes off him. "You look different, Rathbone."

"So?"

"Yeah, he does," agreed Sid, who sat back in his chair and rubbed his chin in thought.

"That's a new haircut, isn't it?" asked Brian

"Kind of," said Rathbone, sporting a slicked-back look, which receded slightly at the temples.

"You OK, mon? You look a bit pale," said Brian, interested, but not concerned.

"Aye."

"And your teeth...they're pointed," Brian noted.

"So?"

"Are they new clothes? You never wear new clothes," said Sid.

"Is that a cape?" asked Brian.

"Aye," said Rathbone defensively. "What's wrong with that, like?"

"That's fooking mint, that," said an approving Sid. "The crimson velvet suits ya."

"Yeah, I know." Rathbone adjusted the high collars of his white shirt.

"Anyroad," said Sid, now bored of fashion chat, "what you been up to, Brian?"

"Interesting night couple of days back, come to think of it. Pulled another one of them snooker slags while on my way to a sixty-six break."

"Seven off me best."

"Fook off, Rathbone! The bitch put me off when I was about to ram home a black to beat you, you little twat! Anyroad, no one ever saw you make a break over fooking twenty. You're full of shit," said a very bitter swordsman.

"Alreet, alreet, what happened with the snooker slag?" asked Sid.

"As I was saying, before I was rudely interrupted, she was proper red hot and, honestly, she was that beautiful—I made sweet love."

"*Sweet* love?" asked Sid, unconvinced.

"*Sweet* love," confirmed Brian, "Foreplay and everything! But something strange happened, like. When I reached me vinegar strokes, she exploded."

"Aye, that's a bit odd." Sid scratched his chin. "Saying that, you ain't exactly careful where you put it. You may have given her a bad dose of summat," diagnosed Dr. Tillsley.

"I don't think the clap can make a lass explode. Well, at least I don't think so. I'll have to nail another bird as an experiment," replied Brian, scienitist.

"Well, at least you finished off, like," said Sid, a glass-half-full kind of bloke.

"Aye, that's what I said to meself."

Sid nodded. "What about you, Rathbone? You been up to anything lately?"

"Not really," he said before heading off to a buy another pint for himself.

"What about you, Sid?" asked Brian, ignoring the flamboyantly dressed Rathbone.

"Been a busy boy, me. Still doing the vampire-hunting thingy. It puts food on the table, beer in the belly, and tabs in the lungs." He lit up another. "Haven't gotta worry about the Benefit Bastards being on me back. These vampire assassins are nothing compared to what them Benefit Bastards can do, I tell ya. Still, I'd prefer me ol' life back."

Rathbone sat back down with his pint and a flourish of his cape.

"Yeah," continued Sid, "I wanna retire from this shit soon. Rich has got some big plans, and as soon as they're done, I'll have enough to call it a day."

"Where're you planning to retire to?"

"That's the problem, Brian. A man of my standings can't be retiring anywhere. I need my creature comforts to be content in the later years of my life. I wanna retire to The Miner's, but how can I if the fooker is closed? I need to get it back. I can't retire without Kev's beer."

"It's shit in there."

"Shut up, Rathbone," said Brian and Sid.

Rathbone's attire caught Brian's eye once more. "Are you sure nowt has happened to you?"

"Yeah."

Rathbone wasn't the sort of man to pass up the chance to brag about an adventure and then exaggerate it ten-fold. However, Rathbone had taken a pasting from one of them vampire bastards, and he was feeling a little bit strange too, so until he thought of a good-enough story to explain his encounter, he was keeping schtum. As for the clothes, after he'd woken up in the alleyway where he'd been attacked, he'd delveoped an undeniable urge to wear a cape.

The door to the near-deserted pub opened, causing the trio to look up.

"Arthur Peasley, the one and only," greeted Brian.

"Howay the lads!" shouted Sid.

Arthur plonked himself down at the table. He was looking good, but he didn't look happy. "She won't stop nagging, man. She's one hard-headed woman. She's only pregnant. What's the big deal? If I gave birth, I'd be back at work the next day."

"Yeah!" said Sid, jobseekers allowance claimant for over twenty years.

"And I wouldn't use it as an excuse to get fat!"

"Yeah!" said Sid, Body Mass Index: 42.

"Man, she's driving me crazy. I'm at work all day, and at night, I wanna wind down and have a few beers with the guys. What's hard to understand?"

"Nowt, mon," said Brian. "I told you this'd happen."

"I thought she'd be different. You know, being a vampire and that, but she's just the same. Nothing I do is good enough."

"Just leave her, then," said Brian.

"No way, man. She's carrying my baby," said the proud future father.

"You'll be able to get custody rights. Although saying that, I'm not sure how that works with vampires. It ain't worth staying with a woman for the bairn," said Brian, absentee father of dozens.

"Just leave it, man." Arthur changed the subject. The oddly dressed Rathbone caught his eye. "You look different, man. And that cloak and bow tie combo really suits you, man."

Rathbone, secretly happy, gave the cape a little flourish so Arthur could catch a glimpse of the red velvet inside. At that moment, Reece Chambers made his entrance.

"Oh fook, not him again," said Brian when Reece was in earshot.

"Eh'up, Rich. Got me tabs?" said Sid, the only man pleased to see him.

Reece threw down another pack of two hundred Silk Cut. Sid eagerly tucked in, offering a pack to the other lads who willingly shared the wealth.

"We are going to have a busy—" Reece stopped mid-sentence when he caught a glimpse of Rathbone. After a moment of realisation, Reece reached under his long trench coat, pulled out a gun, aimed it at Rathbone's heart, and without a moment's hesitation, pulled the trigger. Blood erupted from the gaping hole which was once Rathbone's chest.

"Watch me fooking pint!" shouted a concerned Garforth, covering his glass with his hand.

Rathbone tumbled out of his chair and lay lifeless on the floor.

"I guess he sort of had it coming, like," said Sid.

"Aye," agreed Brian, "always been a bit of a twat."

"He's a vampire!" screamed Reece. "How the hell did he become a vampire?" He pulled a short sword from the inside of his coat and walked purposefully towards the lifeless vampire.

"Leave him alone, mon. He's had enough," said Sid, sipping his beer.

"He's one of them. We must kill him," said Reece without remorse.

"He's one of *them lot*?" said a fear-stricken, homophobic vampire hunter.

"No, Sid!" said Brian. "Although he might as well've been for the amount of fanny he got."

Reece pulled back the blade to perform the *coup de grace*. He'd always wanted to kill the horrible, greasy little bastard, and now, he was well within his rights to do so. This would be one of the most pleasurable executions he'd perform in many a year.

He struck, bringing down the blade with all his might. Rathbone, coming around, saw the blade flashing through the air, rolled to the side, and the fatal blow missed the mark. He jumped to his feet and bared his fangs. He coiled, ready to strike, until he noticed the bloodstains that covered him.

"You've fooked up me cape!" he squealed before turning nasty. "I'm gonna 'ave you!"

Rathbone had never been a good fighter, but now, he had the strength of the vampire. He leapt at Reece, but wasn't fully in control of his new vampire superpowers. Missing his target by a mile, Rathbone dived across the pub, through a door, and into the urinal of the gents.

"There's piss on me cape!" came the screams. "There is *piss* on me cape!"

Arthur, Sid, and Brian burst into laughter at the thought of the urine-soaked vampire. Reece wasn't laughing. He aimed his pistol at the toilet, waiting for Rathbone to emerge.

Jimmy was white as a sheet and close to a breakdown. His pub was a rough dive, but this was a nightmare. His business had been destroyed by the mere presence of these social misfits, and when the regulars find out there'd been a gunfight with a vampire...Jimmy burst into tears.

"Reet then, no more playing silly buggers. Rich, put the shooter away."

"No, Sid. He's a vampire. He must be killed."

"Rich, we all know Rathbone is a twat, but he doesn't deserve to be shot again. Put the gun away. He ain't done any harm to anyone."

"Not yet, but he will. The thirst will take him. He won't be able to help himself. If I don't pull this trigger, someone else is going to die."

"Looks like we have ourselves a situation," said Arthur.

The door to the toilet opened.

7

RAPUNZEL'S NIGHTCLUB. Gunnar remembered back to the night when he'd met with Ricard and Richmond. If only he'd stayed here rather than meeting with his kindred spirit Gabriel, they would've never bumped into Tillsley on that godforsaken night. If they'd only known what he was then, between them, they could've taken him down.

Too late, thought the vampire.

He sat in the same seat he'd occupied on that dark night. Richmond, too, sat in the same place as before. Only Ricard's seat was empty. For all the bullshit the old vampire had spouted about protecting humans, his two sons had probably murdered more than Gunnar had himself. Sparle could've been used as a weapon, and the vampire race could've ruled as kings once more, but no. Ricard was gone, leaving Richmond as the only one left alive whom Gunnar could call a friend.

"How do you fare, brother?" asked the African vampire, dressed as elaborately as ever with his long dreadlocks spilling over his fur coat.

"Better for this," said Gunnar, acknowledging the fine whisky.

"It's good stuff, my friend."

"It always has been." The whisky brought back memories which pulled his mental state in all directions. The peace of sitting here with Richmond, a friend dear to his heart, was counterbalanced with the loss of Gabriel and Ricard.

"Why the change in the look, Gunnar?"

"I can't be bothered, anymore," he said tiredly.

Richmond shook his head. "Not just the hairstyle and beard. There is something about you. You look like a lamia who is feeding. The veins in your neck bulge, your eyes are wild. You even smell different. What has happened to you?"

"What hasn't happened to me?" he snapped back.

Richmond put his hands up, apologetically. "Are you going to be all right for tonight's meeting?"

Normally, Gunnar would've begged for forgiveness from his close friend, but Gunnar was no longer normal. He was in constant agony, and it was only equalled by his rage. It took all his will to control it. "Of course I will."

"And what are you going to do with Vitrago out of the picture?"

"I don't know, Richmond. I don't even care. I'm only here to catch up with old friends."

Gunnar heard the old vampires enter the nightclub building, the echoes of their great footsteps served as a reminder of the size of these animals.

"Gentlemen!" Richmond greeted the five vampires as they entered the safehouse within Rapunzel's. "Welcome, once again."

The largest of the five, a menacing giant, shook Richmond's hand, completely engulfing it. "Peace be with you, Richmond." The words of the enormous vampire did not suit him. Muscles bulged from beneath his smart clothes, and his face was carved out of wood. He was of similar stature to Vitrago. However, his eyes did not burn through you like the old Bloodlord's.

Gunnar did not get up to greet him. He knew Daedlus Karnus well. Although he hadn't the displeasure of meeting him since the Agreement was set. The history between the factions of Vitrago and Karnus were famous. They were well matched, but Vitrago, Gabriel, and Gunnar combined were too great an adversary for anything in the old world. Gunnar was the only one of the three left alive; however, this wasn't the same Gunnar Ivansey. Now, he was a different force entirely.

"Ivansey," Karnus offered him a nod of his head, which was returned by his former rival.

Richmond shook the hands of the other vampires, all ancient and powerful. Gunnar ignored all of them. Each was bound with muscle and each had a killer instinct to surpass the animal kingdom's most voracious predators, but Gunnar was so much more. Daedlus Karnus was the only threat here.

"Please, take a seat," said the host before preparing drinks. Richmond knew them all personally, and he could call each of them friends. He'd confided with Gunnar beforehand. Richmond hoped to mediate this meeting. He believed the outcome of this next hour would affect the direction of the world.

After each vampire was refreshed, Richmond began. "Look around you. This is the first place that peace should be made. The Lamian Consilium no longer exists and unity between the species has been declared. That means nothing if it's not agreed by you six individuals." He took a sip of his whisky.

"Vlastisluv Branko from the Americas, Elias Cai from Australasia, Farai Killato from Africa, Basilio Gorka from the Far East, Daedlus Karnus from the Middle East and Gunnar Ivansey from Western Europe. You all know Britain is the stronghold of vampirism. You all lusted for power here, but Vitrago held fast to the Agreement. In your own lands, you have the power to do as you wish. Here, it is different. Here, there are rules."

"From what I have heard, Ivansey hasn't heeded such warnings," spoke Elias. He was the only one of the five to take pride in his appearance with his stylish blonde hair and impeccable clothing, but it did little to hide his enormous frame and the murderous intent in his eyes.

Gunnar smirked when Richmond tensed in his seat. "We're not here to discuss the past, Elias," said Richmond. "Today is a new day. Here we decide on the direction of our species."

Daedlus Karnus laughed. "What has this new age done to you? Politics and Richmond are two things that have never mixed."

Richmond sighed. "Ricard is dead because of politics. He was a fool to hide Sparle, but he was executed to send a message. His flame was extinguished only to make the politicians look good. We need him now. We need him to guide us. I do this for him."

"Very noble," said Daedlus Karnus, "but would Ricard approve of bringing six of our nature together? What if we decide to rip this country and then the world to pieces? The Agreement was set for Vitrago's benefit. He was the reason the abomination was established."

"Because of Ricard, we live a relatively free life," said Richmond. "Vitrago was merely the reason that talks were held."

Vlastisluv Branko, another giant, interrupted the disagreement. "Ricard is irrelevant now. As you said, Richmond, we're here to discuss the future, not the past. Why did you call us?"

"To ensure we move as one and that we don't waste our efforts fighting each other. We must do what's best for the vampire race."

"The vampire race doesn't deserve to be saved. The line is growing weak," said Basilio Gorka. He was slighter than the other vampires, but the tightly corded muscle on his arms showed that his speed would give him an edge in combat. "Vitrago took all the strength from the Coalition when his vanity attacked Sparle. Why should I care for new blood? Why should I care for others of my kind? A vampire's life is a lonely existence. Only the kill brings satisfaction."

"Then go back to your lands and kill," said Richmond. "There, you will bring no harm to the rest of the world."

Basilio Gorka laughed. "But the sport is here. Without Vitrago, only humans stand in our way. The old times are close, Richmond."

"We can't win." All eyes turned to Gunnar.

"No?" asked Basilio Gorka.

"If we could, do you think Vitrago would've agreed to a bullshit Agreement? You will die if you think you can bring back the old ways."

"Then why are you advertising your presence to the world?" asked Daedlus Karnus.

"Because I don't care."

Richmond held his hands up. "Cool it, everyone. This country is in turmoil. It hasn't recovered since the Firmamentum and the death of Vitrago. We must work together to ensure our survival. Only then can we, as a group, initiate a new epoch in our species' history."

"Rousing speech," said Basilio Gorka sarcastically, "but that relies on us getting along. Now, I believe that would be possible, but *he* happens to be here."

Like Daedlus Karnus, Basilio Gorka had history with Gunnar, who had beaten him to within an inch of his life last time they met. "You shouldn't take that tone with me, Gorka. I might have to finish the job I started all those years ago."

"You can try it, Ivans—"

Gunnar launched himself at Basilio Gorka, knocking him from his chair and tearing at his face until he could see a bloody skull. Through the years, Gunnar relied on his speed to defeat opponents, but not now. He fought like Sparle, feral in combat. Without pause for breath, he drove down his elbow hard, crushing the vampire's head between the floor and the bone of his arm. Incessantly, he hammered down until there was nothing left but gore.

Gunnar rose to his feet, covered from head to toe in bone, brains, and blood. No one had tried to stop him. No one said a thing. To the others, it was one less rival to contend with.

Richmond stared at the floor, saying nothing.

Not even the survival of his race could quell the demons now controlling Gunnar's tortured soul. Only the pain of others brought him satisfaction.

He threw himself at the nearest vampire and was lost in darkness and blood.

As soon as conscious thought was his once more, he instantly wished it would leave him forever. Gunnar shook his head to clear the red mist. Richmond looked up at him, his eyes growing dim with his last moments.

"What have I done?" Gunnar whispered.

Richmond's throat was no longer there. There was no windpipe, and Gunnar could see his friend's spinal cord through the bloody mess. He could also taste blood.

"What have I done?" he said again.

Richmond reached up and gripped Gunnar's hand.

"I didn't mean...Richmond...I didn't mean..."

Gunnar felt his friend's grip relinquish.

Rage began to take over once more. He felt it rise from his belly, wanting to overpower him. "NOT AGAIN! NOT AGAIN!" Gunnar fought it. And, miraculously, he held it at bay. But it was all too late.

He looked around him. The walls were painted with blood. There was no life left. How had he managed to kill all of them? How could he kill someone he loved?

His testicles. He was a slave to testosterone.

He needed that name. He destroyed the chemical plant for the name that could help bring him peace. If not...was death the only way to rid him of this curse?

8

THE DOOR OF THE BADGER'S TOILETS OPENED WITH AN EERIE CREAK. In the doorway stood Peter Rathbone, vampire. His fangs were extended and his eyes glowed red with bloodlust. He let out a low, guttural growl that could only be unleashed by one of the damned. He would've looked menacing if he didn't have piss all over his cape.

Pointed at the forehead of Middlesbrough's only vampire, was Reece Chambers' pistol. His hand did not tremble. The pistol was cocked and his finger was a millimetre away from unloading a bullet directly into his target's brain.

Drunk at the bar were Sid Tillsley, Arthur Peasley, and Brian Garforth. They all had a beer on the go and were enjoying the show. They felt they should really be stopping the whole ordeal, but Reece and Rathbone were both unpopular, and watching them beat the crap out of each other was a no-lose situation. If it got really nasty, they'd step in...probably.

"Another round of beers over here, Jimmy," called Sid.

Poor Jimmy was a nervous wreck. If your pub didn't have regular gun-slinging fights, you could be forgiven for being a bit nervous around a hoedown, especially when it involved a vampire.

"Jimmy, three beers!" Sid banged his fist on the table, which fired the barman into action. The only thing more dangerous than a shootout with the undead was a beer-less Tillsley.

"Are you gonna stop this, Sid?" asked Jimmy hopefully.

"I'm on me day off, lad."

"Is Rathbone really a vampire?"

"Well, he didn't used to be, but he's got a cape now, so I guess he is, like. Don't worry, mon, this'll be a good scrap."

Without warning, Reece fired the pistol. The bullet was true, and Rathbone's brain exploded over the toilet walls.

"Reet, he really has had enough, now" said Sid.

"*Had enough?*" said a white-as-a-sheet Jimmy. "He's fooking dead!"

"Not yet," said Reece, advancing.

Arthur stood in the way and threw some karate poses. "He's had enough, man. You don't wanna take another step."

"Stand down, Peasley. Rathbone is a vampire. He's not the human you knew. He must die."

"Not today, man."

"Yeah," agreed Sid, "we ain't letting you cut his head off. At least wait until he gets up to some mischief before killing him."

Reece lowered his weapon. He could deal with Rathbone later. The most important thing at the moment was keeping Sid sweet.

The toilet door slammed open.

"You fooking twat! You shot me in the head!"

BOOM!

Rathbone staggered back into the urinals once more, but it was a glancing blow. "Reet, that's fooking it!" Rathbone came out fighting, but not like the noble vampire.

Rathbone opened up with artillery—not to inflict damage—but psychological warfare. Historically, the heads of enemy soldiers were catapulted at the advancing legions, but Rathbone had a nastier surprise.

"You dirty bastard!" shouted the spectators as urinal blocks were launched at Reece, who was a tough cookie, but even he shied away from piss-soaked urinal blocks. Reece overturned a bar table and fired pot shots from cover.

Jimmy wept into his hands. Punters would never come back, and he owed a lot of bad people a lot of bad money. He was only twenty-six, but like most kids on the Smithson Estate, he'd left school with no qualifications, making his money by wheeling and dealing. By robbing a bit of from his ex-bird's mum and borrowing a bit from some unsavoury characters, he'd managed to afford the lease for The Badger and was making a tidy sum. That was until these bastards made it their new home. They were killing him both financially and physically. He used to be a good-looking lad, but the stress was taking its toll. No more. It was time to act.

"I'm gonna call the police!" Jimmy yelled from behind the bar.

He was ignored.

"I bloody mean it!" Jimmy gained confidence and at last someone listened.

"You call the bloody pigs," shouted Rathbone from the toilet. "That fooker shot me! That's out of order! As soon as he's out of ammo, he's gonna pray for the coppers to save him!"

Reece smiled to himself. He had enough ammunition to take down an army.

"No coppers, like," said Sid. "We don't need them meddling with me work. I don't know if this killing vampires thingy is legal."

"You're right, Sid," said Reece as he reloaded. "No cops. We'll deal with this ourselves."

"You don't really wanna kill Rathbone, do you?"

"Why not?"

Sid scratched his head. It was a good question. "Well...he's a good...errr. He does a lot of work for...ermmm." Sid gave up. "It just isn't nice, like."

"He isn't human anymore, Sid. He's a vampire. He'll be a murderer within the week." He took a moment to fire another bullet at Rathbone, who had taken the opportunity to peek around the toilet door after hearing a lapse in the gunfire.

"You blew my ear off! You bastard!"

RATHBONE REGROUPED. The toilet looked like a murder scene. It would've been worse if the lads hadn't stopped Rich coming in to cut his head off.

"Wanker!" Rathbone cursed. He felt an itch and an ear started growing out of the side of his head. Vampiring was turning out to be pretty handy. It had sorted his piles out a treat, and he now had a ringpiece as smooth as a Polo mint.

He only had a couple of urinal blocks left. He hoped to make a direct hit and get some piss revenge. His cape hadn't dried yet and it was making him mad.

He looked in the mirror, and boy, did he like what he saw. His high collar on his pure white shirt really brought out his jawline and his new pointy teeth. A black waist coat contrasted the deep crimson lining of his cape. He really did look fooking mint. His hair was slicked back over his head, and yeah, he did look a little pasty, but there was something about him that looked a little bit hunkier.

"Fook this for a game of soldiers."

He wasn't going out like this. No way. With this new look and these new powers, he had women to shag and blokes to punch. First up was that twat Rich, but there was no way he was going to get past the cannon he was brandishing.

What to do... He needed to give himself a fighting chance. If he could avoid a direct shot to the brain, he had a chance. He looked around.

"Perfect."

Jimmy had left his helmet for his pushbike in the gents. That may just give him the edge. What else could he use...

REECE WAS AT A STALEMATE. It was too dangerous to go into the toilets. Even though Rathbone didn't have control of his powers, in a confined space, he was dangerous. Reece's patience was being tested. He longed to sever that bastard's head from his neck. He took a small, round object out of his pocket, much to the dismay of the barman, and even the lads were a little taken aback.

"You can't throw a grenade in there, Rich. That's taking it a bit too far," objected Brian.

"Aye," said Sid. "Explosives shouldn't be used in pub brawls. It ain't cricket, mon."

"Fight like a man, man!" scolded Arthur.

"You can't throw a fooking grenade! This is my pub! You'll destroy it!" screamed Jimmy. "This is madness!"

"Madness?" asked Reece, contemplating. He paused, and then nodding he made his choice. "THIS IS MIDDLESBROUGH!"

RATHBONE COULD HEAR THE COMMOTION REGARDING THE GRENADE. He didn't know if he could regenerate from a grenade blast. It wasn't worth the gamble.

"I'm coming out!" he yelled.

Rathbone edged around the toilet door, hands in the air, hoping Rich wouldn't fire.

"What the fook are you wearing, Rathbone?" asked Sid.

"Jimmy's bike helmet. I don't wanna be shot in the head again."

"Ya dirty, greasy bastard, getting ya grease in me helmet!"

"What have you got in your hand?" asked Brian.

Rathbone hid the toilet brush behind his back. "Nowt."

"Get down on your knees and drop the brush," ordered Rich.

"Canna we talk about this?"

"I won't tell you again."

Rathbone looked to the heavens. He had no choice. It had been more than ten years since the seventy-two break in Merlin's Snooker Hall, and now, as it was then, it was not fear that gripped him, but restlessness, a heightened sense of things. Sid's cigarette smoke kissed the sweat on his chest and neck. Bairns called, complaining even though they had all the Space Raiders they could eat. The steady breathing of the three hundred women in the bingo hall round the corner ready to sleep with him at a moment's pause.

Every one of them ready to sleep with him.

His helmet was stifling.

His cape was heavy.

Both dropped to the floor.

"Your weapon." Rich nodded at the toilet brush dripping from Rathbone's hand.

Rathbone complied and fell heavily onto his knees, allowing his cape to fall free.

Three hundred women ready to sleep with him.

In a moment, he acted.

His helmet was stifling. It narrowed his vision, and he must see far. His cape was heavy. It threw him off balance, and his target was far away.

He launched it.

The toilet brush flew straight and true. Like the spear of a Spartan, it honed in to its target with filthy accuracy.

Everyone in the pub froze with open-mouthed disbelief, and Rich would live to regret leaving his mouth open when the toilet brush landed in it.

"Nice shooting, baby!" said Arthur.

"That's fooking horrible, that," said Sid. "I only just used that bastard to push down the mixed grill I had last night."

It was just vengeance for a pissy, pissy cape.

Rich vomited long and hard.

Rathbone legged it.

9

IT HAD BEEN A SHORT DRINKING SESSION DOWN THE BADGER. After Rich and Rathbone's scrap, Arthur had to go back to her indoors, and Brian decided that Sid's sex drought had gone on long enough. It was time to take matters into his own hands. Brian knew that, as Sid's best friend, it was his duty. He invited Sid back to his place where they continued to drink until they had shared intimate secrets and confessed inner fears. Brian led Sid through to the bedroom. Sid followed with an air of trepidation. This was unchartered territory for both men.

"Brian, I've never done anything like this before."

"It's OK, Sid. I'll guide you. There's no need to be nervous."

Sid nodded, but didn't look convinced, scratching his head awkwardly and rubbing his face with a shaky hand.

"You OK, mate?"

"I don't know, like. I don't even like talking about this sort of thing and can't believe I'm actually gonna try it. What if people find out?"

"No one has to know, mate. No one has to know."

Sid lit up a Marlboro to calm his nerves, and the next three because he loved smoking. He offered one to Brian.

"Marlboros hey?" said Brian, impressed.

Sid nodded. "Aye, earned a job lot of them for landing a sweet jab-cross on some arsehole vampire who'd made some shit selections on the jukebox at a vampire party me and Rich crashed a while back."

Brian didn't ask any more questions. "Sit down there," he said soothingly, indicating the waterbed.

Sid stopped in his tracks. "W...what do you mean?"

Brian smiled. "Just try to relax, pal. Take a seat."

Sid obeyed, wobbling on the liquid mattress. "Maybe this won't be so bad. As you know, I've had a terrible drought with the ladies. I thought being a vampire hunter would've landed me a wealth of stunners, but it hadn't. Fook all. Maybe this is the way. It's the new millennium and you have to be open-minded."

Brian sat on the bed next to him. This was going to be awkward for the both of them, but it was going to be worse for Sid, as he'd never even touched one before. "Are you ready?"

Sid puffed out his cheeks. "Aye, mon."

"Good. Now, take it in your hand."

"I don't want to!"

"Sid, we've come this far. You haven't had sex in over two years. You need something. Now, take it in your hand."

Sid closed his eyes and, ever so slowly, moved his hand towards the tool that would finally bring him satisfaction. He winced as his hand made contact. "It's much smoother than I'd imagined."

"Now, move your finger to the end. Yes, that's it, that's perfect. Apply a little bit of pressure to the tip. Yes. See, that isn't so bad, is it?"

"I...I guess not. What do I do now?"

"It should be obvious, Sid. Just move up and down....whoaaaa! Slow down, you don't wanna break it. I only have one."

"Sorry, Brian, I haven't done this before."

Brian patted Sid on the back. "That's OK, mate. After today, you'll be able to work anyone's, not just mine. But you'll always have mine, Sid...unless I've got a lass round, 'cos that would be a bit weird."

"Aye," laughed Sid. "What would a lass say if you got her back here and I started playing with your thingy?"

Brian laughed. Humour was always good at calming awkward and potentially hostile situations.

"OK, let's try something a little more advanced. Let's try entry. You'll need a bit of coordination."

"I don't think I fancy that, Brian."

"I know it's strange, but give it a go. I want you to gently apply pressure with your index finger—gently, now—and you're there. Just press..."

"Straight in. I'm straight in!" said a satisfied and excited Sid. "Is it always that easy?"

"If I'm all set up properly, then yeah, you can dive straight in. Bet you weren't expecting that, were you?"

"I weren't, mate. I thought it would be a lot more painful than that. I have heard a lot of bad things about it, but now I'm here and doing it, I think I can really get into it."

Brian gave Sid another pat on the back. "Do you want to go a little bit further?"

Sid took a deep breath. "Yeah, let's do it?"

"Reet, move your hand down there," guided Brian, "and click on that bloke."

"Eh?"

"Go on, Sid, double click the button."

"Ain't that a bit, you know, err...*them lot.*"

"'Course it ain't, mate. How can it be? Just 'cos it's a fella, doesn't mean it's dodgy, like."

"Can't I click on a woman?"

"No, mon, it's what they call a 'home page.' All Internet sites have 'em. That fella is Danny Speed. He set up the whole 'boro Internet dating scene."

"Reet, here goes."

Sid's beady, little eyes lit up as beautiful 'boro belles filled the screen. Then his face hardened with a determined look. "When can I nail these birds, Brian? How much do they cost?"

"Easy there, big man. They ain't hookers. This is just like dating a normal lass, but you haven't gotta go through all the shite of meeting 'em first. You still have to take 'em to dinner, buy 'em drinks, and talk to 'em, unfortunately."

Sid scratched his bald dome. "Is that what you're meant to do with lasses?"

"Well, yeah, 'course it is. What do you normally do?"

"You had me driving out to car parks looking for action. I have been doing that for six fooking months now."

Suddenly, Brian felt extremely guilty. He'd never expected Sid to carry on with the whole dogging thing. Poor lad had no luck with the ladies, and he had even less luck with the dogging. If Sid had never gone dogging, he would never have smacked that vampire and would've avoided all the shit he was going through now. "You had any luck?" Brian asked hopefully.

"Fooking none. Loads of *them lot* and fooking perverts, mon."

"Perverts, Sid?" Brian hadn't heard him use the word before.

"Aye, fooking perverts. I thought I was on for a jump last week. I did everything reet: flashed me lights at the reet time, washed me ol' man. I did everything. I went up to this lass's motor and had a look through the window. She was a stunner, I shit you not, and not just that, she showed me her lady garden."

"What did ya do?"

"I tried the door and it was locked, but before I could punch the window through, she started pointing at me ol' man. As you know, I ain't shy, so I showed her a bit of the magic."

"What happened?" said Brian, sensing trouble at mill.

"Well, there I was at the passenger's window, when some fooking pervert shows up on the fooking driver's side!"

"Oh no."

"Made my blood boil, it did, and to make matters worse, she preferred the look of his ol' man to mine! She fooking ignored me over some fooking pervert."

"What did you do?"

"I did what any man would've done, I had a word. The bird weren't impressed and she fooked off." He shook his head. "I don't get it, Brian. Women, they love boxers, they love pro rugby players, they love the hard men in the films, but when I give some twat a pasting in a car park, they get all upset and phone the rozzers."

"You didn't get arrested, did ya?"

"Nah, I got the fook out of Dodge. No rozzer is gonna catch me in the new motor. It's fooking lightning."

"You don't miss the Montego Estate?"

A pained look crossed Sid's face, but he dismissed it with a wave of a giant paw. "There ain't a thing finer than a 1987 Nissan Bluebird four-wheel drive turbo. Yeah, Brian...TURBO!"

Brian was knocked back by a gust of bad breath blown at him with the shout of "TURBO." He picked a bit of Sid's dinner from his cheek before wafting his hand, trying to clear the air of a smell he didn't want to recognise. "I hate it when you shout 'turbo' at me. I know what fooking car you drive."

"TURBO, Brian. I never thought I'd drive Sunderland's finest. Anyroad, I got out of there before any coppers showed up. Enough of all that. My dogging days are done."

"Good. I don't want you traipsing around them car parks at night. You'll be an easy target for them vampire bastards."

"I don't give a fook about them, Brian."

"You'll be an easy target for *them lot too*." He knew that would sober him up. He was right.

"I will never go dogging again," vowed Sid, deadly serious.

Brian gave Sid another pat on the back. "That's good, pal. Now, it's time to bring you back to humanity. A few more computer skills and you'll have free rein on the ol' Internet."

Sid still wasn't completely convinced. "I've heard there're a lot of weirdoes on this ol' Internet thing."

"I ain't gonna lie to you, Sid, there're a lot of weirdoes on the Internet, but there are loads of red-hot sluts too."

"I'm in."

"Where were we? Oh yes, the sluts. Now, I'm gonna level with ya, the women you meet online ain't gonna look like the birds currently on the screen. The birds on screen are there to entice you."

"It worked. How can I shag 'em?" said Sid, looking on with fire in his eyes.

"Have a play. Try clicking on different women to see their profiles. I'll go get us some fresh tinnies."

"Reet you are," said an excited Sid.

Brian walked through his bachelor pad. It was only a small flat, but each room was designed for shagging. Everything was carefully arranged so that there was minimal distance between Brian and his prey. Subliminal messages were discretely displayed to make sure the ladies were thinking of nothing but cock, from the tasteful artwork of phallic-shaped fruits, to the close-up, full-colour photograph of his genitalia.

Brian took a couple of four-packs back through to the bedroom. They wouldn't go warm as he had a fridge next to his bed where he kept a couple of bottles of bubbly chilled in reserve for lady callers.

"Have you found 'owt, Sid?...SID!"

Brian dropped the ales and jumped onto the bed where Sid lay unconscious. Brian slapped Sid round the face, trying to wake him, fearing the worse as the big man wasn't the healthiest of fellas. Brian put his head on his chest to check for a heartbeat and the reason for Sid's lack of consciousness became apparent.

Two, middle-aged, fat, hairy men were going at it, hammer and tongs, on the computer screen. Brian shook his head.

How did Sid stumble upon a hard-core gay porn website?

Brian closed the computer window and Sid instantly regained consciousness. "Find me a lass, Brian."

Brian jumped at Sid's instant revival. "Sid, what happened?"

"What're you talking about, mon?" asked Sid, bemused.

Brian realised that Sid's Gay Defence System had erased the last five minutes of his life and that no bumming had taken place on Brian's PC, or anywhere else on the Internet for that matter.

"Right, let's get you a woman." It was best to pretend nothing had happened. "We need to register you online. The first thing we need to do is to give you a username."

"What's a username, Brian?"

"A nickname. People will be able to identify you online by it. You want something witty, something punchy. Any ideas?"

"'Sid'?" suggested Sid.

This was going to be tough. "Maybe something a bit catchier, a bit sexier maybe?"

"'Monstercock'?"

"That may be where you're going wrong, mate. You need to be less obvious and be a little bit more mysterious with your innuendos. Get me?"

"How about 'Monstercock'...but with a question mark on the end?"

"We'll stick with 'Sid'," said Brian who began to type. "Fook, it's taken."

"What do you mean?"

"Someone has already registered 'Sid' as their username. Means that you can't be 'Sid.' You can be 'Sid1' if you want?"

"I don't wanna be 'Sid1.' My name is Sid. I wanna be called 'Sid.'"

This wasn't a trivial thing for Sid. The ferocity of the stare the computer screen was receiving was testament to that. "There isn't much we can do about it. It doesn't really matter what you're called. It's all about the patter. Great. I have registered you as 'Tillsley the Tease.' Now we have to make a list of your likes and dislikes. What shall we put as your likes?"

"TITS!"

"We need to be a little more classy, a little more discrete."

"TITS!"

"No, Sid, we need to entice the ladies."

"TITS!"

"Come on, think outside the box."

"TITS!"

"How about—"

"TITS!"

Brian sighed. "OK, I'm gonna write 'socialising.'"

Naturally, Sid interrupted, "That better be a posh word for looking at tits, Brian."

"No, Sid, basically it means you like going out for a drink."

"I don't wanna be going out for drinks with lasses. I wanna be nailing 'em."

"Sid," Brian looked his mate square in the eye. "I'm gonna be brutally honest with you. You're not gonna get a woman if you continue with this sort of attitude."

"Brian, mon, you're confusing the hell out of me. The last time I saw you pull, you backed some doris up into a corner while swinging your tadge 'round like a helicopter and told her you were gonna stamp on a puppy's paw if she didn't touch it. What's all this posh shite about?"

"I'm glad you asked. Firstly, with that lass, I was creating an illusion. I would never really stamp on a puppy's paw. I just wanted her to believe that I would have if she didn't touch me tadge. Creating an illusion is fine. It's just like pretending you're a fighter pilot or spraying your boxer shorts with deodorant. Secondly, this is different to pulling birds down the 'boro. The Internet is a much classier place, and the girls need a bit of romancing compared to the lasses downtown."

"Is the Internet a bit too classy for me?"

"Nah, you'll get used to it, and I'll be there to help. So where were we? Ah yes, your likes. We need to think of a few more things to entice the ladies. How about holidays? All lasses love holidays."

"I don't, mon. Unless it's a lad's away day to Scarborough or Skeggy, because then, it's fooking champion."

"No man from the North likes holidays away with the missus, but you don't wanna be saying that on your Internet profile. You've gotta say things that they wanna hear."

"I think I get it." Sid chafed his hands together, ready do get down to business. "Reet. Put down that I like animals. They love all that shit. Remember the crazy bitch I was dating?"

Brian distinctly remembered Sheila Fishman, and he wouldn't have called it "dating." Sid touched her tit once, through her jumper. She tried to get him banged up for benefit fraud and helped a vampire try to murder him. "I can, but you have to be careful with all this stuff. You still wanna come out of all this looking macho. You don't wanna look like, you know, one of *them*..."

Sid raised a hand. "Say no more! Put down that I like tits. I don't want them getting the wrong idea."

Back to square one.

"Look at this, Sid. This is my profile."

"That ain't you! That's Arthur!"

"So?"

"What happens when they turn up and the fella they think they're meeting ain't there?"

"Half the time, they fook off. However, most of them have lied about their pictures too, so they're sort of guilted into staying. They know I lied, I know they lied. It all evens itself out in the end."

"I didn't know you were Evel Knievel's nephew."

"I ain't Evel Knievel's nephew."

"Fooking hell, Brian! I didn't know you were the world's most well-endowed dolphin trainer!"

"I ain't ever trained a dolphin."

"I didn't know you enjoy long walks and cosy nights in."

"That's the biggest lie of all."

Sid rubbed his scalp. "Fook me, Brian. I don't know about all this. It's all based on lies. I've only ever lied to the Benefit Bastards and the rozzers, but that's allowed. I just wanna be meself, and that ain't getting me anywhere."

"Easy, big fella. You're a rough diamond. You're a good person, Sid Tillsley, and I won't have anyone say different. You're too good for all the slags in the 'boro and all the slags on the Internet."

Sid waved his hand. "Oh, you're just saying that!"

"No, I'm not. We're not on this site to find you a wife, but we are gonna get you a jump, and this time without paying for it. I'll sort your profile out, and then you can tell me what you think."

"Cheers mate. Good timing too as I'm desperate for a dump." Sid awkwardly clambered off the waterbed and waddled out of the room.

Brian grimaced and prayed that Sid's visit to the khazi would end well. Brian had placed several wire coat hangers in a bin next to the toilet. Hopefully, they'd be enough. Most plumbers in the area, including Arthur, refused to go near any toilet within Sid's known territories. Kevin had actually installed an extra-large waste pipe in The Miner's to cope with the monstrosities that sailed down it.

Several minutes and several agonising grunts later, the toilet flushed. A minute later, the toilet flushed again. A minute later, the toilet flushed again.

"Fooking 'ell! Have you blocked it?" Brian yelled through the flat.

"No." The toilet flushed again.

"You lying bastard! Use the coat hangers!"

"I wondered what they were for. Reet! Have at you!"

Brian listened to Sid making rapier-like swishing sounds. "I feel like Zorro."

"Zorro didn't break up shit, Sid."

The toilet flushed. "Howay the lads!"

"Thank fook."

"Brian, the coat hanger won't flush."

"You idiot." Brian hadn't thought of the best way of disposing of the offensive weapon. "Chuck it out of the window, mon."

"Right you are...Shit!"

"What's happened now?"

"Have you got any washing outside?"

"Yeah, why?"

"You may need to wash it again."

"Fooking 'ell! Just wash your hands and come and have a look at this profile I've made for you."

A minute later, the two Internet Casanovas were sat on the bed looking through Tillsley the Tease's dating profile. Sid was impressed.

"Brian, that's brilliant. The picture of me looks just like Tony Soprano."

"That *is* Tony Soprano, you daft bastard."

"Aye, you're right. I didn't think I had hair."

Brian laughed. "The picture isn't a bad likeness."

Sid excitedly read his brand new profile. "'Former heavyweight boxer?' Brian, you know boxing damages your brain cells."

"Sid, in all fairness, you've been in a fair few slugging matches in your time. You killed that sixteen-foot vampire-monster thing."

"Glass jaw, mon."

"Didn't you scrap twenty vampires at the same time last week?"

"Glass jaws, mon."

"You've never had a scrap with anyone who you thought was hard, then?"

"I was cut up on a roundabout by Kendo Nagasaki once. He put up a fair fight, like."

Brian didn't pursue the subject. "Anyroad, you gotta show the ladies that you have a sensitive side as well as having the tough-guy exterior. They'll be gaggin' for it. What do you think of the rest of your profile?"

"Animal welfare worker? What the fook is one of them."

"You know, RSPCA officer, that sort of thing. I told you that the lasses need to see your sensitive side too. They wanna have a man who is in touch with their feelings while having the ability to knock any fooker out."

"That sounds like me, Brian."

"Aye, Sid, it is. Problem is, your idea of being in touch with your feelings is probably a little bit different to a lasses. It's a piece of piss, really. Just tell the birds you saved a bin liner full of kittens from drowning, or you untangled a pony's cock from some barbed wire."

"Reet, I get ya."

"You're all ready to go. I've put your advert on the website, and now, we simply wait for some lasses to send you a message. Still wanna go through with it?"

"Aye!"

Brian pressed the ENTER key with a flourish. "Sid Tillsley is on the Internet!"

"Howay the lads!"

"You can entice some lasses in one of the chat rooms, if you like," suggested Brian.

"Eh?"

"Basically, everyone's computer is connected to one place, and if you type something, everyone can see it. What happens is that you get chatting to someone, and then you end up connecting directly to their computer and having a private natter. Sometimes, you can even get lasses to send pictures of themselves to you."

"I'm up for that."

"No probs." Brian tapped away at the computer and placed Sid in a chat room that he knew, from experience, was full of desperate housewives. "All you have to do is type what you wanna say and press that key there to send it. It will take some getting used to, but don't worry. Reet, I'll get some more tinnies."

Brian left Sid tapping away at the keyboard and smoking a tab. All the guilt of Sid's horrific dogging escapades disappeared, and Brian was confident that the big man was going to find a decent bird to bang. Behind the booze and violence was an old romantic. He picked up the beers from the fridge and went back to see how Sid was getting on.

Brian walked into the bedroom to find Sid unconscious...with two, middle-aged, fat, hairy men going at it, hammer and tongs, on the computer screen.

"How the fook does he do it?"

10

YOU COULDN'T CUT THE ATMOSPHERE WITH A KNIFE. It was too thick. A truce had been called between Rathbone and Reece. Each warring faction detested the other. Reece had sworn to kill any lamia, no matter what the consequence and hated Rathbone because he was a vampire. Also, the greasy, horrible, little bastard had thrown a toilet brush into his mouth, making him violently ill.

Rathbone hated Reece because he'd shot him in the head several times. Reece also had a better wax jacket than he did.

There was only one man who could mediate a meeting like this and that was the smartest man on the Smithson Estate, Brian Garforth. Neutral ground, The Badger, was the place for parley, and Jimmy the barman was hoping the encounter wouldn't end in another gunfight.

Sid was here as the enforcer, charged with breaking up any dustups. He'd already put down about ten pints of Bolton Bitter and was picking up pace, so it was unlikely he could be called upon to sort out any trouble.

The two sworn enemies sat at the end of a long bar table. Rathbone had a pint of Redcar Bitter in front of him, and Reece had his usual bottled mineral water. Brian was using his intelligence. It was what he did.

"Rich, you're not to shoot Rathbone anymore. Rathbone, you're not to put your hands on anything in the toilets except toilet paper, hand soap, and paper towels. And, when you've finished with them, you are to dispose of them in a clean and hygienic fashion. Are we all clear?"

Rathbone pointed at the hunter. "He's the one who keeps bloody shooting me."

Reece shrugged. "You're a vampire. You deserve to die."

"I haven't done 'owt wrong."

"Well, that ain't entirely true, is it, Rathbone?" said Brian.

"Well...no, but as a vampire, I haven't done anything worse than I did as a human."

Brian nodded at Rathbone's truthful comment before putting the ball back into Reece's court. "Fair play. Rich, what do you say to that?"

"I've no idea why he's a vampire. Nor, for that matter, have I any idea why Sid can kill vampires with his bare hands or how Arthur has impregnated one. What I do know is that the piece of shit sitting in front of you is a killer. Maybe his instincts have not kicked in yet, but soon, he will crave blood, and when he does, innocent people will die."

"You canna blame me for stuff I haven't done yet," Rathbone whined.

"Lamia, do you have any desire to kill?"

"It's 'Rathbone,' twat, and yeah, 'course I have the desire to kill, but I've always had that."

"He's reet," Sid confirmed. "He's always been an evil, little bastard."

"So, why would anyone care if I killed him, right here, right now?" asked Reece, coldly.

Even the smartest man on the Smithson Estate was stumped. "Well...he's...err...Sid?"

Sid downed his entire pint and called for another, pretending he hadn't heard. Brian was on his own. "Well...err...You can't go around killing people."

"He's not a person; he's a vampire. Sid kills vampires all of the time. What's different about this?"

"Well, Rathbone's got a mother in a home that he has to visit," said Brian.

"Can't stand the bitch. Haven't visited her in years." Rathbone never did himself any favours.

"For fook's sake, Rathbone," said Brian.

Rathbone looked askance at Brian. "What the fook is your problem?"

"I'm trying to help you, mon. You ain't making this easy."

"I'm gonna get another beer." Rathbone went to the bar for a single pint of best.

"Thirsty, vampire?" Reece smirked.

"Aye, dickhead," he said as Jimmy passed over a pint.

"You cannot satisfy your thirst can you? No matter how much you drink?"

Rathbone looked down at his empty glass. Unknowingly, he'd finished the whole pint. "Now you come to mention it, yeah. Is there a bug or summat going round?"

"You desire blood, vampire. It's the only thing that will satisfy the unquenchable thirst."

"Rathbone is a well-done sort of man. He ain't going near any blood," said Brian.

"He won't be able to help himself," said Reece, shaking his head. "He's one of them now. He's dead already."

"No, I'm not."

"You are. You just don't know it yet."

Rathbone shook his head and ordered another pint of Redcar while Brian had a quiet word with the vampire hunter. "Rich, you really have to stop it with all the Hollywood bollocks. You sound like a reet twat when you come out with it."

Reece tried to pretend the comment didn't irk him.

Rathbone sat back down at the table of parley. "Look, can't you just fook off?" the vampire asked. "You've been hanging round here for far too long, and you've stopped getting the beers in too."

"I'm in partnership with Sid. We hunt vampires. Isn't that right, Sid?"

Sid ignored him until two hundred Camels went airborne. "Whatever you say, Rich."

Kristjan Andrus, an Estonian vampire, had made the mistake of being recognised by Sid, who was convinced the vampire had pushed in front of him in the queue for the teacups at Alton Towers. A vengeful right hand had set the record straight.

Brian didn't like Rich or Rathbone, but he had to live with both of them. And, due to his incredible I.Q., it was his duty to sort this out.

"Reet, this is what's gonna happen: Rich, you ain't gonna kill Rathbone, and I'm gonna tell you why."

"This better be good." Reece settled back into his chair.

"You can learn a lot from Rathbone. You've never had a chance to study a vampire like this. Studying Rathbone may lead to new ways to kill them."

Reece contemplated the proposition, which, astonishingly, made sense. He could kill Rathbone later, but the knowledge he could acquire... "You just saved your friend's life."

"He's not my friend!" said Brian and Rathbone indignantly and in unison.

"Very well. He'll live as long as he's useful. However, if he even comes close to harming another human being, he will be dead in a heartbeat."

"Then we're reet," said Brian, with finality.

Rathbone, however, wasn't impressed. "What the fook do I get out of this? That's crap. What's stopping me putting another toilet brush in his fooking—"

The force of the bullet to the chest took Rathbone off his chair.

"You've got a deal," groaned Rathbone as he got up, dusted down his cape, and offered out his hand.

"I'm not shaking the hand of the damned," said Reece, holstering his weapon.

Brian raised his eyes heavenward. "Fine, Rich, shake my hand and I'll pass it on." Reece obliged, and then Brian offered his hand to Rathbone, who gave it his trademarked, limp-wristed, sweaty wet fish.

"Ow, that...ow...that fooking burns, mon!" Rathbone was out his chair quicker than when he was shot off it. "What the fook have you got on your hands?" He ran to the toilets to run his hand under cold water.

"What's up with him?" asked Sid, returning to the table now that the awkwardness was over and done with.

"Not sure," said Brian looking at his hand, and then it dawned on him. "Oh, shit!"

"What is it?" asked Reece.

"It all makes sense now!"

"What!" demanded Reece.

"It's me jizz! Me jizz kills vampires!"

"What are you talking about?"

Brian regaled the story of the snooker slag from Merlin's and how she'd exploded when he gave her the gift of his seed.

Cogs whirred in Sid's brain. "So what just happened with Rathbone, then? It must mean that…"

Brian didn't want to explain why he had semen on his hands, but Sid had put two and two together and was about to knock out five because it was queer.

"Sid, first thing—stop thinking. Second thing, I'm gonna explain everything, even though I'm not the sort to kiss and tell." Brian told the tale of the morning's steamy encounter with Jimmy the barman's mother. Brian had the decency to start off with discretion but couldn't help himself as the crowd was gagging to hear more. Well, not the entire crowd. Rathbone was still in the toilet, desperately washing his hand, and Jimmy the barman was crying inconsolably…not that anyone tried to console him. Reece wasn't listening. He was too busy worrying about the sexually transmitted diseases currently working their way from his hand to more susceptible parts of his body. Only Sid sat enchanted by Brian's tale. It was just like reading the dirty stories in *Tits*.

"…So yeah, funnily enough, it ended up all over me thumb!"

Sid roared with laughter and clapped his appreciation, while Jimmy the barman considered taking his own life.

Reece wondered what set this group of down-and-outs apart. What was the link? Each of them affected vampires in a way that was linked to their physical attributes.

Sid had been a hard-case since he was a kid. He was always the toughest guy around. Arthur was a man whom women were drawn to. Were they attracted to his fertility or his looks? How could he impregnate a different species? The only reason Reece hadn't hunted down Lucia was because he wanted to see what genetic marvels the hybrid child would bring. The weasel, Garforth, his diseased genitalia should've killed him years ago. How could his semen kill vampires but not the local population of bored housewives? And finally, the greasiest, most horrible little bastard Reece had ever met: Rathbone. Instead of dying, he'd managed to survive and annoy from the grave. What did these men have in common? Were there more like them? Could he use them as a weapon? Garforth was right about Rathbone, studying him would yield a wealth of knowledge. Reece realised that all four of these friends could bring untold treasures, but his rudimentary lab couldn't give him the answers he sought.

"You're all barred! You're all fooking barred!" sobbed Jimmy.

"Don't be like that, lad," said Brian. "It was only a bit of fun. You canna deny your mother a little bit of fun, can ya? After all, she's a widow."

"No, she ain't! My dad's in fooking hospital!" Jimmy shouted through the tears trickling down his face and onto his lips.

Brian rolled his eyes. "Come on, Jimmy. He may as well be dead."

"You're barred!" It was all Jimmy had left.

"Right you are, Jim," said Brian, ignoring him.

"Pint of Bolton, please, Jim?" requested Sid.

"Fook off!" sobbed Jimmy.

"Right you are, Jim" said Sid, who made his way round the bar and pulled himself a pint. "Ale, Brian?"

"Aye."

Sid obliged and pulled another pint. He dropped a fiver on the table by Jimmy and patiently waited for his change. Poor Jimmy. His business was ruined, as was his family life. He took for the beer and threw the money across the bar.

"That's the spirit, lad," encouraged Sid. He did feel a bit sorry for Jimmy, but he should keep his beer better. That was what made Kevin Ackroyd untouchable. His beer was immaculate. That sort of behaviour demanded respect. The fact that both his mother-in-law and missus were absolute horrors probably had something to do with it too.

Meanwhile, Reece was thinking long and hard about how he could turn Brian's "gift" into a weapon. "Brian, did you wash your hands after it came into contact with your semen?"

"'Course I did," said an offended Garforth until he thought a moment. "Well, I wiped my hand on the curtains, like. Does that count?"

"Not really." Reece grimaced. "Brian, I need a sample of your..." He stopped mid-sentence and saved himself a broken jaw. Sid wouldn't be able to understand that the chemical and biological testing of another man's semen wasn't an act of rampant homosexuality. For Reece, this really was hard work sometimes.

"Sample of me what?" asked Brian, as Rathbone returned from the toilets.

"Nothing. It isn't important. I'll be back." And with that, he got up and went to the bogs.

"Thank fook he's gone," said Brian with a relieved sigh.

"Aye. I was just about to kick the shit out of him," said Rathbone.

"Sure you were. You're scared shitless of him."

"Am fooking not!" He flourished his bullet hole-ridden cape around himself defensively and added pathetically, "He keeps shooting me in the head."

"He has been rather rude," admitted Sid, lighting up one of the cigarettes Reece had given him. "He does keep me in tabs, though. He canna be all bad, like."

Rathbone wasn't getting the sympathy he thought he deserved. It was tough being a vampire. He went to the bar and pulled himself a pint of Redcar. Unlike Sid, he didn't give Jimmy any money. The beer went down in one. It didn't fulfil him. He fancied something a little more...metallic.

"Hey guys," said a dishevelled Arthur Peasley, entering the building.

"What's that on your head, Arthur?" asked Brian.

"Eh? What do you mean?"

"Looks like a thumb-print to me!"

Sid erupted with laughter while Rathbone pointed and jeered, glad that someone else was getting a rough time of it.

"Arthur is that a pinny you're wearing?" asked Sid, eager to jump on the bandwagon.

"No," said a confused Arthur.

Sid continued unabashed, "Because you do all the cleaning and cooking and stuff." There was a brief moment when everyone tried to work out if this was actually a joke or not, but when Sid looked around hopefully, people joined in the hilarity.

It just left Rathbone to finish off the mocking of poor Arthur. "Ya hen-pecked prick."

"You all right there, Arthur?" Brian returned the group to relative normality.

"She's at it again. The woman is making my life a misery." Arthur pulled at his hair in frustration and the newly created style took cool to a new level. "Now she wants me to paint the spare room and turn it into a nursery. She won't leave it alone. She moans about the nursery then the toilet then the nursery then the toilet. What have I got myself into?"

"Just kick her out, then," suggested Brian.

"I can't," Arthur moaned. He was a good man at heart. "Jimmy, pint of Bolton over here." Arthur noticed that the barman had his head in his hands and was crying at a rate to cause dehydration. "What's up with Jimmy?"

"He's being a big pansy," said Brian. "What do you want? I'll get it for ya."

"If it's a free bar, you might as well make it a pint and a chaser."

"FREE BAR!" shouted Sid and ran, as best he could, in order to take advantage of the landlord's generous offer.

While Sid was at the bar, Reece returned from the toilets. "Brian, a private word."

"Eh?" said Brian. Their mutual disdain wasn't something they hid.

"I have a business proposition for you."

"What have you got in mind?" said Brian, after they'd moved far enough away for Sid not to here. Even though Brian hated the vampire hunter, he was minted.

Reece took out a packet of condoms causing Brian to recoil. "I've thought of a way of using your powers against the vampires. I need two of these, used, for samples. One I will analyse to see if I can find a chemical the vampires are allergic to. The other, I will test as a weapon."

"It's a bit weird, like," said Brian, sneering up his face.

"I will give you a hundred pounds for each one."

"Deal," said Brian, his sneer replaced by a smile. He offered his hand.

Reece declined it. "I'll get to it then." Brian took the three-pack off to the gents for some quiet time.

Sid, Rathbone, and Arthur came back from the bar carrying trays full of top-shelf spirits and pints of ale.

"Where's Brian?" asked Sid.

"He's gone to the gents," said Reece.

"Ah well, he'd better hurry up, because I'm gonna need to use the facilities in a bit."

The lads started knocking back ale at a mighty pace, which concerned Reece, considering the importance of the mission he and Sid were about to undertake. Reece was soon to strike deep into the heart of the vampire nation, but only if his weapon of mass destruction was sober enough to fight.

"Take it easy, Sid. We have a long day tomorrow."

"I'll be reet," said the big man, whisky in one hand, brandy in the other. "Here comes Brian. Brian, mon! You're missing out on all the booze. You alright?"

Brian limped over to the table, obviously in discomfort. "Rich, can you give me a hand getting the beers in, please?" he asked.

"Yes, of course."

The two men went to the bar. One walked, one limped. "What's wrong, Brian?"

"I canna do it, mon. I've always hated these things with good reason, but I never thought that the fookers would be so painful. Contraception is the fooking word. I couldn't even get a semi on."

"What are you on about? They shouldn't be that uncomfortable. Not unless you're massive...down there."

"That, I ain't," Brian turned around to check that no one was looking. "Look at it!" he said, pulling down his trousers and pants.

Reece looked away in disgust. The man's genitals looked like they were suffering from a dose of leprosy. But something made him look again—and burst out laughing.

Brian pulled his pants back up before the other lads looked around. "What you laughing at, ya twat?"

"It's not meant to go on your testicles."

"How am I meant to know where the fooking thing's supposed to go?" Brian said. "I'm a real man. Why would I wear one of these things? That's where your swimmers are. I thought that crushing 'em in a bag of pain would keep 'em in there."

"Go try again. I'm sure you will find the experience more comfortable." Reece struggled to hold in his laughter. Smartest man on the estate, indeed.

Brian bit his tongue and headed back to the toilets.

"I thought you were getting the beers in," called Sid as Brian went past.

"Fook off!"

The lads continued to put booze away while Reece nervously watched Sid pick up the pace. Rathbone, who was drinking at a rate that would kill a human, was lapping him.

"Still thirsty?" asked Reece.

"'Course. It's a free bar."

"You look tired, Rathbone. You look thinner too. Do you feel ill?"

"Fook off." But Reece was right. He wasn't feeling quite right when the other day he'd never felt better.

Brian returned a few minutes later. He had a bit of a knee-tremble going on. "Can you help me get another round of drinks at the bar, Rich?"

"Certainly."

"Fooking champion, mon," said Sid.

Once they were out of earshot and he knew that the lads wouldn't see, Brian pulled out the merchandise.

"What on earth is that?" asked Reece, eyes wide with amazement.

"It's me...you know...stuff."

"It's the wrong colour."

"Eh?"

"And why is it glowing?"

"'Cos it's fresh," said Brian, matter-of-factly.

"What's that smell?"

"Do you want it or not?" asked Brian, losing patience.

Reece handed over five twenties. He then took out a handkerchief and offered it to Brian who put the tied, but oozing, prophylactic inside before handing it back. "I need one more."

"Fooking 'ell, mon, I ain't getting any younger. Give me a minute," begged Brian. "Help me with the beers first." He walked around the bar.

"Sid has his most dangerous mission coming up. If he goes into battle and isn't on form, it could well be the end of him."

"Sid can handle 'owt when it comes to a punch-up. Let the big man have some fun for once. You're always on his case. Come on, bring some ales over."

Reece felt a cold, clammy, burning sensation on his leg. A wet patch was visible on the pocket where he'd put Brian's used condom. The fabric of his trousers began to steam.

"That's disgusting." He withdrew a rubber glove from his coat, pulled it on, and removed the offending weapon from his trouser pocket. The prophylactic had almost completely perished. He placed the tissue in a glass while trying not to gag from the smell and covered it in some tin foil he found behind the bar. He hid the glass in the pub's fridge with the non-alcoholic beverages, the only safe place on the premises.

"What good are them things gonna do?" Brian asked as he pulled another pint. "If they break that easy, no wonder they have such a bad rap."

"If you can fill another one before Rathbone leaves, I'll give you two hundred for it."

Brian knew Reece was up to no good, but to Brian, two hundred notes was two hundred notes. "Consider it done. Now, let's get these beers back."

"About time!" said an impatient Tillsley. "We've a lot to drink to. After tomorrow, most of me hard work will be finished with, and the next day, I'm going on me first date in two years."

"Howay the lads!" shouted Brian and raised his glass, which was acknowledged by Sid and Arthur. Rathbone didn't bother. He was too thirsty to toast Sid's getting lucky and finished his pint before the others even started theirs.

"I told you that the ol' Internet dating would pay dividends, fella," said Brian.

"Who is she, man?" asked Arthur.

"She goes by Sunderland Sue, and funnily enough, you or Brian haven't nailed her."

Both Arthur and Brian looked shocked.

"Good luck, man," said Arthur. "I'm sure you'll be fine and dandy. Just love her tender, and she'll be back for seconds."

"Cheers, mate. I canna wait."

"Worry about tomorrow, first, Sid. It's dangerous to think of anything else," warned Reece.

As one, the lads raised their eyebrows. "What's so dangerous about tomorrow's mission?" asked Brian.

"I cannot divulge any information."

Brian held up his hands in dismay. "Well, how the fook can he keep his mind on the mission, then?"

"If he goes in drunk, he will die. It's as simple as that. There'll be hundreds of vampires ready to destroy us at a moment's notice."

"Sid'll be reet," said Brian. "Last time we went to the 'boro/Newcastle derby, he ended up in the wrong stand, the daft bastard. If he can survive that, he can survive anything."

"So that's why everyone was rather rude," said Sid, finally understanding why a thousand people had simultaneously attacked him.

Meanwhile, Jimmy the barman had stopped crying and now stared at the table where the four drinkers sat racking up an enormous bar bill. He'd adopted the thousand-yard stare. The lights were on, but no one was home.

Rathbone followed Arthur to the bar and pulled a bottle of whisky from the optic. He was still thirsty and wasn't even a little bit merry. A bottle of spirits would surely get him on his way.

Sid took himself to the toilet, leaving Brian and Reece alone once more.

"Three hundred for the condom."

"Alreet, you just got the last one. I ain't eighteen anymore. I ain't even got any stimulation."

Reece was desperate to try out an idea he'd formulated on how to use Garforth's vampire-lethal semen. "Will a thousand pounds stimulate you enough?"

"I could be pulling nowt but a floppy for a while, but I'll give it me best." He took two blue pills to make sure and, as soon as Sid was out of the toilets, went to war. The fact that Sid only needed to urinate gave Brian a fighting chance.

A half hour passed before the swordsman returned, limping. He looked drained. He was drained. He'd been to heaven and back three times that day, twice flying solo, and a man of his age wasn't meant to perform such sexual heroics. He raised a thumb to Reece.

With the specimen captured, Reece had to move quickly before the toxic semen/venom ate its way through the rubber. He gloved up once more. Luckily, the other lads were too drunk to notice. He got to his feet, met Brian at the toilet door, and handed him the money.

"Quick, put the end on there."

"What are you up to?" said Brian, looking at the pencil Reece held tight in his hand.

"Just do it!"

"Alreet, keep your hair on."

Reece pulled back on the condom to make a dirty catapult. This was the danger zone. If the semen ate through the rubber, it might break when he pulled it back to cock the weapon. Feeling the strained tension in the rubber jonny, he knew he only had seconds... and seconds were all he needed.

"Hey, Rathbone!"

"Eh? What do you—Oh, shite!"

Flying straight and true, the deadly condom was on course for Rathbone's forehead, who stood transfixed by his airborne nemesis.

Nevertheless, the reactions of the vampire were now his. He moved just in time, *Matrix*-like, and watched the condom fly by. But traces of the noxious liquid hit him in the face and he fell to the floor screaming as if he'd been drenched in acid. However, the condom still had metres of potential energy left within its rubbery spirit.

Karma is a funny thing. This group of men had ruined Jimmy's pub and therefore taken away his livelihood. They'd stolen hundreds of pounds of booze from him. One of them had had sex with his mother while his father was terminally ill in hospital. What had he done to deserve that?

The answer: He didn't look after his beer.

Fate and Karma had one more punishment in store for Jimmy the barman.

Poor Jimmy the barman.

"It's in his eye. Why the fook isn't he blinking?" wondered Brian.

"What the fook is going on?" asked Sid.

"Yeah, man," said Arthur. "Why is Rathbone in agony? And what the hell is that over Jimmy?" The condom had completely dissolved. The only thing in view was a strange, glowing, viscous liquid covering the barman's face.

Jimmy started twitching. The burning sensation brought him slowly back to the land of the living. Luckily for him, he didn't know what was covering his face. Unluckily for him, Brian Garforth was standing by.

"Hahahaha! He looks just like his mam."

Everyone has a breaking point.

Jimmy reacted like a madman, but his actions weren't against the offending gentlemen, they were against his beloved pub. Grabbing the baseball bat from below the bar, he went to work.

"MY BEER IS SHITE, IS IT? MY BEER IS SHITE, IS IT? MY BEER IS SHITE, IS IT?" he screamed as he smashed the beer pumps and the lines to smithereens. Beer sprayed everywhere.

"Yeah, it fooking is!" Brian wasn't first on the waiting list for a job at the Samaritans.

"WELL, YOU WON'T HAVE TO DRINK IT EVER AGAIN, WILL YOU?"

The lads watched as Jimmy decimated the spirits shelf with wild flurries of the bat. Most people would've been nervous of a maniac with a bat but not these lads. They were used to it.

Reece was a happy man. He could see the potential in his newfound weapon. Rathbone was still on the floor. If he'd been hit with the full force, he would be dead for sure. Reece needed to perfect the launching device and use a material that wouldn't be destroyed by whatever it was Brian produced.

The lads left the pub, shaking their heads at the booze that had been wrongfully murdered. It was the saddest Reece had seen them since The Miner's was shut. At least there'd be no more boozing and Sid would get a good night's sleep and, hopefully, wake in a relatively healthy state.

"THAT'S RIGHT! NO MORE DRINKING IN HERE! NO MORE SMOKING IN HERE! YOU CAN'T DRINK WHAT ISN'T HERE! HAHAHAHAHAHA!"

Jimmy's manic laughter didn't end. The lad was heading for the loony bin.

"End of a good piss-up, that," mourned Sid.

"Sure was, baby," agreed Arthur. "I may as well go back home and get yelled at."

"I'm going to bed," announced Brian. "Three times in a day ain't good for ya, like."

"Reet," said Sid, "I'm off to get meself a kebab before bedtime."

Reece hoped it was out of Sid's system before tomorrow night where he would undertake the most ambitious mission of his life. He would enter the lion's den and come out a hero. Reece needed help for such an audacious adventure, and he had it in spades. If Sid completed the mission—and survived—Reece would barter for a few treasures, which could help him understand what these four lads were and how he could use them for the battle ahead.

11

"I HAVE DONE THY BIDDING, MY MASTER. Now, give me the fucking name, or I will find out who you are and rip out your beating heart." Gunnar had started sarcastically, but his temper flared, and he'd spat the end of the sentence down the mobile phone that had been left for him all those weeks ago.

He'd destroyed the vampires' chemical plant, because his controller at the Coalition had demanded it. Now, they had to pay the price for his services.

He sat alone on top of the spire of St. Teresa's Church, Chesterfield. Over the last few days, he'd travelled south from Rapunzel's Nightclub in Newcastle, running through the hills, swimming across rivers, and scaling buildings as he went, trying to burn the excess energy that relentlessly fuelled his body. He ran to try and free his mind from the guilt of killing his only remaining friend. The agonising pain of his testes accompanying every step was a vicious reminder.

He gripped the phone so hard that the plastic cracked. "Give me the name, or you're going to have a news crew within the hour wondering why every member of this church I'm sitting on has been crucified. Give me the fucking name!"

He felt the darkness creep over him. *Hold strong. Hold...*

"Edward Limkin, Nottingham," said the muffled voice.

"Let's hope for your sake that he comes up with the goods." Gunnar put the mobile phone back in his pocket. Edward Limkin, the man who would bring him peace. There was light at the end of the tunnel, and then a time for grieving, followed by a life fuelled by nothing but revenge.

First, Tillsley, then the world.

Gunnar sat on the church roof, trying to gather his thoughts. He'd nearly blacked out again while screaming down the phone at his puppeteer from the Coalition. It was getting worse. He lost control quicker every day and for no reason. He needed to find the strength to stay calm when he met Edward Limkin. Gunnar hoped that calm lay somewhere inside him.

He jumped off the church roof and the wind whistled through his hair. His knees didn't buckle when he hit the ground. He had power beyond his wildest dreams but no means to wield it.

"What are you doing here?"

Gunnar's head snapped round quickly. He didn't know anyone was in the churchyard. "I'm doing whatever the fuck I like," he said to the approaching old man.

The man sighed. "Laddie, that's no way to talk in the presence of God." He gave Gunnar a sorrowful smile. "What's the matter?"

Gunnar noticed the dog collar. "Nothing your god could put right. He has no place for my kind."

"God has a place for everyone in the Kingdom of Heaven, my son," came the polite retort.

"I'm not your fucking son!" Gunnar snapped. *Hold on,* he told himself and fought the blackness that closed in on him. If he couldn't control his temper at a mere turn of phrase, what chance did he have when confronted with Edward Limkin?

But, the old vicar wasn't discouraged. "Want to come inside out of the cold and talk about it?"

To Gunnar, God-fearing folk were cattle, just like all the rest. Would they believe their sacred books if they knew that demons walked the earth? The vampire was the ultimate force. Would God have made a lesser being in his own image? Gunnar considered the slight clergyman, and a wry grin formed.

"Father, forgive me." He relaxed his stance. "Let me tell you my troubles." He followed the clergyman inside. He'd rarely visited a church or any other place of prayer. The architecture of the empty building was impressive. He couldn't take that away from the monkeys.

He couldn't imagine living for a meagre seventy years while enduring illness, disease, cancer, poverty, and wars resulting in the loss of millions, and all the time thanking your Maker for it. However, for these fragile beasts, the torment was over in the blink of an eye. He endured the loss of loved ones for hundreds of years. At times like these, he saw death as a gift.

Edward Limkin was his chance, but only if he could harness his emotions. That was the reason he sat in confessional with a Roman Catholic priest. It was time to test his restraint with a human, and a man of the cloth should be the least obnoxious of the vermin.

"Tell me what ails you, my lad." His voice was mildly comforting.

"I have murdered my best friend, Father."

"Why did you do that?"

Gunnar smiled. The priest's voice was calm. Gunnar may as well have been making pleasantries about the weather. Either the priest dealt with a lot of compulsive liars or this was a rough neighbourhood.

"I lost it. When I lose control, there's nothing that can calm me."

"Calmness can always be found, my son. The eye of the storm is tranquillity while chaos dances around it. God always offers a hand—"

"Your god has nothing to do with it," he snarled back, a moment of anger but not enough to open the floodgates.

"Look inside yourself, lad. There's an inner peace in all of us, an inner sanctity. Even if you don't believe in Our Lord, every religion speaks of it. I can smell the evil on your breath. I can sense the demons lurking inside you. Look within yourself and find an ounce of peace. Find one happy moment and cling to it."

"I have no..." Gunnar trailed off. He was going to mock the priest, but anything was worth a try. Anything that could help him hold on to a thread of sanity was worth a shot. Meditation was something he hadn't practised for centuries. Why hadn't he thought of it sooner? Because the pressure in his testes had masked all sane judgement.

He needed to practise. He needed to meditate before he met the man who could save him. The vampire burst out of the booth, out of the church, and into the night. He made eye contact with the statue of Jesus as he went. These were the queerest of times.

12

BWOGI RELAXED BACK INTO A GRAND THRONE and swilled a glass of fine wine. This should be a time to relax and enjoy the festivities. The Occursus was finally here.

The Occursus was only held once a decade, and this was the most extravagant celebration of the event the world had ever seen. Planning had started a year in advance, but after the Firmamentum and the appearance of Sid Tillsley, the Coalition had decided to plunge a great deal more money into the project to raise spirits and, hopefully, avoid war.

Bwogi had commissioned the reconstruction of Ardvreck Castle, a sixteenth century masterpiece that hugged the coastline of Loch Assynt, Scotland. The castle had burnt to the ground in the seventeenth century, and its remote location made it a perfect spot for the festivities. Originally, Slain's Castle was the choice, but with the plummeting morale of the vampire nation, the scale of the event had escalated, and Slain's position in the middle of the busy city of Aberdeen made it too much of a risk. It was a shame, as the magnificent castle was credited as Bram Stoker's inspiration for his novel *Dracula*. Bwogi knew otherwise.

It was Ricard, the old genius, who "commissioned" Stoker to write a novel about the vampire as a brilliant piece of propaganda for there were a number of incidents threatening the Agreement at the time. The writings of Stoker caused the number of false allegations of vampirism to rise exponentially, diluting the real stories and leaving the authorities no choice but to dismiss everything as public delusion. If only things were that simple in the age of the video camera.

The reconstruction of Ardvreck Castle was a triumph. A large chunk of the investment would be raked back, as the castle would be converted into a hotel with golf courses hewn into the surrounding countryside. A few centuries ago, this would've become a vampire stronghold, but those days were well and truly gone.

Five hundred vampires were invited to the event, and it would be the largest congregation ever recorded. It was a sign of strength at a time of weakness. For every vampire present, there was a human who would wait on them—and probably wondering why there was no food to serve. At midnight, they would find out. The finest musicians in the world entertained the crowd. Naturally, they were lamia.

Bwogi closed his eyes. He'd never heard anything quite so enchanting.

It wasn't every day that one could listen to a millennia of experience coming from a handful of individuals.

He sat on a balcony overlooking the great hall below where all the guests were comfortably enclosed along with most of the humans. The restoration encompassed all the original features of the castle yet with a modern feel, and the result was stunning, even by a vampire's standards. The restoration represented the Coalition's goals: mixing old and young. In the crowd mingling below, the old, powerful vampires stood out like beacons. There were more here than he'd originally hoped for, and it sent a signal to the younger generations: There was unity in the vampire nation.

Tonight, Bwogi had a chance to relax. He was tired. So tired. He sat alone and savoured the peace. The security for the event was, most likely, overkill. A no-fly zone had been declared on a ten-mile radius of the castle. A ship, courtesy of the Royal Navy, patrolled the coastline. A circular defensive ring, enforced by the British Army, was deployed five miles from the castle, and a hundred vampires patrolled the grounds. Bwogi had to admit that Sanderson did his job well. Gunnar Ivansey would not trouble them this evening.

"HOW MUCH FOOKING LONGER HAVE I GOTTA HIDE IN THIS BASTARD?"

"Sssshhhh! Keep it down or they'll hear us," Reece whispered desperately to an uncomfortable Tillsley.

"So fooking what? I thought the plan was that we start smacking 'em. Why can't I start now?"

"There are five hundred of them in there, and a hundred patrolling the grounds. We'll be dead before we reach the castle, so less with the mouth."

Sid complied but broke wind with bass-heavy gusto, which, unfortunately, was pitched at the resonant frequency of the crate they were both hiding in.

"What was that?" came the muffled voice of the driver of the van that carried them. He slammed on the brakes.

"Sid, you idiot! What the fu—*gak*!" Reece dry-heaved.

"Sorry, mon. I think that kebab from last night was a bit off, like."

Moments after stopping the vehicle, the lorry driver was pulling off the lid of the crate, and Reece escaped the worst possible death by asphyxiation. He took a huge gulp of fresh air. The driver and his assistant took in the situation, and then the stench reached them. Mercifully, Sid's fists hit them before they could consciously breathe in any more of the noxious gas.

"Thank fook for that. That was a stupid plan, Rich."

Reece began to reprimand the smelly vampire hunter. "We've only just got past the roadblock. If the guards see our van's stopped, we're dead. Quick, get into his clothes."

Sid shrugged. "I don't know what you're so worried about. Once it all kicks off, they're all gonna come running anyway, and then we'll have to start smacking people." He climbed into the van driver's overalls, who was, luckily, as unhealthy as Sid.

"We have an escape plan. Don't worry."

"I weren't worrying. I'd just prefer to get it over and done with."

After dumping the two bodies into their now-abandoned crate, the two hunters made their way up to the castle. Reece drove.

"Right, we're nearly there. Let me do the talking, and for god's sake, try not to fart again. Hang on..." He suddenly remembered Sid's last comment. "You agreed to this attack thinking I didn't have an escape plan? Why would you agree to a suicide mission?"

"I'm running out of tabs," said Sid, lighting up a Dunhill. He'd come into a tidy little number for sticking the nut on Pasco Myghal, a particularly violent vampire. Sid could've sworn he went to his house party a couple of years ago and had picked out the vampire for a kicking after he'd made the mistake of putting the ready-salted and the mixed-flavour crisps in the same bowl.

Reece took the tradesmen's entrance to the castle, causing Sid to chuckle as they drove past.

"How d'ya know where you're going?"

"It's all planned, Sid. I know everything about this place, its guests, and its geography. It would've been easier if we hadn't been discovered, but I have accounted for every eventuality."

"How the fook do you know all this?"

"Let's just say I'm getting a lot of help from an inside source."

"Is it Brian?"

"No, Sid, it isn't Brian." Reece shook his head slowly at Sid's stupidity. "Do you really care?"

"Good point." Sid went back to not caring.

"Right, here we go. We have to check in with the guard over there near the main entrance."

Reece gradually slowed the van. He and Sid both had baseball caps pulled down low so the guard wouldn't see their faces. Reece wound down the window. "Got a delivery for you, pal," he said in a Scottish accent.

Sid gave him a funny look, not expecting the voice change.

"What are you carrying?" the guard asked, his vampirism stood out a mile, and it was exactly what Reece expected.

"Fireworks, pal."

The vampire looked down the list on the clipboard before nodding. "Good, you're on time. Now, let's see some identification."

"Terry has our identification," said Reece, giving Sid a knowing nod. The vampire checked down the list to make sure that Terry was one of the drivers.

Unsurprisingly, Sid didn't twig.

"Terry," said Reece, slow and deliberately, "give the man our identification."

"Who the fook is...ahhh!" said Sid with a dropping penny, giving the side of his nose a tap. "I get ya." Sid got out of the van and gave the vampire the identification of the unconscious deliverymen.

The vampire looked at it and his brow furrowed. He looked up to a grinning Tillsley. "Oh, fu—" said the vampire, before receiving an extreme close-up of a very, very big fist.

Reece nodded his appreciation. "Sid, pick up his radio and clipboard and let's get these fireworks delivered. The less commotion we make, the easier our job will be."

Sid carried out his orders to the letter and got back into the van, looking smug. "What do you think, Rich? I was like Roger Moore there, weren't I, mon?"

"Yes, Sid, very James Bond. Keep it up." *Stupid twat,* he thought.

Once inside the castle, they delivered the fireworks to the castle's gardens. Reece was determined for them to stick as rigidly to the Occursus's plan as possible, and if the fireworks didn't turn up, questions would be asked.

After dropping off the fireworks, the two went back to the van to pick up another crate that Reece had smuggled aboard. They moved around the service corridors of the castle without difficulty, but Reece's easy ride came to an end when he reached an obstacle his partner found insurmountable.

"You're having a fooking laugh," said the stubborn mule.

"What are you talking about?"

"I didn't sign up for no fooking assault course. I came here for a fooking ruck and for some good money. You'll be expecting me to do fooking star jumps and press-ups like that Mr. Motivator arsehole."

The problem was one short, shallow flight of stairs.

"Sid, we have to go up there. It's just one flight, please!"

Sid's face turned heart-attack red. "I hate Mr. Motivator, and I ain't climbing no fooking stairs, especially carrying this fooking crate."

Reece closed his eyes. He was so close to his target, he could have cried. Meanwhile, human servants scurried about, not paying much attention to him and Sid dressed in their stolen uniforms. Reece would've known their fates even if he wasn't privy to tonight's fatal events. Most of the staff were of Asian and Eastern European origin, illegal immigrants smuggled in from abroad. They were untraceable and just kids, barely twenty years old. No one would bat an eyelid when they went missing.

The contents of the crate Sid carried had taken all of Reece's skills and innovation. He knew it'd be impossible to take any metal into the castle, so he'd relied on the twentieth century's greatest invention: Kevlar. He had constructed battle suits for himself and Sid. He'd made some Kevlar blades, too, but they still had to rely on Sid's fists, an airtight escape plan, and a little extra help from three kilos of Semtex to get them out alive. The British Army's sniffer-dogs had gone wild at the crates where Sid and Reece had hid. However, no search took place as they were officially carrying gunpowder and the guards were expecting the dogs to react.

Reece planned to use the Semtex in conjunction with a gas leak he would rig from the kitchens. However, to access the kitchens, he needed to climb these stairs. He didn't expect this sort of fuss, though in hindsight, he should've done.

"Sid, come on. These are the only stairs you have to climb. I'll give you a pack of cigarettes for every stair."

Sid considered the offer. "Alreet, you have a deal."

"Good. Let's go."

It was slow going, and the spectacle of a complaining Tillsley brought unwanted attention. Five steps in, Sid made an announcement. "That'll do me, Rich. I think I'm gonna take me hundred tabs and call it a day, like."

"What're you talking about? You said you'd do it."

"No, *you* said I could have a pack of tabs for every stair. You never said there was a minimum stair requirement," replied the sly ol' fox.

"Climb the fucking stairs, or we're in trouble."

"I don't think I like your tone, Rich." The offended gentlemen sat down.

"Is there a problem?" came a voice from the top of the stairs.

Shit, thought Reece. Just what he feared: a vampire.

"Yeah, that prick is being a twat," said Sid, eloquent to the last.

IT WAS ALMOST MIDNIGHT AND TIME FOR THE FEEDING FRENZY. Bwogi wouldn't take part. Even as a young vampire, he never had a voracious appetite and only needed to feed every few months. Some of the vampires below were restless and a few had already taken their fair share of the staff. If only they could control their bloodlust, then the species wouldn't be in this predicament.

And that was what made the Coalition's job so difficult. They needed to control and suppress the vampire, but they couldn't deny the birthright of a species. Haemo, though, could do just that, and Bwogi was the reason the project had been re-initiated.

Augustus joined Bwogi on the balcony. "Having fun?"

Bwogi laughed. "I've embraced the much-needed rest. It's been a difficult year, has it not?"

"What a ridiculous understatement. Look at them down there. They've no idea what's happening, not even the elders."

The sounds of laughter and merriment could be heard over the delightful music. The vampires mingled; the old with the young.

"That's why nights like these are so important, Augustus. Nights like these make it seem like everything's OK."

"But it isn't, is it?"

"No," Bwogi said sadly, "but nights like these will buy us more time."

"The inevitable is coming, Bwogi, and Haemo is not what the lamia needs. It will destroy the very essence of vampirism. We should not pursue this madness. Even if it is administered, revolt from even ten per cent of the population would bring the war that we fear."

"Haemo is our friend, not our enemy," Bwogi calmly replied.

THE VAMPIRE WAS A YOUNGSTER, BUT A THREAT, NONETHELESS. He wasn't important enough to be at the party, so he was here as a guard. The firearm pointing at the arguing heroes gave that away. "ID, NOW!" he yelled.

"Terry, show the man our ID." Reece prayed that Sid wasn't going to be an arsehole.

"I ain't called fooking Terry!" said the arsehole.

Reece turned to give Sid a look, which he hoped would indicate they were in trouble.

Sid stared back defiantly.

Reece heard the click of a safety catch being removed. Two of the female staff stopped to watch the commotion from the bottom of the stairs.

He made his choice. He reached into his pocket, turned, and unfurled a Kevlar blade weighted with a granite handle at the vampire at the top of the stairs. Years of practise were justified as the heavy granite drove the blade deep into the frontal lobe of the vampire's brain. Since the vampire was young, it would take him a long time to recover from an injury so physiologically damaging. The two girls at the bottom of the stairs turned and ran for their lives, but what they'd witnessed sealed their fate. Reece dispatched two similar knives, one after the other. One girl fell, lifeless before she hit the floor. The other girl had a split second to realise her friend was in trouble before her life was extinguished with a knife embedded in her brain.

"They ain't vampires!" cried Sid.

"Oh no! I thought they were," Reece lied. "Quick! We have to hide their bodies."

"What about him? He's a vampire. Look, he's still twitching."

"He won't be able to function for a while. I'll finish him once we've cleared up the mess. Sid, I'm sorry I asked you to climb these stairs. I will double the money for the evening, but we need to cover up these terrible events."

Sid trudged down the stairs, shaking his head. He picked up the first girl he came to. She couldn't have been more than eighteen years old. "This ain't right. I don't want to do this if kids like these are gonna get hurt. Poor lass." He went to pull the knife out of the back of her head, but Reece stopped him.

"No! It will hold the blood in."

Sid muttered something under his breath before throwing her gently over his shoulder.

Reece sensed his mood. "I don't think I can live with myself if this happens again, but we're here to protect these people. We're here to rescue them. At midnight, they're all going to be killed by the vampires. We can't save them all, but we'll save as many as we can."

Sid picked up the other victim, a blonde girl who looked even younger. "Fook me," he said forlornly as he placed her over his other shoulder.

Reece dragged the vampire down the stairs, letting his head hit every step. "Good, there's hardly any blood. There's a utility cupboard farther down the service corridor. We can dump the bodies in there."

"How do you know that?"

"I've memorised the blueprints of the entire castle. If you follow my plans—exactly—this will be easy. There'll be no need for any more of us to die." He had never been able to manipulate Sid emotionally before. Hopefully, he could do it again.

"Alreet then, but I want twice the money, and I want it to go to these bairn's families."

"Of course. I'll give them more than that, I promise." Reece fibbed.

Once inside the utility cupboard, Sid lay the girls down gently before Reece unceremoniously ripped the knives out of their skulls with a sickening crunch. Sid shook his head.

"And now for this bastard." A demented grin split Reece's face. He was going to delight in this. This was the closest he'd ever come to torturing a vampire. "Sid, keep guard outside. This will take a couple of minutes."

"I can finish the poor sod, if you want. He won't feel a thing."

"No," said Reece excitedly. "I'll see if I can get any more information out of him. If anyone comes, knock twice on the door."

Sid shook his head, but he didn't know how Reece had suffered because of the vampire. He shut the door. He didn't have to justify himself.

Minutes later, he came out of the cupboard, wiping the blood from his knives, and struggling to hold back a manic grin.

"Everything is going to plan. That was a little bonus. Now, we need to set up the explosives in the kitchen. Sid, you need to climb the stairs. It's the only way we're going to save the others."

Sid sighed and nodded.

"Let's go," said Reece. "Grab the crate."

The two made it to the kitchen without bumping into any more vampires. A few servants passed them down the corridor, but they were too busy to notice the unusual pair. The kitchens were deserted, much to Sid's disgust. He rummaged through the vast fridges and the pantries in vain. It only took Reece a few minutes to rig up his explosive device. "Right, that's it."

"Won't somebody notice if they come in, like?"

"We're going to seal the doors. There's no food, as you or I would call it, at this party. All the people we've passed, all five hundred humans, will be vampire food once midnight strikes."

"Reet." Sid punched his palm. "It's time that I started smacking people."

"Hell, yeah! First, we need to get into our battle gear."

"Yeah!" agreed Sid.

Reece pulled the Kevlar battle armour suit out of the crate. "What do you think?"

Sid sneered his nose up. "What the fook is that?"

"It's battle armour. It will stop a magnum bullet."

"Fooking poncy shite. What the fook do I need that for?" Sid took off the van driver's overalls and the big jumper he'd been sporting to reveal his awful leather jacket. Underneath the jacket, the stitching of a T-shirt Reece hadn't seen before was being tested by Sid's mighty belly.

"'Frankie Says Relax?'" quoted Reece.

"Aye. Fooking mint, ain't it?" said the proud owner.

"Do you know where that comes from?"

"I got it down 'boro market. Whoever Frankie is, he sure knows how to roll."

Reece struggled to hold in his laughter. "Sid, you should put the armour on. That room is going to be crawling with vampires packing assault rifles. One lucky shot and you're dead. The suit will give you a much better chance. What protection is that jacket and T-shirt going to give you?"

"It makes me look fooking cool and manly. Them vampire fannies will see me and know I mean business. They'll be too fooking scared to shoot straight."

"I didn't think 'shooting straight' was the look you were going for in that T-shirt." Reece smirked.

"Eh?"

"Nothing."

"Reet, what's the plan?" Sid pointed to a door. "Shall I walk that way and start hitting people?"

"Oh no. I have something special in mind."

13

AUGUSTUS AND BWOGI BOTH SAT ON THE BALCONY overlooking the festivities. The conversation between the two members of the Coalition had become heated.

"How can you possibly believe Haemo will solve all our problems? We should not pursue it," said Augustus

"Haemo is a masterpiece of the scientific age. Garendon has developed a drug that will suppress a vampire's need to feed. It is, in essence, a cure."

Augustus frowned. "You tread a dangerous path. It's not wise to suggest that we suffer from a disease."

"If the Agreement is compromised and the world is made aware of our presence, then that's the line we will take." Bwogi moved to the edge of his seat, passionately arguing his cause. "We'll be forced to fight for our lives on a political battlefield. If that fails, we will live a life of exile."

Augustus rubbed his jawline. "I wouldn't let the other vampires hear you talk this way. The kill is everything to many of us. Some would rather die than be a slave to a drug."

"Us?" questioned Bwogi.

Augustus dismissed it with a wave of his hand. "Ivansey will become a martyr if this goes too far."

"If not Ivansey, it will be someone else. Without Vitrago, we are vulnerable to any warlord who wants power or anarchy."

"Tillsley can act fast, Bwogi. He's a quick fix that can be wiped out afterwards."

"Not yet. He will catalyse unrest. We can deal with this alone. After tonight, we will put together a team of the best we have."

"I'm not sure that will be enough—" Augustus cut off abruptly. "Ssshh! Someone's coming up the stairs."

Bwogi and Augustus changed the subject. This wasn't the place to discuss Coalition business, but during such troubled times, it was difficult not to.

Apart from Ivansey and Tillsley, the last person Bwogi wanted to see took a seat next to Augustus.

Borg Hemsman was a political powerhouse in his day and also a mighty warrior, but time had taken its toll on him, as did the birth of his daughter. The male vampire often died during childbirth, because the female needed to feed off the father's blood to fuel the birth. Borg would've died if he wasn't so strong, but the ordeal had weakened him permanently. His thick brown hair was heavily streaked with grey, and his face was lined with the worries of parenthood. His aquiline nose and his unusual eyes, black, emotionless pits, meant he wasn't as fair as other lamias. However, he commanded a handsome, yet intimidating presence. He was a big vampire, but he no longer packed the muscle of his younger years, and his tuxedo hung loose around the arms and shoulders. In his prime, he would've been a physical match for Michael Vitrago.

"And what were you discussing before you heard my footsteps?" There was no joviality in his voice.

"Good evening, Borg," said Bwogi calmly. "Just Coalition matters."

"I see. I don't suppose you were discussing the whereabouts of my missing daughter?"

"We have some of our best trackers searching for Lucia, Borg. She will be found, but we know she's safe," Bwogi tried to sound confident. Lucia was the only reason why Borg wasn't involved in the Coalition. The love for his daughter meant Borg never interfered in her business.

"How marvellous you have your best people on it, Bwogi," he said sarcastically. "I can sleep at day knowing the mighty Coalition is doing all in their power to bring my daughter home." He nodded towards Augustus. "Who is this?"

Augustus stood up and offered his hand, which was ignored. "I'm Augustus."

"So you sit on the Coalition and uphold the Agreement for the good of the lamia?"

"Yes, I do," said Augustus confidently.

Borg shook his head. "Vitrago was a fool for imprisoning the vampire race. If he'd tried it two hundred years previous, I would've ripped out his heart. However, I was powerless to oppose him, and when Lucia's passion for politics became apparent, I stepped away." He looked into the distance.

"You should be proud of Lucia. She's a fine councillor."

"Spare me your empty words, Bwogi. If you don't find her, I might have to fill her shoes," he snarled.

Bwogi tried to keep the shock from his face but failed.

"I'll leave you to discuss your Coalition's proceedings. I want to sit in comfort while my old friend addresses this pitifully weak excuse for a species. Do not fail me."

Borg turned on his heel. When he was out of earshot, Bwogi said, "He's the last thing we need." He slouched in his chair after the confrontation.

"Lucia's father. I've heard of him before. Surely, he can't barge his way onto the Coalition?"

"He can make our lives...difficult. We must find Lucia. What else can go wrong? At least Ivansey hasn't showed up."

The castle bell rang out midnight and the guests and servants meandered to the edges of the great hall. Pontius, the oldest of the vampire race, slowly made his way to the centre of the clearing. He looked old and frail, like an eighty-year-old human. In truth, he was thousands of years old.

Now, it was Augustus's turn to slouch into his chair. "What bullshit will this old fool come up with now?"

"I don't know," said Bwogi. "He's still bitter that we disbanded the Lamian Council. Whatever he says will be controversial. Unfortunately, Borg will back up his words. I'm just glad Lucia turned out the way she did."

A single bell tolled, bringing with it the attention of the party. Pontius stood in the centre of the hall with his hands raised for silence. The crowd drew back to the sides of the hall, and the ancient began to speak.

"Lamia, not in my lifetime has there ever been a greater gathering of us. I'm proud to see you here on this most special of occasions. The Occursus was the beginning of our domination, and we rightfully celebrate it, even though we have endured a hard year. The Firmamentum was something I hoped never to experience again. I didn't think we would get through it without the Agreement being shattered, but we did." He raised a glass of blood to the congregation, resulting in a mighty cheer from all. "The Agreement must stand. We are not strong enough to rise up and take the world. Brothers and sisters, we are weak. Michael Vitrago wasn't killed by Sparle; he was killed because of his own vanity.

"Now is a time for hibernation. I look around and see the potential for warlords of the old age to walk the world once more. Only then can we regain our power and bring back the blood."

Again, the crowd roared. Bwogi and Augustus looked on and both laughed without mirth.

"I can't wait for him to die," said Augustus through a rictus grin.

"Nor can I. It's fascinating. He gives the same message as we do, yet for completely different reasons."

"Some of the youngsters look up to him. The only thing he's done of any worth is not die. He's managed that by avoiding any conflict over the past two thousand years. And for that reason alone, we are treated to displays such as this."

On cue, the musicians started to play while an audaciously decorated cake was wheeled out that required three servants just to push it. On top of the cake sat four, stunning, young female vampires wearing nothing but their smiles. Everyone applauded as the cake was wheeled over to Pontius.

Bwogi whispered into Augustus's ear, "It makes it even worse that I have to do this." Bwogi stood up. "My friends!" he cried, raising his arms to attract the crowd's attention.

Gradually, all turned to acknowledge him. The look on half the audience's faces, including Pontius's, told Bwogi that they wished he'd jump from the balcony. "Over the past millennium, Pontius's guidance has been essential in leading us through the industrial and technological revolutions that have made our existence ever more difficult. This is just a little something to say thank you."

Bwogi sat down as the four stunning vampires on top of the cake jumped off and draped themselves around Pontius.

Augustus looked on in disgust. "Look at the perverted grin on his wrinkled, hideous face. They're going to have the worst night of their lives with that sick bastard."

"We have to give the crowd what they want. Wait until they see what comes out of the cake."

"SID, STOP IT! YOU'LL COLLAPSE THE CAKE!."

"I canna help it, mon. I'm fooking starving."

Hidden inside Pontius's giant cake sat Reece and Sid, crouched on their hands and knees, top to toe, wrapped around a great metal cylinder that would spurt blood from the top of the cake to indicate the start of the feasting.

"Stop munching it down so fast. I don't want you breaking wind in here," said Reece, rightfully worried.

"Are you sure this is gonna work?" asked Sid between mouthfuls. "It seems fooking daft to me. Can't I just start smacking 'em?"

"They're expecting a fountain of blood to erupt from the top of this cake. Only their blood will be spilled tonight. You'll get your chance then."

Sid clutched at his belly. "This cake is giving me gut ache."

"Then stop eating it, you fat bastard!" Reece bit his tongue—too late.

"Did you just call me a fat bastard?" said an outraged fat bastard.

"No, now shut up or they'll hear us. We're being moved into position."

Reece was aware of the barrage of bullets waiting to hail down on them from the guards stationed on the balconies of the great hall. He wouldn't be able to kill any with the gun he'd picked up from the vampire guard, but it didn't matter, this was psychological warfare. Just their presence here would strike deep into the heart of the vampire nation.

"Ah, shit."

"What? What's the matter?" asked Reece worriedly.

"I've got one coming."

"You've got what coming?"

"This cake is really rich." Sid rubbed his belly again, which was letting out some pained groans. "And that kebab has done me a wrongun."

"Oh, no! Hold it. You've only got to hold it for a minute."

"I don't know if I can. It's heading south, like. It's building up momentum," his voice was becoming increasingly strained. "I hope I don't follow through..."

"Sid, we need the element of surprise or we are both dead."

"Oh, this'll be a surprise, mon. This is gonna be one helluva surprise...Owwww..."

"Hold it. Please, just try and hold it!"

"I...can't...hold...ahhhhhhhhh!"

Vrrrruummmmmmmmmmmm!

Sid's arse blew one side of the cake away.

The decimated cake did little to hide Sid Tillsley's builder's bum. Before the vampires had time to act, or even pass comment, the room was full of a noxious gas, forcing them to grab at their noses and giving Reece and Sid the few seconds they needed to start the chaos.

Sid got to his feet awkwardly, slipping on cake, and waded into the nearest group of vampires, windmilling haymakers. By the time the guards let off a shot, Sid was mingled in vampire bodies and flying ash. Reece hid in the cake and awaited an opportunity to blow the bomb that would cause a big enough distraction for them to escape into an underground cavern leading to an old mine shaft.

He couldn't help admire the sight of Sid depleting the vampire nation. There was pandemonium as the human servants ran from the conflict along with the younger vampires, fearful of the legendary killer. The older, powerful, and proud vampires tried to push themselves to the front in an attempt to bring down Sid and earn themselves a place in lamia history.

As for Sid, he was just happy to finally be scrapping. Each vampire that fell victim to a big right hand brought him more tabs. He couldn't knock them out quick enough.

BWOGI'S CLUTCHED AT HIS SKULL WITH BOTH HANDS, hoping to wake from a nightmare.

"Tillsley!" yelled Augustus, leaning over the balcony to get a better look, disbelieving his eyes. "How did he get here?" He turned his attention to some of the guards stationed on other balconies around the great hall. "Someone shoot him!"

"HOLD YOUR FIRE!" screamed Bwogi. "He's near Pontius. A stray bullet may kill him at his age."

"Is that a bad thing?"

"Like you said, the younger generations love him, Augustus. Losing another vampire icon might finish us off. As soon as Pontius is clear, give the order to finish this, once and for all!"

UNFORTUNATELY, FOR THE VAMPIRE NATION, Sid was making his way towards the beautiful, naked women, and Pontius was in the middle of them. Sid had incorrectly identified one of the vampires as Blowjob

Barbara, a forty-something Internet divorcée from Hartlepool and was hoping that she'd read his last email:

A-up pet

hop u lik Me mussels. i lik ur tits so we r reet. I lik UR Name bloJOb BARBABabABARA. I lik uR tits.

TiLLS9LEY #the TeeSe

It had taken him two hours to type it out. This was a great opportunity to end the drought. A big ol' vampire crossed his path.

"I have been waiting for this for a long time, Tillsley. You will die on the end of my blades." Orhunt Lyeurn had been an associate of Vitrago's and had dismissed the opportunity to join the team that was sent against Sparle. He was a powerful vampire of the old ways. He unsheathed two blades, not dissimilar to the ones used by Vitrago in his battle with Sparle.

Sid had learned that knives hurt. He'd been stabbed a lot this year, and it pissed him off. "Put them fooking knives down and fight like a man."

Sid grabbed a vampire who was trying to run to safety and used the vampires' momentum, swinging him round and launching him at his armed adversary. Orhunt Lyeurn gracefully, and mercilessly, cut through the rapidly approaching vampire with two powerful slashes of his razor-sharp blades, dicing him into pieces. Sid countered by throwing a big slab of birthday cake that struck the vampire between the eyes, temporarily blinding him. As he tried to clear the offending confectionary from his vision, Sid launched one low. The characteristic double pop of exploding vampire gonads confirmed that the strike was true. As Lyeurn doubled over with shock, he met a monumental left uppercut. The combined force took the vampire's head clean off before it exploded into dust.

"Barbara!" Sid managed to say when he reached the vampire beauty. "Did you get my email?"

The naked vampire bared her fangs at him while the others surrounded and protected Pontius. "Kill him!" screamed the ancient one.

"Fook me!" yelled Sid as the four naked women leapt at him. Sid wasn't a fast runner, but he was a wily old fellow. He was used to women attacking him and was adept at avoiding their scratching nails and ball-breaking fists and knees. However, when four naked, vampire vixens jump at you, it's worth taking the odd scratch for a little slap and tickle.

Sid allowed himself to be taken to the ground and proceeded to have the time of his life. He squeezed and poked everything, absolutely everything. This enraged the vampire women who pummelled him with punches and knees that didn't affect him. He wore a cricket box and only suffered the mild irritation of a tightly contained erection.

"Scratch his eyes out!" shouted Pontius, which caused Sid to instantly dislike him, especially as he was surrounded by naked beauties. Sid concluded that the old man must be famous; it was the only explanation. Realisation dawned on Sid.

"That's fooking Bruce Forsyth!"

Sid hated Bruce Forsyth, the ancient, English television presenter. The girls went for Sid's eyes, and he had to act, otherwise he would be blinded and unable to see any more titties. He got to his feet with the women still hanging from him. He grabbed one of the scratching beauties, looked for a safe place to throw her, and found one: the cake.

One, two, three, four naked, oiled, buxom vampires landed in the lower tier of the gigantic cake, away from Reece who was safe in the upper tier with the blood cylinder. It was time for Sid to give Bruce Forsyth a piece of his mind. He also wanted to give him a swift jab for that dancing programme on BBC1, which Sid thought was shite and full of *them lot*.

"Hang on a minute," said Sid, realising there were four naked, oiled, buxom vampires wallowing in a giant birthday cake. He turned on sixpence.

"Howay the lads!" He executed a perfect belly flop into the cake and onto the naked vampires.

"OPEN FIRE!" shouted Augustus when Sid was clear of Pontius. Bullets hammered down from the surrounding balconies and Sid forgot all about the naked vixens (after one last grope). He clambered onto the upper tier and hid behind the blood cylinder with Reece.

"I'm gonna kick the fook out of Bruce Forsyth."

"What are you talking about? Actually, never mind. I'm going to detonate the bomb. Our work here is done. This attack will rattle the vampire world. Cover your ears and follow me closely. You see that small door over there?" Reece pointed at a door twenty yards from where they hid. "That's our escape route. Once through, I want you to barricade the door until I can open up the cellar. Clear?"

"Yeah, mon, but I have some unfinished business," said Sid, his head popping up between gunfire and looking around.

"There's no time. It's too dangerous."

"I've gotta do this. I owe that fooker good."

"Who?" said Reece, as a bullet whistled past his ear.

"Bruce fooking Forsyth. I fooking hate that dancing shit."

"Bruce Forsyth?" Reece looked up from the detonator. "What are you talking about?"

"That ballroom dancing programme where *them lot* prance around with lovely ladies when they have no intention of banging 'em. Unnatural it is!"

"What are you talking about?

"The prick is over there!" Sid pointed at Pontius who was now protected by half a dozen guards.

"Pontius!"

"Who?"

Reece immediately recognised the eldest of all the lamia. This would be another nail in the coffin of the vampire race. "You have to kill him, Sid."

"I don't wanna kill him, like. Just give him a jab."

Reece theorised that a jab from this monster would most likely kill the elderly vampire. "That'll do. The gunfire will stop when you get near Ponti...I mean, Forsyth. Once you hit him, I'll blow the bomb, you run back here for cover and then to the escape route. Here, take this." Reece took off his Kevlar jacket.

"I don't wanna wear that shit."

"Just hold it over your head until you reach Forsyth. I'll fire this cylinder as a diversion." Reece inched his way up the edge of the cylinder, trying to keep it between him and the gunfire. "Ready, Sid...GO!"

It wasn't the fastest sprint in the world, and it would've been quicker if Sid hadn't lit up a tab after standing up. Reece opened the valve spraying blood far and wide into the congregation, giving Sid the diversion he needed. A second later, bullets ricocheted off the jacket he held over his head like an umbrella. He made it to the vampire guards and lamped vamps in a way that only Sid could.

"You ain't going anywhere, Forsyth!"

Sid ducked past knives and nightsticks and landed solid punches as he went. He only had one target in mind. Within moments, he'd reached it and picked up the ancient by the scruff of the neck. Sid pulled back his fist. He really hated *Strictly Come Dancing*.

"STOP!" screamed Bwogi. "Back off—everyone!"

Sid looked up and recognised Bwogi from when he stood in front of the Coalition. Bwogi had promised Sid that Lucia would bare all if Sid helped them fight Sparle. The vampire still hadn't come up with the goods. Sid shook his fist. "YOU'RE STILL OWED ONE OF THESE, PAL!"

"PUT HIM DOWN!" shouted Bwogi

"NO! I HATE BRUCE FORSYTH!"

"HE'S NOT BRUCE FORSYTH!"

"Eh?" Sid slowly relinquished his grip.

Over the past few months, Reece had learned the hard way that it was possible to inspire instant emotions in Sid, instant, violent emotions. It was time to use it to his advantage.

Putting on a thick, Scottish accent, Reece yelled, "YOUR T-SHIRT IS WELL GAY!"

"NOOOOO!" screamed Bwogi as Sid defended his T-shirt's honour with a big, big right hand.

BOOOOOOOOOOOOOOOOMMMMMMMMMM!

The castle shook as Reece detonated the bomb. It took Sid a moment to react to the situation, peeved that someone had the audacity to even think his T-shirt was...you know. Most of the vampires didn't react to the explosion; they were too busy lamenting the death of their icon after Sid's brand of justice.

"Sid, NOW!" screamed Reece.

Sid waddled over to the cake and then followed the escape route. A few vampires made the mistake of getting in his way before gunshots chased him to the door that Reece had told him to run through. Slamming the door shut, he leant back against it. No one could shift the weight of his fat arse.

Rolling back a rug on the floor, Reece revealed a trapdoor. He opened the hatch before grabbing hold of a bookcase adjacent to the doorway. "Sid, get ready to move when I push this in front of the door. Ready...Now!"

Sid moved just in time as the bookcase slammed down on the castle floor. "Quick! Put the rest of the furniture in front of the door," Reece instructed. "I'm setting a charge on the trapdoor. Once it blows, they won't be able to follow us."

Sid threw everything at the door in an attempt to stop the vampires who were close to smashing through the heavy oak.

"Sid, through the trapdoor!"

Sid ambled down to the underground corridor and after Reece.

"A few more feet and we'll be there," he said.

The vampires broke through the doors and dived through the trapdoor, but it was too late. Reece detonated the bomb, bringing the cavern crashing down on top of the vampires while ensuring the hunters' escape.

"How far have we gotta walk?"

"Half a mile until we reach the mine shaft."

"Half a mile?" Sid considered going back and taking his chances with the vampires.

"There'll be quad bikes waiting. They'll take us past the guards."

Quad bikes sealed the deal. Sid started walking.

"Good work, Sid."

"Yeah, yeah. Anyroads, how did you know about all this?"

"I told you. We have inside help." Reece laughed. *And with Pontius dead*, he thought. *I am owed big time.*

14

LUCIA LONGED FOR HER REAL HOME and the company of other vampires. She missed going out, and it was difficult here where she stood out a mile in this town of hideous people. She did her best to ignore the glares of the women and the lewd comments of the men. It was best not to make a scene. It would only take one sighting for her whereabouts to be known. One sighting would lead her father here and that would be the end of Arthur and possibly the baby. She lived this life for the sake of her family.

Shopping for provisions was something she never had to do as a vampire. Anything she needed was brought to her and funded by the huge sums of taxes vampires were forced to pay. Shopping proved to be a depressing task. She'd ventured into a supermarket—once.

Lucia had never dealt with pensioners before, and one trip to the supermarket convinced her never to venture into their known territories again. They stood in the middle of the aisles, talking inane gibberish, complaining incessantly about the price of everything in the shop. Then, when finally at the checkout, they would price check every single item that was put through the till before triple checking their change while telling the rest of the shop about their cat Pickles who had a funny turn, their relatives who were slaughtered in the war, and how "Johnny Foreigner" was taking over the country. Old people had driven her away from the supermarkets and into local stores where the dregs of society stalked the night.

The Judicial System, as implemented by the Coalition, had meant her prey sometimes included common criminals, wretched human beings. However, people who regularly used local convenience stores were in a league of their own.

Tonight, she was shopping for tea for her man. He didn't stop complaining about her cooking, and she tried so hard. He was a monster sometimes, but she still loved him dearly.

This corner shop was better than most. The old woman inside seemed nice enough and didn't drone on too long about the "good ol' days" of hardship, poverty, death, and disease. Lucia pushed open the door.

"Eh'up, our pet," said the shopkeeper.

Lucia smiled. She'd never worked out why old women put a strange, blue dye in their hair. Lucia had never returned small talk, but the lady seemed nice enough, not pushing herself into her personal life like some of the other shopkeepers had. The old lady just stood behind the till, staring out of her gaudily framed glasses, smiling.

"What can I get you, love?" she asked in a warm voice.

"I just need some vegetables and any sources of protein you might stock."

The old woman smiled. "You all right, love? You never say much?"

Lucia smiled. "I'm fine. Do you have such provisions?"

A confused look crossed the old lady's face at the unusual word. "I'm Gladys, love. What's your name?"

"I'm sorry, Gladys, I'm already late. If I can just buy the things I need, I shall be on my way."

Gladys walked around the counter. She was the shortest woman Lucia had ever seen, and her dress sense the worst. Lucia had not come across a pink fleece embroidered with poodles before.

Gladys looked up at the towering vampire with a huge, semi-toothed smile. "What's your name?"

"Lucia," she said. It had slipped out, but the woman had a motherly aura. She felt strangely at ease with Gladys's arm linked around hers.

"Do you want a cup of tea, pet?"

"I'm fine, thanks. I need to be on my way."

Gladys stroked her arm. "Don't you worry. I'll put you a basket of things together, and you can tell me your problems."

"I haven't got any problems, Gladys. I'm fine."

"You've shacked up with young Arthur, haven't you?"

"How do you know that?"

"Oh, word travels fast around these parts. No secrets in the 'boro."

Lucia would've been suspicious of anyone except the little old lady in front of her.

"He's quite a catch is our Arthur. A few of the girls round town were quite upset when you nabbed him. Think they're a bit jealous, like, but who can blame them. You're absolutely gorgeous."

"Thank you." Lucia wondered if they'd be so jealous if they knew how disgusting he could be around the house.

"Men are all the same, you know."

"I don't understand." Lucia watched the little old lady gather vegetables from around the store.

"I see hundreds of people every week, love. You learn a lot about people doing a job like this. I've seen that look on every married woman's face who's been in here. Men. Can't live with 'em, but you can't live without 'em. But, it ain't all bad, is it?"

"I guess not."

"My Burt, God bless his soul, he could be a right ol' *you know*, sometimes. He'd come back from the football with a skin full and I knew he'd be a handful. He could be the loveliest boy in the 'boro, but he could be a right—" she looked around to make sure no one could hear, even though there was no one there, "bugger."

"Things were a lot better until this started growing," Lucia said, pointing to her belly.

"I heard you were preggers."

"How?"

"News travel fast, I told ya. And that fella of yours is a proud father."

"Really?" said Lucia, both eyebrows shooting upwards.

"Oh, aye. He'll make a great dad, pet. There you go." Gladys handed her a bag full of shopping. "Call it a fiver."

Lucia handed her the money. "Thanks, Gladys."

"You can always chat to me, our kid. Remember, times can be tough, but he's a good man at heart and will be a fine father."

"Thank you."

Lucia walked home content. Gladys was the first person to show her any sign of affection in months. Gladys had given her hope, something she'd been without. Arthur would change. Once the baby came, everything would change.

15

SANDERSON TRIED HIS BEST NOT TO LAUGH. He couldn't believe his ears. Sid Tillsley had jumped out of a birthday cake and punched and killed Pontius, the oldest living vampire. It sounded like something from a disastrous, trashy novel. The Agreement was well and truly up shit creek now. Haemo was the only option they had left.

"How could this have happened?" demanded Bwogi, rubbing his forehead so hard he was in danger of breaking the skin. Sanderson had never seen a vampire suffer from stress until now. "Sanderson, you told me that security was sufficient!"

"I believed it to be, but I wasn't heading security, was I? You put someone else in charge at the last minute." He enjoyed the flash of anger that crossed Bwogi's face. "Best ask your man on the ground."

"Rempstone?" asked Caroline.

"Well...," began Rempstone. This was the new boy's debut. Sharp suit, clean shaven, perfect blonde hair, bright white teeth, not a pimple in sight.

Sanderson would've disliked him under any circumstances. He chuckled to himself at Rempstone's nervous manner. Starting off with a long pause reeking of uncertainty wasn't the greatest of starts to Rempstone's career.

"Things have not gone quite to plan, not that we ever planned for such a scenario. Tillsley and Chambers escaped through the underground passages running deep under the castle where they had transport waiting. Chambers would've needed classified information for such an escape plan. This confirms that we have a leak within the Coalition."

Sanderson refrained from a slow handclap. "Fucking genius," he mumbled under his breath.

"Are you suggesting it's one of us?" asked Sebastian.

"What other explanation is there?" asked Rempstone. He was Sanderson's replacement because he was the complete opposite: calm, cool, collected, and a company man. Sanderson wasn't naïve. He knew that full-blown war wasn't the answer, but sometimes, it was best to let a soldier make the decisions. Now, they had an office jockey leading soldiers, lions led by donkeys. This kid had never seen war. He went straight from public school to officer school. Great A-Levels but couldn't fight his way out of a paper bag.

"Maybe Chambers hacked into our systems," suggested Pervis.

"No chance," said Sebastian. "We're impenetrable. I personally designed our system. There's no chance Chambers has the skill to bypass it. The best hackers in the world work for us, and I'm better than them."

Sebastian was right. No one could hack his systems...not unless he let them. Sanderson's suspicions grew.

"Maybe he's extracted the information, somehow. Is anyone missing from the agency, apart from Lucia?" asked Pervis. The sweat on his brow said he was worried that he might be next to meet a grizzly end.

"Rempstone, make the necessary enquiries," ordered Caroline. "The attack on the Occursus was catastrophic. If there's a leak, then the traitor's hate of the vampire race and their lack of vision may bring down the Agreement."

Fuck off, thought Sanderson as her penetrating glare paused and then passed him.

"How is the clean-up going, Rempstone?" asked Charles.

"Once it was obvious that we wouldn't catch Chambers and Tillsley, some of the younger vampires...lost control."

Sanderson almost laughed aloud at the awkward choice of words.

"The choice for such a remote castle has been our saviour and the body count hasn't been too high, but it's the spread of the killings that have made things so difficult."

"How did you regain order?" asked Sanderson.

"We didn't. The bloodshed finally waned. We lost a lot of army personnel and were lucky there were no surviving witnesses. It was akin to a riot, if truth be told. Only the dawn saved us."

Sanderson nearly choked when he heard the words. "Kid, did you just say we were *lucky* we lost all our fucking soldiers?"

Rempstone looked Sanderson direct in the eye, and without a hint of remorse said, "Yes. It's for the greater good."

Sanderson bit his lip while every muscle in his body tensed so hard, he felt the onset of cramp. Somehow, he restrained his tongue. "You fit right in here, kid."

"And what does that mean?" snapped Charles.

"It means these soldiers have lost their lives, leaving their loved ones to grieve, and you lot don't give a flying fuck." Sanderson replied, spittle flying, restraint was a distant memory.

Bwogi intervened, raising his voice before Charles tried to rip into Sanderson. "We must show our brothers and sisters we are still strong. They must know their actions carry consequences."

"We can't punish all of them," said Augustus.

"We must," said Bwogi. His fist slammed on to the table in a show of authority, but his quivering bottom lip ruined the effect.

"Dead wood snaps," said Caroline calmly, the weight of her opinion carried her words. "We must be flexible. We show leniency this time. We need every lamia on our side. Things have gone from bad to worse."

"To lose a beloved vampire such as Pontius is a crushing blow to the vampire race," said Bwogi.

Sanderson wanted to say that Pontius was a horrible, sadistic old bastard who was better off dead, but he held his tongue.

Bwogi placed his head in his hands. "We cannot ignore the demand for Tillsley's head. We cannot think of sending him to kill Ivansey."

"It may all be too late," said Charles.

"The Agreement is doomed," wailed Bwogi. "Only the Haemo project can save us. We must enforce it as soon as it's available."

"Enforce is not the word," said Caroline. "We need to *market* Haemo. The upheaval now is nothing compared to what we'll have to deal with when we announce our plans."

Sebastian, whom Sanderson noticed had been quiet for most of the meeting, sat in his chair, shaking like a nervous ball of energy. Finally, he unleashed. "Haemo is complete and utter madness! You cannot do such a thing." His fangs extended in protest.

Sanderson's pulse raced. Seeing Sebastian lose it gave him an adrenaline rush, making him want to cut the head off the murdering bastard. Sanderson would bet his life on that vampire being the leak.

"The drug should quell the vampire's want to feed," said Garendon, unaffected by the hostility around him. "The feral drives will be suppressed if there's no physiological need for blood."

Sanderson considered whether Garendon was a vampire at all.

"They'll still need to take the drug in the first place. They still have to make that choice," said Caroline.

"Ivansey destroyed the plant," said Augustus. "It's not an option. There's no need to discuss it."

Sanderson was enjoying this meeting. Seeing the vampires on the wrong end of a Coalition decision was a first for him, and he liked it.

"Research should continue," said Bwogi. "It may be our only chance of saving the species."

Augustus growled, gripping the table, visibly straining against his anger. "If the vampire nation knew we were even considering developing it—"

"And that's why they can never know, not until it's ready," said Caroline, a sea of tranquillity.

"There's a fucking leak, remember!" Augustus snapped back, but it didn't faze Caroline.

"If it's administered, members of this Coalition will hold special privileges after the implementation. They will be exempt."

"That's...that's got nothing to do with it," said Augustus, his demeanour relaxing.

Sanderson shook his head and couldn't help but goad the vampire. "I'm sure it hasn't."

"Shut up, you..." Augustus trailed off when he saw Sanderson's grinning face.

"How long until we can manufacture Haemo on a large scale?" asked Charles.

"We are confident in the drug," said Garendon, "and taking it will mimic the effect of ingesting blood. Amazingly, we still don't entirely understand why vampires need blood. We can't monitor it due to the speed of which it is digested. Although, this speed does give us a clue as to why we can regenerate.

"Haemo exhibits remarkable properties that allow a vampire to generate energy from its own bloodstream."

"What are the side effects?" asked Augustus.

"So far, the test subject has suffered no side effects and is completely normal. That's if you consider me normal."

Sanderson laughed. Garendon wasn't like the other vampires. His thirst was for knowledge, not blood. Sanderson was even starting to like him.

Garendon offered the briefest of smiles before continuing. "The formulation I developed was being scaled up in the plant Gunnar destroyed. The formulation was an intravenous injection, which means the vampire would either cooperate, or be shot with a dart-gun."

Sanderson lounged back in his chair and daydreamed about the best job in the world.

"It won't work," said Sebastian, wild-eyed.

"Yes, it would be problematic," admitted Garendon. "I'm investigating...other avenues."

"Just do whatever you think is necessary," said Bwogi. "No expense spared!"

"I concur," said Caroline.

"Please tell me you're joking?" cried Sebastian.

"We may not have a choice!" Bwogi replied with added fire. "Get to it, Garendon."

"As you wish."

"Tillsley and Chambers need to be killed, now," said Bwogi. "We need to broadcast this to the vampire nation. Four hundred years ago, we would've hung, drawn, quartered them, and then took their remains to the corners of the lands."

"And you're usually against violence," said Sanderson.

"Don't mock me!" shouted Bwogi, his fangs descending. "We have to show strength. We have to support a vampire nation that is baying for blood."

"But we can't allow them to run amok like at the Occursus with innocent people dying as a consequence," said Caroline. "What of our spies in the Northeast? What of Helena Ichvamovich?"

"We've heard nothing from her. Nor have the lamia who travelled to the Northeast with her," said Augustus. "I fear the worst."

"And what about the leak?" asked Sanderson.

Caroline shook her head, a small twitch of her cheek showed uncertainty.

"Haemo is our main concern," she said, "and the fact we haven't had a lynch mob at our door implies the leak isn't concerned about Haemo." She took a second, rapped her fingers on the desk and made a decision. "Sebastian, you are the information expert, search the systems and the phone lines, and if you find anything, we need to act. We need to set an example."

"You're asking *him* to do that?" Sanderson didn't know whether to laugh or cry.

"What's wrong with that?" growled Sebastian. His fangs still hadn't retracted from his previous outburst.

Bwogi shook his head. "Both of you, pack it in. We don't even know where this leak is manifesting. What *is* certain is that killing Tillsley is vital, even more so than bringing down Ivansey. Does everyone agree?"

Round the table the vote went, and every member of the council, vampire and human, nodded their head until it was Sanderson's turn. "When Ivansey turns up, you're gonna wish you had ten Sid Tillsleys."

16

SID LOOKED IN THE MIRROR and saw two very attractive Sid Tillsleys. One of them wished they hadn't drunk so much; the other wished they'd drunk a lot more. This was Sid's first date in years, and he needed to be a little oiled so that the conversation would flow. All blokes knew that women couldn't resist the slightly drunken patter of a Lothario. And besides, he'd earned a significant bit of dollar from the night before, and it would've been wrong not to celebrate with a few more than normal. Rich was so happy that he'd smacked Bruce Forsyth, he'd given him a few extra quid on top of what he agreed to send back to the families of the bairns that'd been killed.

The big man had made an effort for the evening. He'd wiped down the leather jacket, and washed his jeans and the Esso Tiger Token T-shirt. Unfortunately, the jeans had run into the T-shirt, making it a light blue and, more dangerously, he'd shrunk the jeans. Luckily, the analgesic effect of the booze meant Sid couldn't feel the pain he was in.

Sid was meeting a lady, an actual lady.

"Sunderland Sue" was one of the classiest ladies on the web. Out of the hundred and thirteen women Sid had examined, only seven did not have an obscene act in their names, and Sunderland Sue was one of them, but more importantly, she was one of the few Brian or Arthur hadn't nailed. And, even more importantly, Sue had approached him!

Sue wasn't a bad looking lass, and Brian was convinced that it was a genuine photo. Her interests were nights out and cosy nights in, fine food and wine, flower arranging, and walks. Agreed, not a perfect match, but she was going to meet him for a date and that was the main thing. Brian had booked them into Gino's restaurant, a little Italian place. Gino was a good lad Sid had known for years, and Sid hoped he wouldn't piss in the soup. He was a little unsure of the etiquette, but Brian had taken him through the dos and don'ts of a romantic meal. It was lucky for Sid he did, because he was astounded to learn that women would not find his "pull my finger" joke in any way amusing when it was obviously fucking hilarious, especially with his novel twist.

Sid was meeting her at the restaurant, and the confidence-building pint, or twelve, made his timekeeping a little off. He bundled into Gino's, almost crashing into a woman waiting just inside the door.

"Sorry, pet," he said to a bottle blonde with a scowl on her face generated by being almost crushed to death by a twenty-five stone monster. She was quite pretty, really, but there was a lot of war paint creating a diversion from her age. She looked familiar...“Fook, it's you!” he said, recognising his date.

“Pardon?”

“I said, ‘Fook, it's you!’”

“I *beg* your pardon!”

Sid wasn't used to the company of ladies. Luckily, he realised he was taking a path that wasn't going to end in titties.

“Sorry, Sue. I've been in a mad rush all day, and you caught me by surprise, like. I'm Sid, and I'm very pleased to meet you.”

Sid waited for the lady to offer her hand, and when she did, he took it gently but firmly enough to show that he wasn't one of *them lot*. She hadn't done a runner; things were looking good.

Gino noticed Sid waiting and pointed to a table at the back of the cosy restaurant. Sid took the lead across the small but busy bistro, with only a minor stumble, and pulled out his date's chair, before taking his own seat.

She weren't a bad looker. She definitely wasn't red hot, as she was dressed far too conservatively. There was absolutely no cleavage on display, at all, but Sid figured there were some pretty impressive bazookas under her blouse. The lass was trying to age with dignity, which sadly suggested he wasn't going to get a jump in the restaurant bogs.

“Are you hot with that jacket on, Sid?” Her accent wasn't strong. She was nearly well spoken. Sid wasn't used to posh.

“A little, like.”

“Why don't you take it off?”

“Because it makes me look handsome, pet.”

“I'm sure you'll look just as handsome without it. You look just like your photo, by the way, except with a little less hair.” Her accompanying laugh was almost mumsy.

Sid beamed. *Just like Tony Soprano*, he thought. “Why, thank you. I must say, you look as ravishing in person as you do on yours.”

Sue only half-smiled. Maybe using the word “ravishing” was a little too much for this classy lady. Ah well, Sid would chalk this one up to experience and move on to the next one.

Might as well get pissed up, then, he thought. “Fancy a drink, pet?”

“A glass of wine would be most pleasing. And it's Sue, not ‘pet.’”

“Right you are.” He nodded. “GINO!” he yelled across the quiet restaurant. “A bottle of wine and three bottles of that Italian piss you drink!”

Sue looked away, embarrassed.

“Sid,” called Gino, in an over-the-top Italian accent, “please, keep it down. Respect my customers and my beer.”

Sid shook his head and told Sue, “He's a Geordie, born and bred, ya know." Sid put his elbow on the table, which received a disconcerting look from Sue, so he moved it off but misjudged the size of the table and nearly fell off his chair. "Fook."

"Have you been drinking?" asked Sue.

"Well, pet, I've had a couple, like."

"A couple?"

"Well, I say a couple. I actually mean twelve pints, but don't you worry, I can still give you a lift home."

Sue shook her head before taking Sid to task. "You get drunk before our date. You don't even make an effort to dress up." She grew flushed with her anger. "You shout across the restaurant, embarrassing everyone, and you have stared at my chest from the moment you met me. Your behaviour is despicable!"

Sid's jaw hit the table. How dare she? He did make the effort to dress up! "Well, you can f—"

Sue leaned forward and whispered, "And it fooking turns me on, you dirty bastard."

"Wha...?"

"You heard me," said Sunderland Sue aka Sue the Sordid Swinger. "You turn me on, and after this dinner, I'm going to take you back to mine and bonk your brains out."

"Wha...?"

She had her back to the rest of the restaurant so she gave Sid a sneak peek at the goods. There were indeed bazookas hiding beneath the frumpy blouse.

For a second, Sid's eyes were larger than Sue's breasts, "Fook me!" he yelled to the disdain of the other patrons.

"Shhh, big boy, all in good time," she teased.

Gino brought the wine and beers over. "For fook's sake, canna ya keep it doon, mon? You're fookin' reet pissin' off me other customers, like."

"Sorry, Gino. Won't happen again. Remember to put the accent back on, pal."

"Fook off," said the Italian stallion.

Sid finished off a bottle of Italian lager before pouring a scandalously large glass of wine for his filthy squeeze. Sue smiled at his eagerness. "I don't want you drinking too much, baby. I want you to perform tonight."

"Don't try and change me, woman," said a serious man's man.

"You're a bad boy, aren't you?" she said, biting her bottom lip.

Another pissy lager missed the spot. "Aye, lass, and you don't know the fooking half of it. How long you been doing the Internet thing?"

"A few years, now. I got divorced from my husband and decided it was time to have some fun. I've been swinging ever since. I don't fook any ol' one. No, I like bad boys, me. I like bad boys like you."

"Howay the lads!" he cried, making more diners wish they'd chosen a different restaurant. "How many blokes you met over the 'net?"

"One hundred and ninety-four. I'm hoping to make it to two hundred by the end of next month," she boasted.

This would've put most men off, but not Sid. Others would've condemned Sue for her promiscuity, but Sid was an equal rights kind of guy. No strings, no ties. She was perfect. Although he was definitely going to wash it afterwards, no matter what Brian's opinion of safe sex was.

Sue knocked the wine back, matching Sid, drink for drink, and the two hit it off like a house on fire. Sid never thought he could have so much fun with a woman while not shagging. Admittedly, three-quarters of the fun he was having was because of the forthcoming shagging, but the lass was a great laugh.

"Dessert, my favourite," she announced as Gino brought out two portions of genuine Middlesbritalian ice cream for the two potential lovers.

"Cheers, Gino. Another bottle of wine and another three of them Italian pissy lagers, please."

"Coming reet up, Sid."

Sue picked the strawberry off the top of her ice cream and sucked it back and forth. It was one of the sexiest things Sid had ever seen in his life, even more than the colour VHS *Tits on Your Telly* Rathbone sold him last month.

"Fook me!"

Sue looked at her watch. "In less than an hour, I will."

"FOOK ME!" A young family left the restaurant for the sake of their child's upbringing. "Is there anyone at your place?" he asked.

"I told you I was divorced, didn't I?"

"Any bairns?"

"One boy, but he's all grown up now."

"House to ourselves then. Champion. What does your lad do then, Sue?"

"He's a hairdresser."

"Barber is a good solid profession. Always useful when you fancy something for the weekend as well, eh?" He laughed.

"I guess that's one way of looking at it."

"Found himself a good woman, yet?"

Sue laughed. "Oh no, I can't see that happening for a while."

"Good lad. I don't blame him sowing his wild oats. It's best to do it when you're young, like. It gets a lot harder with age."

"It was the other way round for me, like. I was married at eighteen. Oh, the wasted years." She shook her head. "Sid, how about we take this bottle of wine back to my—"

Sid was already on his feet and struggling into his coat. "You got beer at yours?"

"Yes, of course."

"How many?" he asked.

"There's a four-pack in the fridge in case of gentlemen callers."

"I'll buy a crate of that Italian piss, then."

FOR THE FIRST TIME IN YEARS, Sid entered a woman's residence without any money changing hands. "This is proper charming, this is, like," said Sid, using the word "charming," which Brian taught him.

Sue's flat was situated in one of the nicer parts of the 'boro and was about a mile from the infamous Smithson Estate. The flat was cosy and couldn't have been more different to Sid's humble, or rather rancid, dwelling.

"Go through to the lounge and make yourself at home."

"I'll just pop these beers in the fridge and grab that four-pack you mentioned," he said excitedly.

"You do that, honey, and open the wine while you're at it. I'm going to slip into something more comfortable. In fact, I'm not going to slip into very much at all."

Sid gave her a cheeky wink before making his way into the lounge, impressed that there were no plates with leftover kebab meat, no underpants, empty tinnies, or animal droppings. He could get used to this. Sue was a knickknack sort of girl, as well as someone who loved photos. There were pictures everywhere.

Guess that's her son, thought Sid, looking at the nearest photo. The lad looked a lot like Sue. *Very close to his mother, by the looks of things,* he thought, seeing them both on the *Sex and the City* tour together.

He scanned through the photos. *Ha! Bit of banter with the lads, being slapped on the arse by a bloke with one of the bushiest 'taches I've ever seen!*

He bent forward for a closer look. *Why the fook is he waving a rainbow flag?* Sid didn't think Sue was Welsh.

He picked another photo. *Why is he having his picture taken outside the box office of* Miss Saigon, Phantom of the Opera *and* Les Miz...Miz...*some bollocks? That's all women's shite. Must be on a date trying to shag a lass.*

When he saw the photo of her son with his tongue down a guy's throat, Sid assumed it must be for a bet where the winner gets to shag a stunner. He smiled. The things lads do when pissed and on the pull.

Hang on a minute...

Sid got to the last photo and a horrible realisation dawned on him. The last photo was of Sue's lad, standing outside the studio for *Dancing on Ice.*

"He's one of *them lot!*"

Sid's head found his hands. Why was nothing easy? Sid longed for some intimate time with Sue, but there was a risk. One of *them lot* had come out of her thingy. Could his old fella come out of there with the same tendencies? He wasn't a scientist, but it sounded likely. The dilemma was causing havoc with his genitalia. The half of him that wanted to make sweet love pumped blood into his extremities, but the half of him that was scared of catching *them lot* pumped blood away, leading to the bizarre physiological phenomena of a lop-sided erection.

"I'm ready."

Sid turned to see Sue wearing nothing but a smile.

"Fook me!" All thoughts of her son being *them lot* disappeared. Sue was an absolute scorcher, and it was time for Little Sid to be pleasured in ways that Big Sid couldn't provide. Both halves of Sid agreed and blood pumped until equilibrium was reached.

The result: an absolute stonker.

Sid ripped down his kecks and jeans in one, no easy feat considering the tightness of the shrunken garments. The power of his erection held his belly in the air, making it hang over either side of his steel.

"Come here, you big, bad bear."

Sid waddled over, like a penguin, as fast as he could. Sue's hand was at crotch level, and he had a heat-seeker locked on.

"Mother! You can't, you just can't!"

The bottom of Sid's world fell out. He stopped in his tracks.

The words came from behind him. Sid turned round; his belly quickly covered his dignity, as the power of love could no longer hold it up.

The destroyer of Sid's fun stood before him, and all the signs were there: clean, ironed clothes with no beer or curry stains. His clothes all matched, too, and he had one of them posh T-shirts on, one you had to buy and didn't get free from pubs for drinking fifteen pints in a night. His hair had been brushed, all smart and styled with a gel like a *them lot* haircut. He even had a nice pair of shoes on to complete the outfit, again, no stains from dropped takeaway. And he didn't have a beer belly. There could be no mistake: the lad was a *them lot*.

All Sid wanted was a shag. His blood began to boil.

"Jason, what are you doing home?" cried Sue. "Where's Paul?"

"He's left me. He's gone back to his wife—again." Jason was close to tears.

Sid experienced a rainbow of emotions that caused a destructive effect on his central nervous system. Only beer, mammoth quantities of beer, could possibly restore order to his scrambled brain. *Pink Alert* had been caught unaware and his Gay Defence System couldn't cope. Sid was only capable of experiencing one emotion at a time, and there were too many stimuli in this room. Things were turning dangerous, especially for Jason.

Sid's one-armed bandit of individual emotions was going to pay out a fight or a frolic, and hopefully, it would be matched with the right person.

Sexual arousal—fear—violence—sexual frustration—sexual confusion—stupidity—sexual arousal—fear—violence—stupidity—sexual arousal—violence—

VIOLENCE—STUPIDITY—VIOLENCE—VIOLENCE.

Jason flew through the first floor window. A few people walking back from the pub looked round to see what the commotion was. When they saw Sid Tillsley with his knob hanging out, staring out of the window with a look of thunder, they wisely walked on.

"JASON! TILLSLEY, WHAT HAVE YOU DONE, YOU MONSTER!" Sue grabbed a dressing gown from the bedroom and rushed downstairs to see what had happened to her beloved son.

"H...h...help me!" called a weak voice.

"Where are you, baby!"

"I'm in the t...t...tree."

Sid had a good think about what he'd done. Throwing Sue's son through the window may have jeopardised his chance of a jump. It was probably a good idea to leave, as there was a distinct possibility that Sue would call the police who would automatically assume that this predicament was his fault.

Sid made a quick exit.

He then made a quick re-entry into the flat, picked up the crate of beer, and made another quick exit.

17

IN FRONT OF GUNNAR LAY EDWARD LIMKIN. It was possible that this human was his saviour. He was the reason the Coalition's precious plant was now a smouldering, twisted wreck. Gunnar had enjoyed destroying the plant, but it still irritated him that he'd followed orders.

The next couple of hours were key. After his chance encounter with the priest, Gunnar spent his time sitting in meditation. He'd always bustled with energy, but it was ten times worse with the pain of excess testosterone.

He'd secluded himself deep in the hills and valleys of the Yorkshire Moors, searching for inner peace. He could see it. When he closed his eyes, he could see a black hole in the distance, a place of nothingness, but in front of that, vivid, flashing colours, psychedelic flames, and torrents of incandescent blood whirled on the backs of his eyelids. He couldn't reach his peace, but he could see it, and knowing it was there was enough. He'd tested himself. He'd placed his hand in flames while searching for calm, and his anger hadn't devoured him. He held on while the flames and the lights, dancing in his mind, engulfed him.

He could hold on, or so he hoped.

Gunnar perched on the end of Limkin's bed, on tiptoes, sat on his heels. This human was the only one with the power to take the pain away.

"Doctor, I have an unusual request."

"What the—" The man woke up startled. "Who are you? Where did you come from?"

"As I said, I have an unusual request."

The doctor looked desperately around for his wife and breathed a sigh of relief when he found her asleep next to him.

"Don't worry, Dr. Limkin, she's asleep. She won't wake until dawn and neither will your children."

"W...why?" managed the terrified Edward Limkin, top urologist of the King's Medical Centre, Nottingham, and private physician to the human members of the Coalition.

"I need you to perform an operation for me. If you don't, then I will kill you, your wife, and children."

Dr. Limkin now knew *what* sat at the end of his bed, but he didn't know *who*. "What operation could a vampire possibly need? You regenerate."

"I need surgery, Doctor," said Gunnar, calmly, breathing rhythmically.

"It's impossible. I don't have access—" His protests ceased when

Gunnar stroked the surgeon's wife's foot and she moaned in her sleep. "OK, I'll do it! I'll do anything!"

"We don't have much time. Unfortunately, you will have to perform the operation downstairs."

"What? You can't be serious," he whispered desperately. "I have none of my equipment to hand."

"Do you have a scalpel?"

"Well...yes."

"That should be sufficient." Gunnar laughed darkly. "Perhaps it's better that I show rather than tell you. Come, Doctor, there's work to be done."

Moments later, Gunnar sat naked on the kitchen table and Dr. Limkin was examining him, wide-eyed. "I've never seen or heard of anything quite like it before. If I hadn't seen it with my own eyes, I'd never would have believed it. Eunuchs, yes...but this?"

Gunnar cracked his knuckles. "All you have to do is remove any trace of my genitalia, and I will be on my way. If you don't..." Gunnar looked pointedly across the kitchen at the stairs to the landing where Dr. Limkin's family slept.

"There is no trace of the penis, no scarring, nothing. Removal of the testes should be a simple operation—well it would be if I had access to my equipment."

Gunnar hadn't considered an operation until he found a mobile phone a month ago. He'd no idea how they'd tracked him. He'd preyed upon a young female, and the second she'd died, the phone in her bag had rung. He'd answered the phone and was offered the deal by a disguised voice on the other end. There was no guarantee the operation would succeed, but he had to try. He remembered when a bullet at the chemical plant had blown off his testes. The moment's rest from the agonising pain had been an oasis in a never-ending desert. The loss of consciousness, the death of Richmond...this had to end.

"How did this happen?" asked the doctor.

"That doesn't matter."

"Have you consulted the elders?"

Gunnar laughed. "Not my style."

"Why me? I've never operated on a vampire before."

"No one has. You are an expert on such matters," he said, gesturing to his genitals, "so you're the most qualified."

"Who told you where I live?"

"I suggest you get on with the task at hand, Doctor. I'm losing my patience."

Limkin took the hint. "I'll need to shave the area."

"Just get on with it."

Limkin examined Gunnar's testicles. "They're so swollen. The ordeal will be excruciating."

"Make sure to remove any nerves. All traces must be gone to avoid regeneration."

Limkin nodded. "Regeneration may take place, even with all traces removed. Your DNA holds the key to your body's structure and that's where the repairs begin."

"My penis didn't come back. Remove more than you need. If you don't, then I will have to wake your wife."

"Very well. But let me warn you, the first incision would be a fate worse than death to a human."

Gunnar sat and meditated. He searched for peace. Every moment the black hole of nothingness waned; flames devoured it, blood drowned it. *Hold on. Just hold on*, he told himself. Blacking out would be the end. *Fight it!*

The scalpel entered his swollen scrotum. There was no denying the agony. He fought with all his might. He was strong. He could hold on...

Thirty minutes later, it was done.

"I removed every nerve. It's all I can do."

Gunnar stretched. "Doctor, you wouldn't believe how good I feel. I thank you for your help, but unfortunately, this is not going to end well for you. I have a message to send to the organisation you work for."

Colour drained from the surgeon's face. "But I did what you asked!"

"Yes, and I'm very grateful. Now, please, give me the scalpel. I want you to experience my pain."

GUNNAR RAN ACROSS THE ROOFTOPS OF NOTTINGHAM. Freedom was his. The burden of his swollen testes was gone along with the pain that had tormented every step. Now, he could run, jump, and soar through the night. Gunnar was free, and now, Tillsley and the Coalition were going to pay.

Suddenly, Gunnar stumbled when he smashed his foot down to leap between buildings. Normally, it would've been a mere skip, but something had stirred. He missed the jump, crashing hard into the side of the next building. It was a long fall to the pavement below. He didn't notice any of it, though. He was groping at his groin.

"No..."

He hit the ground and his shoulder blade shattered under the immense force. He didn't care, something far worse was happening. He could feel lumps. They were regenerating, and fast. By the time he got to his feet, his shoulder was healed and his scrotum was unfurling in front of his eyes.

"Alright, lad, put that away. Pissing in public is illegal and an eighty-quid fine."

Gunnar took in his surroundings. He was just off a busy road and could see various pubs and clubs in the distance. If his predicament with his gonads wasn't so demoralising, he would've laughed. Now, two police officers were walking down the alley towards him. They must have heard his fall.

The police were off limits to vampire feeding. The Coalition came down hard on any vampire who strayed too close to these pathetic, power-crazed humans. But, Gunnar wasn't just any vampire, and the Coalition was going to share in his tragedy. "Eighty pounds you say?" he said almost jovially.

"You can pay now or come down the station."

The policeman wasn't what Gunnar had expected. He was courteous and pleasant and his partner was a tiny woman. What good could she possibly do in a fight?

His throbbing testes interrupted his train of thought. They were back, fully functioning and filling fast. Tillsley, the Coalition, and every fucking monkey had caused all this. The deaths of Gabriel, Richmond, and Ricard, the only people he held dear, would never have happened if Vitrago hadn't agreed to sell out the vampire race. Well, fuck the Agreement. Fuck everything!

Cool it!

"If I give you eighty pounds, will you let me fuck your partner?"

The policeman grimaced. "OK, that's enough. You're coming down the station to sober up. I'm arresting you for being drunk and disorderly."

Gunnar put his hands behind his back so the policeman could handcuff him. The policeman, not knowing who or what he was, pushed Gunnar aggressively against the wall and roughly put the cuffs on. Gunnar did not resist, allowing himself to be treated like a common criminal.

"Let's go, sunshine."

GUNNAR RAPPED HIS FINGERS IMPATIENTLY on the back of the chair he sat in. His hands were still in cuffs, forcing him to sit forward. He paid no attention to the two officers who sat at the other side of the table and instead looked around the sparse, boring room where he was being formally cautioned.

"You are charged with, vandalism, resisting arrest, and assaulting a police officer." The station's arresting sergeant waited for Gunnar to protest at the made-up charges, but he just smiled. The officer clicked his tongue irritably.

"What're you smiling at, you arsehole?" said the second policeman.

"Cool it, Harpe," said the sergeant under his breath.

Gunnar had finally found an object of interest. "Is that a CCTV camera up there?"

"Yes, it is. Now, what's your name?" demanded the sergeant.

"Gunnar Ivansey," he said slowly, grinning insanely at the camera.

"Address?"

"I have many properties scattered across the world."

"Really?" said the sergeant sarcastically, rolling his eyes. "What's your date of birth?"

"I was born on November the thirtieth."

"And the year?"

"Oh, I can never remember. It was centuries ago."

"Put this smart-arse in a cell, Harpe," the sergeant ordered. "We don't need to waste any more of our time. Let's see if he's more cooperative in the morning."

Gunnar laughed. "But there won't be anyone here in the morning."

"Any why not?"

"Because I will have killed you all."

"I'll add threatening a police officer to the list, then," said the officer.

"You might want to add the murder of Dr. Edward Limkin and his family too."

"Take him to the cells, Harpe. Damn nutjob."

GUNNAR SAT IN THE CENTRE of his seven-foot-square cell, legs crossed, eyes closed, meditating. He was trying to cut the mind-body connection to his testes and focus on the black abyss.

The door to his cell opened, and four policemen equipped with riot gear bundled into the small space. They quickly surrounded him with their shields. He felt a few blows to his legs and body with their nightsticks, but these pitiful humans couldn't harm him. He held his meditative position.

"Can I help you?" he asked casually.

"You're coming with us, you murdering bastard."

"Certainly," he said politely. It was well worth taking this abuse from these pathetic creatures who thought themselves better than the rest of the cattle. Their time was running out. The Agreement wouldn't protect mankind for much longer.

The police marched him through to the interrogation room where they tried to force him into a seat under spotlights. He didn't comply with the aggressive behaviour. "Would you like me to sit down?"

The baton to the back of his knees answered his question but did not make his legs buckle an inch.

"Would you like me to sit down?" he repeated, slower, patronising.

This time, the baton was aimed at his face.

Gunnar snapped the chain of his handcuffs, caught the baton, and yanked it out of the policeman's hand before graciously offering it back to him. Gunnar appreciated the uncertainty in the officer's eyes before the human regained a dash of courage and snatched the baton back.

"Sit the fuck down," said a plain-clothed policeman.

"As you wish." Gunnar complied.

The four policemen in riot gear stood close behind him, weapons drawn. He could sense their fear. It made him feel warm inside. Because of the spotlight, he couldn't see the faces of the two interviewers in front of him, but he could tell they were in plain clothes.

"Why did you kill Edward Limkin and his family?" asked the man who had told him to sit down. He had a deep, gravelly voice. It sounded as if he was forcing it slightly, trying to sound like the stereotypical bad cop.

Gunnar smiled. "It amused me."

"You a drug addict?"

"Drugs are not beneficial for your species," he said with fake concern.

"'Our species?' Is that not the same as your species?"

"No, officer, I am a vampire."

There was a moment of silence before the policemen laughed. "Another fruitcake," said the second interviewer, a well-spoken young man.

"OK, *vampire*...is that the reason why you killed Limkin and his family? Did you drink their blood?"

"No, actually. I already told you, I tortured and killed the family for my amusement. It is sport to me."

"Killing children is sport to you?"

"Yes."

"Defenceless, innocent children?"

"You are but a child to me, officer. This entire police station has as much chance of stopping me as a single child. It's the effect that children have on you, which makes them so interesting. The lengths that a human will go through to protect their young still amazes me, even after all these years."

"You sick freak," said one of the riot officers.

Gunnar turned to the outspoken officer. "Yes, possibly, but I've seen how you treat your livestock. We allow you to run free, and look how you use your insignificant time on this planet: You spend it drunk, on drugs, glued in front of a television set."

"Limkin was a brilliant surgeon. Why murder him?" asked the young interviewer.

"As you said earlier, I'm a sick freak," Gunnar said without a note of humour.

"Your days are numbered, son," said the older man.

Gunnar cocked a brow. "Really? But I was looking forward to killing every man, woman, and, hopefully, child in this building."

One of the riot officers went to strike Gunnar in the head, but the young, well-spoken interviewer intervened.

"Harpe! Not yet. We need to question him first."

"Harpe," said Gunnar, turning to face his potential attacker. "You again? I'll save something special for you."

Harpe couldn't help himself. He brought the baton down hard on

Gunnar's skull. Blood splattered across the shields of the riot police. Gunnar didn't blink. It was his biggest test so far, and he'd held on.

"Do you feel better now, Harpe? I can't wait to meet your family."

Harpe snarled and pulled the baton back and went to strike Gunnar again but stopped in his tracks as the wound healed in front of him. The blood congealed, the skin sealed, and within seconds, it was if it was never there. "In...In...Inspector Graynge, the wound just disappeared."

"What are you talking about?" asked Graynge, the well-spoken interviewer.

"His head healed. I...I saw it," said Harpe.

Inspector Graynge stepped out of the darkness to investigate. He was young, handsome, and would leave a good-looking corpse if Gunnar was lenient.

Gunnar laughed. "Hallelujah, it's a miracle! Inspector Graynge, you mocked me for claiming I was a vampire, and now, this man is claiming that my head healed in front of his very eyes." He fixed Graynge with a stare that was anything but holy. "This puts you in a dilemma."

"Which is?" said Graynge.

"If Harpe's telling the truth and my head knitted back together, then it means I am also telling the truth, and I am a vampire. If I'm telling the truth, and I am going to kill everyone in this building..." Gunnar bared his fangs and jumped to his feet. "THEN WHAT ARE YOU GOING TO DO ABOUT IT?"

Inspector Graynge fell backwards while the rest of the policemen withdrew as far as they could from the menace whose face had distorted with fury. Gunnar's voice, a guttural growl, came from man's darkest and oldest nightmares.

Gunnar sat back in his chair. "I am Gunnar Ivansey. I am a vampire."

"Everybody out!" commanded Inspector Graynge.

18

THE SOOTHING SOUND OF WINGS' "Band on the Run" played through the speaker system of Sid's Nissan Bluebird Turbo.

"Stuck inside these four walls...Not been fooked forever. Never seeing no big...tits again.
Big tits...mama...Big tits...mama

If I ever see tits again,
Gonna make some time to play,
Blow a great big raspberry,
All I need is ten pints a day,
If I ever see tits again.

Well, the rain exploded with a fooking crash as we
(break to light a fag),
And the first one said to the (mumble with lyric confusion) *WILL BOTH BE HAVING FUN!* (sung *forte* to make up for not knowing lyrics),
SID ON THE RUN! SID ON THE RUN!
And the jailer man and Sailor Sam were searching lasses' bums
For that SID ON THE RUN, SID ON THE RUN
SID ON THE RUN, SID ON THE RUN

There ain't many things better than a drunken sing-along. A few ales, a few changed lyrics and missed notes were no harm to anyone and all part of the fun. Drunken sing-alongs at eighty-five miles an hour on an A-road were, admittedly, a little more risqué. Sid was a bad boy to be drink-driving, and he'd finished the crate behind the wheel. If truth be told, he wasn't just feeling blue in the ball department. He was feeling a little guilty for throwing Sue's son out of the window. Normally, his *them lot* confrontations were defensive. He knew he was out of order on that one.

He put it all behind him, because tonight, he was going to get some loving. What could possibly go wrong after drinking twelve pints of ale, going out for a boozy meal, and then drinking a crate of Italian lager while depressed? Nothing. Sid parked up in the layby.

"Fooking...Interslag...date...shite!" he chastised. The Internet was for weirdoes, and Sid had had enough of it. He wanted to pull a lass the good old fashioned way: dogging. This spot was notorious for some filthy action. Not that he'd got any in the past, mind.

There was a car up ahead, and the woman in the motor was gonna get it. Sid fell out of his Nissan Bluebird, certain that he'd used all the right signals. He'd flashed his lights a few times and bibbed his horn. But, he couldn't quite remember where he was or what he was doing, or if there was a woman in the motor up ahead.

"Fook. Why is—*hic*!—everything shhideways?"

Sid noted he was on the ground before regaining the gift of drunken logic. His car was nearby. He was drunk. He was out in the country. This could mean only one thing: "Dogging! Yeeaaahhh!"

Awkwardly, he made lewd thrusting actions while still on the ground. With the help of the Nissan Bluebird, he made it to his feet. He eyed up the car that was going to be the lucky receiver of his attentions and tried to remember why he picked this particular vehicle. The interior light was on, and he was pretty sure that meant there was a woman inside ready for some loving. What else could it be?

"If any fooker turns up shhhowing off, he'shh gonna get a fooking ssshmack," Sid grumbled, remembering the incident last time he went dogging. Sid meant business. His flies were down and his old fella was out.

"Reet...here...awww, fook!" He clutched his stomach.

Sid wasn't used to Italian food. Tomatoes are used extensively in Italian cooking but not in the diet of the average Middlesbrough resident.

He looked around desperately for a toilet. Allowing Mother Nature to have her way wasn't an option since decimating a pair of Y-fronts put most ladies off.

"Fooking...foo...YES!" Sid raised his fist triumphantly when he spied a toilet farther down the layby. He ambled over, clenching like he did during the prostate exam that had ended with four concussed doctors and a virgin Tillsley ring piece. He barged his way through the door of the small, smelly, grimy gents...

"Hello."

Sid blinked as he was confronted with a middle-aged man stood just inside near a cubicle. The guy was lucky not to have his face taken off by the swinging door. Sid didn't have time to ask questions as to what the man was up to. "Howay, mate, I need to use the—*hic*!—cubicle."

The man looked down. Sid hadn't buttoned up from earlier. Sid'd never been a shy one.

"'Shcuse us, pal. I need that cubicle."

"I see that you do." He laughed. "Fancy a wank?"

Sid launched a big right hook on instinct. However, with his old fella out, his pants half way down his backside, and an indecent amount of alcohol, he didn't have his usual control and he missed the gay chancer by a country mile and punched his way into the cubicle of the toilets. Sid fell through the door and grabbed onto the toilet seat.

The commotion sobered him a little, and he panicked. He was exposed, butt naked, and...prone. He tried to get to his feet but was too drunk, and his skin-tight jeans made moving difficult.

"OK, pull your pants up, buddy. You're nicked for engaging in sexual activity in a public lavatory."

"Wha...?"

"I've seen enough. Man, you weren't even subtle. Pull your pants up," said the undercover officer, frowning at the sight.

"I was going for a shite!"

"A likely story. You bent over the toilet with your pants around your ankles and wiggled your arse in the air."

"Wha...?"

"Make yourself decent. You're coming down the station. There's been far too much indecent sexual activity going on in these toilets of late, and we've been getting complaints. And by judging how eager you are, I should imagine you've been servicing the entire Northeast."

"You think I'm a...?"

Sid passed out.

AS HAD OFTEN BEEN THE CASE OVER THE PAST YEAR, the Coalition called an emergency meeting at the Great Hall. Since they were in a constant state of emergency, they were simply meetings now. Sanderson hated everyone. He spent more time sat on his arse than doing some good on the streets, on the battlefield. He'd transferred many of his duties to Rempstone, but they still insisted he attended these talking shops. However, this was one he was glad to be a part of. The Coalition was being debriefed by a human agent. The stress was visible on her stern face.

"We have a situation," she said. "We believe Gunnar Ivansey's in police custody at Nottingham Central Police Station. He was arrested earlier this evening for assaulting a police officer. Since being arrested, he's confessed to the murder of Dr. Edward Limkin."

Fearful gasps escaped all the human councillors. This was too close to home. The name of the Coalition's private physician had been leaked. They were right to be frightened, but Sanderson wasn't, he was excited about having a lead on Ivansey.

"What are you smiling at?" said Charles, disgusted at Sanderson's lack of tact.

A violent fire burned in Sanderson's eyes. "This is our chance to nail the son of a bitch. It's gonna be a trap, but traps tend to backfire when a crazy son of a bitch like me comes at you with his favourite grenade launcher."

Pervis was whiter than usual. "He'll come for all of us. We aren't safe. He'll do to me what he did to Rickson! He'll kill—"

"Get a grip, man!" reprimanded Caroline, ever the emotional rock.

"Another nail in the coffin." Bwogi slumped with the weight of the world driving him even farther under the table.

Sanderson sneered at the pathetic individual. "Let's get one thing straight. We have that piece of shit locked up in Nottingham Police Station. Yeah, he knows what he's doing, but we can finish him."

For once, Augustus backed him up. "Ivansey is not the physical specimen that Sparle was, but he's more unpredictable than the beast. We must finish him now we have the chance."

"He must've turned himself in. By now, there'll be CCTV, official records, and photographs," said Bwogi.

"They can all be erased." Sanderson felt a pang of guilt saying it. "Records and...people can be erased. We have him cornered; let's destroy him."

Caroline shook her head. "He isn't cornered. He can leave Nottingham when he wants, and he can leave in a sea of blood. How can we corner him without losing hundreds?"

"It's a small price to pay, Caroline," said Augustus.

"A small price to pay," repeated Sanderson grimly. "It sickens me to say it, but he's right. I would sacrifice myself a thousand times to put an end to that animal."

Bwogi rubbed his cheeks. "It isn't just the people in the police station we need to worry about. We'll need heavy firepower, even if we send in vampires. Everyone within ten miles will hear the battle. Where, in the city, is the police station?"

Sebastian tapped at a few buttons on the console before him, and a large screen dropped down from the ceiling. He got up and walked over to a computer terminal, which had risen from the floor. As he tapped away at the keyboard, a map of Nottingham appeared, giving a bird's eye view of the police station and the surrounding area. Sebastian's groundbreaking work in technological advancement caused Sanderson to trust him even less.

"If we take him out," said Sebastian, "there's going to be a quarter of a million people hearing about it."

"We can't hide that," said Caroline, shaking her head.

"This will bring international attention," warned Charles.

"Have you considered the consequences of letting him go?" warned Augustus.

"We still don't know if we're able to kill the bastard in the first place," said Sanderson "Yeah, we have a team in place, but they aren't warriors of the old code. Our team isn't in the same league as the one Sparle ripped to pieces. But Tillsley could take him."

"We've ordered his death," said Charles, "and besides, he's probably drunk in a bar somewhere."

"Actually, he's in the custody of Cleveland Police Force," said Rempstone.

Sanderson's head snapped around to Rempstone at breakneck speed. "And how do you know that?"

Rempstone pointed to his earpiece. "It literally just came through."

"Send him," said Augustus. "Send him, and once he's finished Ivansey, kill him. No one will know."

"No," said Caroline. "It's not why the Agreement was started. And what of the leak? Details of the Occursus were passed on to Chambers. It seems that whoever wants to bring the Coalition down is not afraid to use Tillsley as fuel to the fire." She turned to Sebastian. "Have you done anything at all to investigate why the world knows our business?" Her sarcasm stung.

Sebastian narrowed his eyes for a second, making him look even more snake-like. "There is absolutely nothing being leaked through our computer systems or any of our phone lines. There's not much more I can do except—"

"Very good," she said, cutting him off with an unimpressed smile. She turned away from Sebastian, who stood at the console, visibly boiling. "If we use Tillsley, the whole world may know by morning."

"We don't know that," said Pervis. "How come the Haemo project hasn't been leaked? We're just *guessing*, for heaven's sake. We have to send Tillsley."

"We may be guessing, but using Tillsley is a huge risk. We must send what vampires we have," said Bwogi.

"And if they fail?" said Pervis, visibly shaking.

Sanderson spoke as the only councillor with real military experience. "After what I saw from the surveillance videos of the chemical plant, those vampires haven't got a chance, not in the tight corridors of that police station. We can back them up with soldiers and the police in the station, but I don't think it'll be enough."

"What do you think we should do?" Bwogi asked.

"We blow the shit out of the station and then think of something fucking fast, or we send Tillsley."

"No," said Caroline.

"Why are you against sending him?" Augustus asked. "He has already rid us of Sparle. Why can't we use him again?"

"Because the battle will take place in a public building," she replied. "We cannot make Ivansey a martyr and the Coalition his murderer. Tillsley has just killed Pontius, a vampire icon. The vampire nation demands his blood. We cannot actively support him. Even if this conversation is leaked, then we face—"

Sanderson interrupted, "We don't know where the leak is coming from. It could be a cleaner, for all we know. We cannot be held hostage to an unknown entity. If Sebastian could do his job properly, then maybe we'd be in a better situation."

"Fuck you," spat Sebastian.

Sanderson enjoyed it immensely but was stunned when the vampire sided with him. "However, you're right. The leak could come from anywhere. We send Tillsley and only use him if we can't deal with the situation ourselves. We kill him afterwards and make out that Ivansey was the hero who brought Tillsley down. No one knows of Ivansey's attack on the Haemo project since that hasn't been leaked. Ivansey's martyrdom can actually work in our favour."

"It's too great a gamble," said Caroline.

"If there's a leak from the Coalition, Caroline," said Augustus, "then news of the Haemo plant will bring the destruction of the Agreement quicker than Tillsley's attack on a renegade. We have bigger issues to deal with. Right now, we have a chance to kill Ivansey *and* Tillsley."

Sanderson was quick to back up the vampire. "We send the vampires first; Tillsley goes in if they can't do the job. Ivansey has to die."

Caroline let out an exasperated sigh. "Very well," she conceded, "on all our heads be it."

19

"INSPECTOR GRAYNGE?"

"And you are?" Graynge turned to see a figure striding towards him down the corridor. Graynge's first impression was that the man was extremely dangerous. Scars streaked his face and the intensity in his eyes was the result of seeing things a man should not have to see. He was older but that just meant his killing career was longer.

"My name's Sanderson," said the grey-haired veteran, lighting up a cigar.

"You do realise it's an offence to smoke in here."

"You do realise I don't give a fuck. I'm here to deal with one of your prisoners."

"I don't need to ask which one. On whose authority?"

Sanderson took out some papers from the pocket of his combat trousers.

Inspector Graynge whistled when he saw them. "What do you need?"

"Is he still here?"

"He's being held in one of our interrogation rooms. We haven't spoken to him since he exhibited some...strange attributes."

"Such as?"

"He believes he's a vampire. We thought him mentally deranged, but then one of our officers hit him over the head with a baton and he didn't blink. The gash in his head healed, there and then. What *is* he?"

Sanderson's face was stone. He took a drag of his cigar. "He's an extremely dangerous individual, but a vampire he's not." He laughed condescendingly. Acting wasn't his strong point. "I need to know which officers have been in contact with him and which officers have been on duty since his arrest. I also need access to your computer and telephone systems."

"Am I expected to run a normal service while you're here?" said Graynge, blowing out his cheeks.

"No. We have called in other local forces."

"It's Saturday night!"

Sanderson's stare intensified, causing Graynge to look away. "We have more important things to take care of. I need one of your officers to brief Agent Keeley, here—" Sanderson indicated to a tall, stern woman with dark hair tied into a tight bun, "as to who's been on duty tonight, and also show Agent Stypes, here"— he pointed to a short, but thickset skinhead—"to your central communications hub."

"How many of you are here?"

"Not enough," Sanderson said fleetingly. "Take me to the interrogation rooms."

Inspector Graynge took Sanderson and his team of operatives, all dressed for combat, through the corridors of the station to the cells and was in awe at the sheer size of the squad members.

"How many cells are in this block?" Sanderson asked, looking through the window of the single door leading to the cells.

"After the reinforced door in front of you, there are three to the left and three to the right," replied Grange. "It's a dead end after that."

"Where is he?"

"Last one on the left."

"The walls that surround the cell, what're they made of and where do they lead to?"

"Bricks. What does that matter?"

"Are there any reinforcements or is it plain brick and mortar? Have you not planned for the break out of prisoners? I need answers. Quick, man!"

"All walls are double-brick and mortar. This section of the station is actually underground, so there's no chance of a break out."

"Good. What about the ceilings?"

"Reinforced concrete. At the back of each cell is an observation room connected by bulletproof, two-way mirrors. These are all linked by a corridor leading to these doors here." Graynge pointed to the doors adjacent to the one Sanderson looked through.

"So this is the only way he can escape?"

"Yes."

"Any other prisoners in the cells?"

"None. We moved everyone after seeing...what we saw."

"Excellent," he said, placing a hand on the inspector's shoulder, leading him away. "Thank you for your cooperation, Inspector Graynge. If you'd be so kind as to accompany one of my agents to the staff canteen, we will give you all the information you'll require."

"That I'll require?"

Sanderson only offered a mirthless smile. "There are some things that are best not knowing."

"Harpe, to what do I owe the honour?" Gunnar lounged, his feet were crossed on the interrogation table in front of him as if he'd just been enjoying an afternoon nap.

Harpe said nothing, but pulled a pistol from behind his back and took the safety off. He'd removed his riot gear and dressed in black-and-whites. Harpe was a thickset man, strong, with stern features and a face that'd seen its share of trouble.

"And what, pray, is that?"

Harpe smiled. "True justice. There'll be no courtroom for you. No bullshit insanity plea. There'll be nothing for you except a bullet."

"Rehearsed that line, have we?"

"Right tough guy, ain't ya?"

Gunnar laughed with genuine amusement. "Your lack of intelligence is startling."

Harpe pointed the gun straight between Gunnar's eyes. "Still think this is funny?"

Gunnar's smile faded. "Actually, no. I'm becoming quite bored of the whole affair. At least the Coalition has finally arrived, which means our acquaintance is almost at an end."

Harpe flinched, but he regained himself. "Yeah, it is. They sent me in here to do this." He pulled the trigger.

The bullet was true and honed in on Gunnar's forehead, but the vampire saw the slug leave the chamber and dodged his head to the side, his hair blown back by the velocity of the bullet. "Missed." Gunnar smiled at the shaken police marksman. This time, Harpe unloaded multiple shots at the taunting vampire.

"You're not very good at this, are you?" said Gunnar, unscathed. "One bullet left. Are you saving it for yourself?"

The gun trembled in Harpe's hand. Gunnar lazily got to his feet. "I'm going to make this really easy for you, Harpe." Gunnar walked purposely towards the mortified policeman and put his forehead against the barrel of the pistol. It was time for Gunnar to test himself to the very core of his meditative powers. "Surely, even you can't miss from there."

"What are you?" said Harpe before pulling the trigger. Brain and skull painted the prison cell.

"SID TILLSLEY, WE FINALLY MEET," said Sanderson, opening the door to one of the offices in Nottingham Police Station. He wasn't surprised to see the greatest-living vampire hunter lazing on a chair with his feet on the table, hands behind his head, and belly hanging out.

"Who the fook are you, like?"

"My name is Sanderson. I've been waiting to meet a vampire hunter for a long time. I'm pleased to have the pleasure, sir."

"What are you on about, lad? What's a fooking vampire?" Sid's acting was worse than Sanderson's.

"Hey, I'm an admirer of your work. And, luckily for you, I have the power to make all the charges against you go away. What was it? Indecent exposure, antisocial behaviour, drunk driving, and let's not forget attempted murder. That's quite a few years in the slammer."

Sid rolled his eyes. "I did wonder why I'd been driven a couple of hundred miles to another police station. Should've guessed it was vampire shit." Sid threw up his hands. "Why does this crap always happen when I'm hungover?" He took his feet off the table. "Alreet, who d'ya want me to hit?"

Sanderson smiled. "Gunnar Ivansey."

"Never heard of him."

"No?" Sanderson said in disbelief. "Your paths have crossed before." He showed Sid a picture of the vampire.

Sid squinted. "Nope."

"Really? You had a fight with him outside The Miner's Arms."

"That don't exactly narrow it down, mate. It don't matter. I'll put the nut on him if it gets me back to the boozer in time for opening hours tomorrow."

"Good man."

"I do have one small request if I'm to get me hands dirty."

"And that is?"

"Tomorrow, when I go drinking down the boozer, I want it to be *my* boozer. The one you lot shut down. Give me The Miner's back."

"Consider it done."

"Fooking champion!" Sid rubbed his hands together.

Sanderson was directly disobeying orders, but he didn't care. He was meant to ensure Tillsley's death, but there was no chance of that happening. That's why he'd play everything by the rules only to make one "mistake." Once Ivansey was dead, Tillsley would "escape." Sid could have his pub back. He could have anything he wanted. He was a hero in Sanderson's eyes.

"Want to know what you're up against?"

"Nah," said Sid, "All I'm thinking of is well-kept Bolton Bitter."

"He's a very powerful vampire."

"I don't give a fook, mon. I'm gonna go in there and smack him with a big right, whatever happens. Although, saying that, an army marches on its stomach, and I'm dying for a bacon sarny."

"I'll have one brought to you. I'll call you when you're needed." Sanderson left Sid to his thoughts. A sick part of Sanderson wanted the initial vampire assault to fail. He wanted to see Tillsley in action, defeating Ivansey in unarmed combat. It was, however, unlikely. Ivansey was trapped like a rat, and hopefully, he didn't know it yet.

GUNNAR AWOKE. He had blacked out, but that was of no surprise considering he'd been shot in the head. Harpe lay twitching on the floor with an inch of the butt of his gun protruding from his mouth. The rest was lodged down his neck and throat. That couldn't have gone in easily.

The Coalition's forces would be here in abundance by now. "I'm sorry, Harpe, the show must go on."

He kicked the reinforced cell door down like it was made of cardboard but wasn't greeted with the automatic weapons he'd expected. In fact, there was no one behind the door at all.

Gunnar smiled at the CCTV camera. "What sort of welcome home party is this?" he said theatrically. On to the next door. He kicked it through as easy as the last, and...nothing.

He shook his finger mockingly at the camera in the next corridor. "I'm starting to get bored, now. You don't want me getting bored, Sanderson."

It had to be Sanderson. He hoped it was.

Gunnar kicked the next door through and finally found the action he craved.

IVANSEY WAS HIT AT ALL ANGLES by explosives hidden in the floor and in the walls. While Harpe had performed his unknown-to-him suicide mission of distraction, Sanderson had rigged the explosives to cause maximum damage to the vampire and minimum damage to the building. They needed to finish him fast. If he was covered in half a wall, he'd be protected from the squad and able to regenerate. The vampires called in for the mission and some of Sanderson's top men charged into the smoky corridor from one of the cells and unloaded magazines into the prone vampire.

"Take his head off!" screamed Sanderson through the intercom. From the station's control room, he watched the events unfold through the cameras attached to the soldier's headsets. On a mass of screens, he could see the battle through the eyes of his men and the vampires.

Stepping in, a human soldier unloaded a shotgun shell into Gunnar's head.

"With the fucking axe, you idiot!" hollered Sanderson, his face inches from the monitor.

The soldier, whose sole responsibility was decapitating the vampire, ran into position.

Sanderson sat on the edge of his seat as the soldier hoisted the axe above his head...Suddenly, the world flipped upside down before the camera lost connection.

"What's going on in there?"

Screams filled Sanderson's headset. One by one, the cameras went dead or hit the ground and stopped moving.

"Someone report!" he shouted as he desperately looked at the cameras and the CCTV camera feed for signs of life. Only one camera was still moving. "UPTON! REPORT!"

The camera stopped and slowly turned. Gunnar filled the screen, while Upton, a good man and a good soldier, screamed for his life. Sanderson could see inside Gunnar's head through the crater inflicted by the shotgun. The brain knitted back together. How could he still function?

Slowly, Gunnar pulled Upton towards him, a show for the camera. Gunnar's head moved to the side of the screen and Sanderson was thankful he didn't have to witness the vampire biting into the young man's face. Upton's screams were blood chilling and, thankfully, short lived. Gunnar grinned at the camera, blood covering his face.

Sanderson grabbed his radio. "Someone get Tillsley!"

"TILLSLEY, WE NEED YOU!" a young agent called.

Sid sat at the table, rubbing his belly. "This is a really bad time, mon. I think the bacon in that sandwich was a bit off, like. I'm gonna need to visit the khazi."

"What! No, we need you—now!"

"I canna help it, lad. I'll hit him after me dump. It's good luck; everybody knows that. Like when you bet on the greyhound that takes a shite when they walk the dogs out before a race, yeah?"

The agent ran out of the office. He didn't have a clue what to do. Not many people did when it came to Sid. Luckily for Sid, the rookie, in his panic, forgot to lock the door.

"Thank fook for that," said Sid and went off to find the little boy's room.

SANDERSON BURST INTO THE OFFICE where Sid was supposed to be. He'd known Sid was missing before he'd opened the door, because the smell of stale beer, body odour, and hangover farts had disappeared.

"You idiot!" Sanderson yelled at the rookie. "Wait here, in case he comes back."

"Yes, sir!"

Sanderson hadn't expected to lose the entire squad in one attack. The vampires in the team were dispatched as quickly as the humans. He was left with no choice but to use the police officers currently under guard by his last two commanding officers. Sanderson sprinted up the stairs towards the canteen. He needed half the coppers to search for Sid while the other half would be used as cannon fodder for the marauding vampire.

He ran into the canteen and quickly barked orders with military precision. "The prisoner has escaped. Inspector Graynge, lead half these officers downstairs to the cells. You have permission, by order of Her Majesty, to use lethal force."

Sanderson walked between the officers. "Everyone to the left, go with Graynge." He sent them to their graves without a second thought. They filed out immediately under direction of the young inspector. "Everyone else, search the building for the prisoner who was recently brought into the station, Sid Tillsley. He's 6'5", obese, bald, wearing a leather jacket and blue jeans. You won't be able to miss him. Search the toilets first. GET TO IT!"

"I'M SORRY, KID." whispered Sanderson, forcing himself to watch Graynge's pending assault on Ivansey. He admired the men who were facing certain death. If circumstances were different, he would've recruited them to his own division. But, he had orders, and he was already leaving Tillsley alive despite them.

Graynge and his team made it down to the cells without bumping into the maniac. There, they were subjected to the stomach-emptying sight of the Coalition's dismembered squad. The grotesque corpses and the agony evident in their faces were an echo of the horror. Some of the coppers cried, some were sick.

Gunnar appeared behind them.

Sanderson was thankful he couldn't hear the screams. But, they'd be waiting for him in his nightmares.

20

EVERYONE LEFT ALIVE WAS IN THE STAFF CANTEEN. Gunnar waited in one of the station's offices. He wasn't running. He was having too much fun. The officers searching for Sid had looked everywhere except the toilet adjoined to the office containing Gunnar. Tillsley had to be in there.

The ten remaining police officers were armed, as were Sanderson's agents. Sanderson had an assault rifle equipped with a grenade launcher. He was going to need it. For once, he didn't have much of a plan. He was going to send the coppers in first. They had to die, tonight. If they could cause a distraction, then maybe he could fire a grenade down Ivansey's throat. Hopefully, the commotion would bring Tillsley out of the toilet. Sanderson relayed the makeshift plans to the policemen.

"Let's get this over with."

GUNNAR WATCHED THE HUMANS, like ants, scurry into the large office he was lounging in. He was hoping for a little more of a challenge. Half went left, half went right and in the middle came Sanderson. His presence made this little venture all the more worthwhile.

Gunnar whistled. "Now, that's a big gun."

Without warning, Sanderson fired. Gunnar watched the grenade leave the barrel. His reactions were so quick, it was only a mild inconvenience to dodge it.

SANDRA, 44, FROM DUDLEY, had an unbelievably cracking set of jugs. Today, *Tits* had come up with some of the finest sets of jubblies seen in many a year. Sid approved and pressed on. He was hoping to get to the end of the magazine before he got to the end of his dump. What he wasn't hoping for was to get blown through the cubicle door only to land in one hell of a shitty predicament.

GUNNAR WONDERED WHY THE POLICE WEREN'T FIRING AT HIM. They were all staring past him. He turned to see something sickening. The grenade Sanderson had fired exploded into the wall housing the toilet cistern and Tillsley had been blown through the cubicle door. If Tillsley had a tail, he would be mistaken for a dairy cow with food poisoning.

"What the fook is going on?" Tillsley, with his trousers still round his ankles, turned around shakily, dazed from the explosion. He looked mighty displeased.

"Toilet time is Tillsley's time and no one else's!...Fooking pricks," he muttered.

Tillsley's soiled behind shuffled away and out of sight. Gunnar heard another cubicle open, a toilet seat drop down, and then a muffled, "Where's me fooking magazine?"

Tillsley reappeared, still with his trousers round his ankles, looking for something.

Gunnar's desire for revenge suppressed the pain from his gonads—and the surreal situation suppressed the need for revenge. Why was Tillsley here? Tillsley stared at Gunnar and then at the policemen, hands on hips, shaking his head. "How the fook am I gonna finish a dump without a fooking magazine?"

Gunnar had seen enough. "Tillsley, we meet again."

Sid squinted. "Who the fook are you?"

"You don't remember me? You don't remember what you did to me? You don't remember what I did to you?"

"Oh aye, I remember." Tillsley's eyes narrowed and he rolled his sleeves up. "You lost my copy of *Tits*."

Gunnar bowled Sid over before he had time to pull his pants up.

SANDERSON WAS INTRIGUED BY THE BATTLE. Ivansey was unlike any vampire he'd seen before. His speed was unequalled, and when Sid tried to hit him, it was like a child trying to swat a fly. Gunnar was never there. It didn't help that Sid's balance was impeded by the trousers hugging his ankles.

Sid struggled with his jab. He couldn't move his feet, and Gunnar easily dodged around him and picked him off with shots of his own. This annoyed the big man, who occasionally threw big haymakers in frustration, but with his trousers around his ankles, his lack of balance took him to the ground. The only thing that stopped the vampire jumping on his back and finishing the job was the vast spread of faeces that had been blown across Sid's arse cheeks from the grenade.

Sid needed help. Sanderson barked the order. "Next time Tillsley goes down, unload into Ivansey!"

It wasn't long until another swing and a miss. The troop of police officers unloaded their weapons, and Gunnar scurried back through the hole in the office wall and into the safety of the toilets. Sanderson sent a grenade in after him.

"SID!" screamed Sanderson. "Get your trousers up and knock him out!"

Sid gave him the thumbs up.

GUNNAR LAY IN A PILE OF RUBBLE, trying to find his calm. He regenerated back to full strength in a matter of seconds. Still, if he was hit with another volley like that, and Tillsley landed a bomb, it would be game over. He had to deal with the guns first, and killing Sanderson would be so much fun.

SID NEARLY HAD HIS INCREDIBLY TIGHT JEANS over the fattest part of his arse. Luckily, the mess was lubricating the denim, allowing easier slippage. The twat who'd lost his copy of *Tits* jumped out of the hole in the wall, dived past him, and into the coppers. He was hard as nails and made mincemeat of the rozzers who were carrying loads of shooters. Yep, a hard bastard, but he was going to get a smack as Sid never got to see the centrefold spread.

"Shit," Sid grumbled as the twat who lost his copy of *Tits* got closer to the fella who was going to give him his pub back. Ambling, as usual, Sid initiated a rescue attempt. The twat who lost his copy of *Tits* had killed all but two of the coppers and a couple of suits and now had his hands around his pub's saviour's throat. Sid arrived meaning business, pushing the pub-saving fella to one side and shoulder charging the vampire bastard into the wall. Sid launched the right, but the vamp dodged out of the way.

"Quick little fooker, ain't ya?"

Sid was still shaking off the explosion but getting sharper with every second, plus the hangover was pretty much non-existent now. However, he was beat up. He bled from a few cuts below the eyes and showed signs of swelling. The ref would've kept an eye on them, but there was no immediate danger of a stoppage.

Still, enough was enough. It was time for "The Special."

"Reet! Have that!"

GUNNAR HADN'T EXPECTED THE SPECIAL...AGAIN. The punch arced downwards towards Gunnar's nether regions, just like six months ago when it had taken his penis clean off. Tillsley's hand fizzed past his trousers. Gunnar's testicles were held firm with tight underpants, and the punch whistled past them. If only Tillsley had caught them, then he would've been free of their suffering. Gunnar sensed Tillsley's movement, and an uppercut followed. Gunnar threw himself backwards to avoid the incoming missile. A hair's breadth of distance made the difference between life and death, and Gunnar felt the searing heat of the punch as it passed. The power was amazing, but so were Gunnar's reactions. Tillsley couldn't touch him.

Gunnar hit the floor but sprung back by kicking his legs up into a flip. He knew that a big right would be waiting for him, but Tillsley would be in for a shock.

SID HAD SEEN THEM MARTIAL ARTS FANNIES do all them fancy acrobatics before. In the movies, they'd hit the floor and spring back up. Sid had always wondered why no one had ever thought of kicking the flash bastards really, really hard in the bollocks. True to form, the wanker landed, and his upper back hit the floor at the same time as his hands. His legs went back and over his head and he kicked himself into the flip. But Sid had a little surprise waiting, a surprise in the form of a vicious, right-footed toe punt to the family jewels.

NEVER HAD A SCROTUM STRETCHED SO FAR. Gunnar collapsed to his knees. His eyes glowed an unholy red. The veins on his neck bulged as if ready to explode. Rational thought was no longer possible. There was no control. There was just pain. His world burnt in pain.

THEORY TESTED, Sid expected his adversary to pass out after the shot to the stones. What he didn't expect was to be attacked with a flurry of razor-sharp nails.

"Fooking hell, mon!" Sid ducked out of the way. Blood gushed from various wounds on his arms where he'd held them up to protect his face. "This one's a fooking psycho!" Sid regained his composure and put his hands up in a boxers guard.

Again, the attack was relentless. The vampire threw wild, scratching swings at Sid before he was even in range. He clawed across the front of Sid's fists, inflicting deep gashes in his knuckles.

Sid grimaced. This was real pain, and he'd never experienced it during a fight before. But, he still had enough left for one more big 'un. He launched the right. The vamp didn't try to get out of the way. The right connected, but it withdrew with the same speed it was thrown. Sid couldn't follow through because of the pain of his lacerated hand. The onslaught continued.

"Fook this for a game of soldiers!"

Grabbing the slashing hands, Sid started headbutting and didn't stop until the thrashing hands slowed. Spinning the psycho around, he picked him up by the scruff of the neck and the waistband of his trousers. His bouncing experience of dealing with aggressive, scratching, 'boro warrior women was coming in useful (although in most cases, he didn't need to headbutt the 'boro lasses). Picking the nearest window, he launched the nutter who fell two stories onto a police car below. His body hit the bonnet, causing a violent whiplash of his head. Sid winced. That would've proper hurt.

"Job done," he said, dusting off his hands. He took another look—and then did a double take. The body had gone.

"Hard fooker, him, like."

Sid lit up a cigarette. It was a premium brand and it tasted good. Two hundred Richmonds were the price for Caewyn Maybon's head. Sid was happy to land the right as he could have sworn that the vampire bastard had taken the last piece of haddock at the chippy the week previous. Sid limped over to Sanderson and took a seat on the floor. That was the hardest scrap of his life, and it was going to take a lot of tabs, and a lot of ale for the healing process to begin. He bled badly. "Fook me," he said before lighting up again.

"You saved my life, Sid. Thank you."

"No problem, mate," he wheezed. "Now you need to hold your end of the bargain and open up The Miner's."

"Consider it done. We need to get you to a hospital."

"You get that pub open and that'll be all the healing I need," said Sid. He looked at his hands. "Ah, fook. I'm gonna need a plaster on these bastards."

"He was different from the last time you faced him, wasn't he?" asked Sanderson.

"Never seen the fooker before. He seemed pretty pissed off with me, like. I must have beaten him at darts before or summat."

21

BANG! BANG! BANG!

"Stop your banging, ya bastards! I'm coming!" came Mrs Ackroyd's shout from behind the The Miner's Arms front door. The four 'boro lads all stamped their feet, trying to keep warm. It was late, but Sid and the gang had to tell Kev the good news. And then try and wangle a few pints.

BANG! BANG! BANG!

"For fook's sake," cried Mrs Ackroyd before opening the door.

At the sight of Mrs. Ackroyd in her beauty treatment and hair curlers, Brian ran away, Rathbone hid beneath his cape, Arthur jumped back into a defensive karate stance, and Sid let go of a teeny bit of poo.

"What do you fookers want?" she cried. "You know there's no ale here."

"Where's Kev?" asked Brian, a little out of breath and jogging back after realising that it was Kev's missus and not the living dead.

"Like you care, Garforth." She crossed her arms. "Since this pub's been closed down, he's heard nowt from ya. Some fooking friend you are."

"Aww, don't be like that, Mrs. Ackroyd," Brian cajoled. "Where's Kev? We've got some good news for him."

"He's down his allotment, again."

"Kev's got an allotment?" said Arthur.

Mrs. Ackroyd shook her head. "How long have you known him? He's been in a proper bad way since he lost his license." She looked at Sid with an appraising eye. "Have you been scrapping again, our Sid?"

Sid looked embarrassed. "Aye, I got into a little one, like. He started it though."

"Did you finish it?" she asked.

"Well, kinda."

"Good lad." Mrs Ackroyd smiled. She always had a soft spot for the big man. "You shouldn't be hanging around with these worthless bastards, Sid. They're a bad influence on you." And with that, Mrs Ackroyd slammed the door.

"Reet, then," said Brian. "Best we go up the Smithson Allotment and find Kev."

Arthur Peasley shook his head. "No wonder the poor bastard spends all of his time up there. His woman nags more than mine."

THE FOUR LADS made their way down the road to the allotments. It wasn't a big patch of land, but it was a nice bit of greenery in the rundown estate, not that it was green at this cold, bitter time of year. It was rare that vandalism took place on the allotments, and it had nothing to do with respect or any nonsense like that. No, the kids around here were absolute bastards. The real reason was because each allotment was heavily booby trapped, and each gardener was equipped with weaponry shipped in from Eastern Europe. This was a classic example of corporal punishment being a fine deterrent against criminal behaviour.

There weren't many allotments, just two central paths with small plots of lands to either side of them, meaning four rows of sheds needed searching.

"Which one do you reckon is Kev's?" asked Sid.

"I've no idea," said Brian. "Let's take a walk and see if there're any signs of the miserable bastard."

"Sounds like a plan, man," agreed Arthur.

"Most of the lights in the little sheds are still on," said Sid. "Have none of these fookers got homes to go to?"

"How many people do you know with an allotment?" asked Brian.

Sid thought long but not very hard. "Well, apart from Kev, no one."

"Exactly, mate. They're a weird breed. Most of them sleep here, you know? They're an untrusting bunch who live for their cabbages and runner beans. They won't talk to you if you haven't got one of these shitty little garden things. Be careful. I've heard tales of these fookers, and this place is most likely booby trapped to buggary and back. Come on, we'll take this side first."

The cold winter's night did not make the cosy-looking sheds look any more appealing. There was something horribly eerie about the trinkets that the Allotmenteers hung from their sheds and outhouses: squirrel skulls, badger furs and, in one case, what looked like human scrotums. The moonlight cast long shadows causing the friends to huddle a little closer together.

A few of the doors opened as they walked past and the occupants came out carrying garden tools that could easily be adapted into offensive weapons. Men who looked like they'd evolved from root vegetables held on to spades, axes, forks, chainsaws, and Chinese flying guillotines. One particularly scary, naked individual wore a knife on the end of his erect member as seen in the film *Seven*, which he thrust, menacingly, at the lads as they passed by.

"They're fooking mental, Brian!" said Sid, in his patented shouting whisper.

"YOU'RE NOT GONNA STEAL MY BEETROOT, YOU TWATCOCK!" an Allotmenteer screamed as they passed by. The man was one of the ugliest people in all of Middlesbrough, and he possessed a strange, giant eye that looked ready to pop.

"Eh?" asked a shaken Sid.

"TWATCOCK!"

"I ain't stealing anything, mon. I fooking hate beetroot," said Sid honestly but fearfully.

"TWATCOCK!"

The psychopath continued to yell the strange obscenity at the four lads until they were a hundred yards away from his door before running back to his beetroot patch to count them for the fiftieth time that evening.

"I don't wanna see that crazy bastard ever again," said Sid.

"Me neither," said Brian. "Hey, I reckon that's Kev's allotment."

The allotment in question was a well-kept and relatively pretty patch of land. There were a few vegetable patches and a simple, but decorated, summerhouse.

The scholar put his brain into gear. He stroked his chin, thoughtfully, like all scholars do when being clever. "It looks like someone normal owns it, at least, and the light's on. It's worth knocking."

"Rathbone, go knock on the door," ordered Arthur.

"Why should I fooking go?" said the lazy, good-for-nothing vampire.

"Because if it's booby trapped, it ain't gonna matter if you get your leg blown off, is it?" reasoned Arthur.

"It will bloody matter to me."

"Yeah, man, but your leg will grow back. If one of our legs goes bye-bye, we'll die."

"So?"

"Don't be an asshole, man. Knock on the door."

"No."

"Go on, Rathbone, just do it," said Brian.

"Fooking 'ell!" conceded Rathbone. "All this for that robbing twat, Ackroyd." He proceeded to climb over the padlocked gate.

"Good lad. I'll get you a pint later," said Sid.

Rathbone walked to the door quickly, wanting to get this over and done with. "You better fooking—AAAARRGGGHHHH!"

A land mine blasted half of Rathbone's leg off. He hopped around for a bit before toppling into a neatly stacked manure pile. "AAAARRHGGHH! There's shit on me cape. There is *shit* on me cape!"

"Landmines," said Arthur. "Where's Princess Diana when you need her?"

Through the agony and the shitty cape, Rathbone still managed, "I...I...shagged her."

"Anyroad," said Brian, ignoring Rathbone, "that ain't gonna be Kev's allotment, is it? He doesn't know how to booby trap 'owt. Otherwise, we wouldn't be able to steal so much of his ale."

"Can you make it over here, Rathbone?" asked Arthur.

Rathbone crawled out of the allotment, and Sid picked him up and acted as a crutch for the temporarily disabled vampire.

"Eh'up, that's gotta be the one," said Brian pointing to an allotment in the distance. "Look, there's a barrel of beer outside."

"That could be Bolton Bitter, Brian. *Bolton Bitter!*" said Sid, drooling like a rabid pensioner. He dropped Rathbone and actually *ran* towards the shed where the best beer in the world waited.

"AAARRGGGHH! You stupid, big fooker!" yelled Rathbone.

"It has to be Kev's." said Brian. "Everything on the patch of ground is dead. He's crap at everything apart from keeping ale."

"The lights aren't on, though, and Mrs Ackroyd said he was up here," said Arthur, who picked up Rathbone and helped him towards the oasis.

Rathbone's newly acquired vampire night-vision told a different story. "I can see movement inside. Someone is definitely in there."

Sid banged on the door so hard, he nearly smashed through the wood. "BOLTON! ARE YOU IN, BOLTON?"

"His name is 'Kev,' Sid," corrected Brian.

"BOLTON!" cried the addict, desperate for his hit.

"Kev, you in?" shouted Brian in between Sid's cries and hammerings on the door.

"I don't think he is," said Arthur.

"I saw movement," said Rathbone. "Arthur, take me round the side for a better look."

Arthur complied, and Rathbone put his face against the window. It was difficult to see anything through the dirty glass. There was a dim light flickering in the background, possibly candlelight. But, there was movement, a rhythmical, gentle swaying of a heavy object. He concentrated on the light and could see a thin line passing across it, almost like...a rope.

"Stupid prat," said Rathbone.

"What is it?" asked Brian.

"He hasn't spilled any booze, has he?" asked a desperate Sid.

"He's only gone and hung himself."

It took a moment for Rathbone's words to hit home. It suddenly got a lot colder.

"Sid, knock the door down!" Brian shouted. Sid didn't need telling twice and a size fourteen obliterated the lock.

A sight no human being ever wanted to see horrified the lads...

GUNNAR OPENED HIS EYES. He'd no idea where he was or why he was covered in blood. Flesh, gore, bones, and unidentifiable human parts were scattered around the room while blood painted the walls and the ceiling. He couldn't work out how many humans had been slaughtered. Five? Ten? How? When? Why?

What happened yesterday?

It came flooding back: Tillsley, the police station, the fight...the kick to his swollen testes. It had sent him over the edge. He'd nearly held it together, but when he'd finally erupted, the red mist clouding his reason had lasted longer, much longer.

Where was he? It looked like a sitting room, but there was no real way to tell due to the carnage. He pushed the human remains from his person and rose to his feet. He was completely naked. A desk blocked a window preventing the daylight that would've killed him. He must have slept all day. His feral instincts still protected him from the sun. Who were these people? He pushed open the room's grand double doors to try and find some answers.

The hall resembled the blood bath he'd just left, but on a monumental scale. It was like a vision of the past. This was his life in medieval times. This would be a life he desired if he could remember any of it. How could he forget this? To only experience the aftermath of your pleasure was a living hell.

The house was huge. It must have been a party. That was the only explanation for the hundred or so humans who now shared this beautiful tomb. However, if this was a party, there would've been music, but there was nothing but an eerie silence. Gunnar walked through the destruction towards the front entrance of the house and the reason for the silence was explained. A mutation of bodies and musical instruments were scattered on a makeshift stage. He bent down and plucked a string of what was possibly a violin, which was impaled in what was possibly a human chest.

He opened the front doors to the countryside and a cold winter wind whipped against his naked flesh. The wind offered small relief as it gently cooled his swollen testes, the cause of the massacre.

The Coalition had a task on their hands covering up this mess along with the police station. Gunnar jogged around the great manor house. There were only a few bodies outside, meaning only a few people had tried to escape. Luckily, he'd had the sense to mop up any stragglers. It would've been his death if he hadn't. There was blood on the ground trailing to some outhouses in the distance. He decided to investigate.

A strange sensation filled his stomach when he reached them, one that wasn't meant to be felt by a lamia: Sickness. The murder in the manor house was reciprocated in the stables, where he now stood. He'd murdered all of the animals. He was a noble vampire, but he'd been nothing but an animal himself. He was no better than a fox amongst chickens. Human sacrifice had a purpose. There was no point to this utter madness.

"THIS ENDS HERE!" he screamed and fell to his knees. His vision began to fade as his testicles pumped hatred into his heart and throughout his body. He had to fight it. He took deep breaths and tried to find calm. Slowly, his vision returned. If he couldn't end this, then he would die trying. There were a few hours to sunrise. A new dawn brought a new day. No longer would he be imprisoned.

Sunlight. There'd be no regeneration from the vampires' bane. He had to resist the urge to hide; an instinct blueprinted into his DNA. He had to face what the lamia feared most. In the wooden outhouse, he punched a hole in the wall and placed his testicles through making it appear as if two large, ripe plums were defying gravity. He hoped a hungry blackbird wouldn't take interest. The burning would be a relief from what felt like fire in his blood. He had to stay strong.

Birdsong indicated it was close. The dawn chorus was beautiful to humans but was the sound of death to the vampire, but now, it brought the chance of life renewed. If he made it, he would make the world pay for what he was about to put himself through.

He pressed up against the side of the wooden outhouse, gripping onto the struts of the building so hard he splintered the wood. Once the sun rose, peace and agony would be his.

He tried to relax and forget about his (or rather his knackers') impending doom. He sought the inner peace inside of him and tried to enter a state of timelessness. Fear gripped him as the sun broke the horizon.

"AAAAAAAAAAAARRRRRGGGGHHHHH!" Even with his eyes tightly shut, white light burnt into his brain, and the pain in his testes emanated through every cell of his body. The white light waned and darkness took over. Loss of consciousness would ruin it all. He had to stand strong. Every molecule of his sack must be removed but he felt faint. "Must...hold..."

Finally, he collapsed. He crawled to the corner of the stables to a tarpaulin and pulled it over him. There was nothing he could do but pass out.

"WHAT'RE YA UP TO, KEV?" asked a rather concerned Brian after the lads barged into the spacious allotment shed.

"What are you doing here!" screamed the startled landlord, clambering to his feet, displaying his naked, portly male form for all it was worth.

Brian wanted to look at the floor where the sights were less...disturbing, but his eyes were drawn to the various contraptions and objects hanging from the ceilings. "We came to...errr...bring you some news."

"Out with it, then," said Kevin impatiently.

"Errr, yeah...errr...don't worry about that, now. What the fook are you up to?"

"Nowt. Now, if you don't mind?" Kevin gestured to the door.

"That's some weird shit, man," said Arthur, shaking his head, scanning the...things.

"Yeah? Is it? Is it fooking really?" Sometimes the best defence was headstrong offence.

"Yeah, man, it is."

"What are all the ropes and shit for, Kev?" asked Brian.

"Realistic movement."

"Oh. Oh, reet."

Sid pointed to an inanimate object. "Are you shagging that?"

"'Her,' Sid, 'her.' 'Am I shagging her?' is what you mean?"

"I...I...don't know what I mean, mon."

"If that's what you meant, then yes, I am, or rather I *was* shagging her until we were rudely interrupted."

"Where did you get it, man?" asked Arthur.

"I got *her* from the Internet, if you must know. As I did her friends."

Arthur inspected Kev's extensive range before focusing on the model suspended by ropes. "Has she got, you know...bits?"

Kevin raised his eyes heavenward and sighed. "Of course she has. Inga has three working orifices."

"Inga?" repeated Brian.

"She's my Swedish sex siren."

"Oh, sorry. What are all the ropes for again?"

"Realistic movement. Observe."

Kevin pulled what seemed like a random rope and Inga the sex doll burst into action by changing from one lewd position to another. With a jolt of another rope, she back flipped into what would be considered by most a very lewd position indeed.

"I see," said Brian. "I had no idea you were so good with...erm...knots. How about putting some clothes on, Kev?"

"I'm fine," he said, running his fingers over his ginger moustache. He hoped that by acting normally, details of this awkward situation would go no further.

"Anyway...," Brian started. "We have some good news. Sid has clenched a deal that means you can reopen The Miner's again."

"Oh, fantastic," Kev deadpanned. He would've been jumping for joy if his customers hadn't caught him shagging a sex doll. "I'm looking forward to celebrating with a free night of booze for all of you—*if* this little incident is forgotten about."

"I think a week is more apt for this one, Kev," said Brian.

"A week it is," said Kev offering a hand. He retracted the handshake when it received nothing but disgusted stares.

Much to Kevin's disdain, Rathbone touched Inga's skin with his disgusting, greasy hands. Kevin bit down on his lip. It was hard to contain the fury as the greasy, horrible, little bastard ran his hands up her back and into her soft, thick, golden locks. Suddenly, Rathbone maliciously pulled off the doll's wig. "Look! It's Sid!"

Unable to cope with the defilement of a sick rendition of his own beautiful form, Sid started windmilling at Kev, and luckily for Kev, Sid's first couple of punches got caught up in Inga's intricate pulley system.

Within seconds, he was a tangle of ropes, prosthetic limbs, and pubic wigs.

Kevin, seeing his second wife being assaulted, and with no fear for his own safety, jumped in, brave as a perverted lion. This resulted in a strange ménage a trois with both men becoming tangled in a web of sexual deviancy.

Arthur, Rathbone, and Brian fell to the floor in hysterics as Kevin and Sid screamed obscenities at each other.

22

"AND HOW DID TILLSLEY MANAGE TO ESCAPE, EXACTLY?" asked Charles, condescendingly. "He isn't the most agile of fellows, and I doubt he's smart enough to lose you."

Sanderson was debriefing the Coalition about the mission that could only be classed as an absolute failure. He didn't mind pulling the wool over the eyes of these bureaucrats, but convincing them that the loss of Tillsley was an accident would be a futile and idiotic venture.

"He saved my life."

"Personal feelings shouldn't come into your job, Sanderson," lectured Rempstone, chin held high, chest puffed out, enjoying the moment.

"You're right." *1-0 you little shit.* "But when you see a man jump in to stop an animal from ripping your squad apart and then he saves your life, you can't help feel a little grateful. But then, you'd know all about field combat, wouldn't you?"

Rempstone's chest deflated as if he'd been punched in the stomach. "We cannot let this weapon go. If we had sent him in first, we wouldn't be knee-deep in shit, right now."

"We cannot be seen to—"

"We are *losing*, Caroline!" He ignored her enraged glare. "Ivansey is an animal unlike anything else. I've no idea what's happened to him, but he's unstoppable."

"He cannot be made a martyr."

"Jesus, woman! It's easy making bold statements when you haven't experienced real conflict. If you won't send Tillsley, you'll need every last man in the SAS, and that's no guarantee you'll take Ivansey down."

"You should have ended Tillsley's life," said Bwogi. "The Occursus is a sacred event, and the attack was seen as an act of war."

Sanderson closed his eyes, trying not to let the madness of the council affect him.

"Garendon," said Caroline. "Please tell us Haemo is on track."

"Yes. In fact, we're doing a little better than that. You gave me permission to look into alternative formulations, and I must say, the airborne route is looking very promising, more efficacious than the injection."

"Airborne? Are you mad?" snapped Sebastian.

"No. This is ingenious," said Bwogi, excited. "An airborne route means the vampire could be subjected to Haemo without even knowing it."

Garendon nodded and continued. "I've always been interested in viruses, and I researched their mutative capabilities during the Second World War when Nazi Germany gave me all the resources I needed to create biological weapons. We made some marvellous advances during that time."

"And committed some hideous crimes," added Sanderson, sickened that he'd actually started to like Garendon.

"No, just science. Through my research, far more lives were saved as a result of the lives lost. I never gave the Nazis access to the weapons. Incidentally, would you have judged me so harshly if I carried out my tests on Nazis? Probably not."

"Garendon, please get to the point," said Caroline.

"Of course." He offered Sanderson a polite smile before continuing. "Viruses are fascinating entities. Mutations are simple to produce and can lead to some novel applications, take the Human Immunodeficiency Virus, for example."

"HIV is a mutation from the Simian Immunodeficiency Virus found in the white-collared monkey," Jeremy Pervis, even when in constant fear, still had time to be the know-it-all.

Garendon laughed. "Yes, that's what we led the media to believe. We created the Simian Immunodeficiency Virus after we released HIV—by accident, I must add."

Sanderson couldn't believe his ears. "You created HIV...and let it out by accident?"

"That's something that doesn't need discussing now. I'm sure I could cure it, if I had the time."

"If...you had...the time?" Sanderson ground out slowly, trying to digest the concept.

"I can't work 24/7, Mr Sanderson. I need to unwind. I also have a passion for geology."

"Well, if you find some time in between looking at your fucking rocks, maybe you can put your mind to ridding the world of a virus that's killed over 25 million people, so far."

"I'm sure I will, someday," said Garendon not noticing the mocking tone. "HIV was created by accident when I was investigating the vampire's autoimmune defence system, in which, we have yet to find a weakness. I was looking at ways of transporting substances into the vampire's blood stream."

"Why would you do that?" asked Augustus.

"Have you ever been drunk?" Garendon asked lightly, a loaded question.

"Of course not. It's impossible for drugs to affect a vampire."

Garendon smiled. "I was working on a way to get drugs into the blood stream without them being attacked by the autoimmune system."

"Again, why would you want to do that?"

Sanderson shook his head and thought, *To get pissed, dickhead. It would be great if you could unwind with a beer instead of massacring a family.*

"I wouldn't," answered Garendon, "but I knew someone who did, and it sounded like an interesting project. That's how I discovered HIV. I managed to mutate a virus that interfered with the human immune system, but I was never able to recreate this in a vampire."

"I guess we should be thankful," said Augustus sarcastically, while nervously biting his nails.

"In a human, the virus can only be passed through the transfer of certain bodily fluids, although it would be quite simple to adapt the virus to an airborne version."

Sanderson now looked on with horror at an individual who was potentially far more dangerous than Ivansey and the entire vampire nation.

"Don't even think about it," warned Caroline.

Garendon shrugged his shoulders. "With vampire physiology, the airborne route is a far more subtle way for a virus to enter the body. With a little work, I managed to design and mutate a virus that could carry small molecules. These molecules would be obliterated, mopped up by the vampire immune system, but not Haemo, as the body uses it like a food source. A vampire's body will actually rip Haemo from the virus."

Bwogi looked at Garendon incredulously. "So you're saying that you can create a *virus* that will quell the bloodlust in all vampires?"

"Even Ivansey's?" cried out the pathetic Jeremy Pervis.

"It's not exactly a virus. Once the vampire's immune system destroys the carrier and feeds on the Haemo, then the vampire will need another hit, so to speak. We will need to pump it into the air on a permanent basis. Haemo works, but I need to develop a virus carrier specific to Haemo itself, and that is going to take time. After that, the scale up may offer further problems."

"And the cure?" asked Sebastian, trying not to appear horrified.

"Well, that's the easy bit. The carrier will be destroyed in the body, but the Haemo will be absorbed. Once the body has exhausted the Haemo supplies, the bloodlust will return. It will be as if the vampire never took the drug in the first place."

The councillors exchanged glances, all of them unsure whether they had just heard Garendon correctly.

Bwogi was the first to speak, and there was hope in his eyes. "So you're saying the effects aren't permanent?"

"I hoped they would be, but no, the latest trials show that the effects of Haemo are, indeed, temporary."

"This is exactly what we've been looking for!" Bwogi gushed. "My god, why didn't you tell us this sooner?"

"I didn't think it was as important," he said, with a shrug. "The main goal of my research was to quell the blood lust."

Sebastian wasn't convinced. "How can you be so sure it will work? I should imagine you didn't expect to wipe out millions of humans with AIDS."

"I'm seventy per cent certain of my hypothesis."

"We can't gamble on seventy per cent," said Sebastian.

"No," said Caroline, "but we should start scaling up production immediately while Garendon performs the necessary safety tests."

"But safety testing is so boring," said Garendon like a petulant child.

"I don't care," scolded Bwogi. "We only go with this if you're one hundred per cent sure that it's not permanent or hazardous to humans or vampires. Does anyone have anything they would like to add?"

"This needs more discussion," said Sebastian.

"Here, here," agreed Augustus.

Caroline sealed the deal. "Its use needs discussion, but its development doesn't. Until Tillsley and Ivansey are dead, the development is to carry on with no expense spared."

Sanderson smiled.

"Yes," Charles said. "This airborne, viral carrier seems very interesting, indeed. Double your efforts, Garendon. In the meantime, let us finally rid ourselves of Ivansey."

"And have we come any closer to deciding how?" asked Sanderson. He really hated Charles.

Caroline took a moment and then relented. "Sanderson, you've got one more chance. *One* chance. And if he isn't dead..." Caroline didn't need to finish the sentence for him to know what she meant. The threat didn't bother him. He respected her more for it.

"You're sending Tillsley?" said Bwogi.

Caroline nodded. "We can go round in circles. We can worry about the leak, but Ivansey must be stopped, one way or another, and Tillsley is the best we've got. Sebastian, you better plug that leak damn quick, because news of the disaster in Nottingham Police Station is going to travel around the country like wildfire. Things are about to get a lot worse."

23

MAGIC WAS IN THE AIR. This was the only time when an all-dayer, in the true sense of the term, could be initiated: 11 a.m. In a moment, the enchanting sound of the great oak door of The Miner's Arms unlocking would inspire wonder and excitement in all drunks within earshot, waiting for the nectar of the gods: well-kept Bolton Bitter.

Kevin Ackroyd kept the best beer in all the Northeast. There wasn't a better combination than Kev's fine landlord skills and succulent Bolton Bitter, a copper colour, with a well-rounded, rich flavour and a lasting, bitter finish. This beer was a champion of champions.

Outside The Miner's Arms stood Sid, Arthur, Brian, and the lads who watched Tarrant. It had been one of the most sorrowful days on the Smithson Estate when Kevin rang time for the very last time. Today, joy replaced that sorrow. Like a drunken phoenix, The Miner's was about to rise from the ashes, pissed and craving a kebab.

Sid was giddy with anticipation of a free day's drinking. Brian had managed to patch up Sid and Kevin's differences concerning Inga with some smooth talking, and the whole event was forgotten as long as the week's drinking was free of charge—but within reason. The lads were only allowed Bolton Bitter, but after their cruel separation, they wouldn't want anything else.

The door unlocked, and out stepped the hero of modern bar keeping. "All right, you lot, calm down," said Kevin, trying not to smile as everyone barged past him to get to the bar.

The Miner's Arms was a special pub indeed. It hadn't been decorated in decades. It was an absolute shithole. It got trashed at least once a fortnight in its infamous, coma-inducing bar brawls. There was hardly any furniture, and what was there was filthy. There was no music either. The police were scared to say its name, but it was extremely popular with rats and flies.

"BOLTON!" demanded Kev's patrons.

Kev proudly strutted around to the service side of the bar. "Certainly, gentlemen, I would be honoured to serve you." He pulled the pumps, and like a waterfall from the Garden of Eden, Bolton spewed forth, bringing intoxication. Every pint was poured to perfection. Every one poured to the exact quantity as deemed suitable by the Trading Standards Committee.

In other pubs across the land, there would've been a toast where everyone savoured the event. In this pub, however, this real, drinking pub, there was no such etiquette. Every man drank as much ale as he could, as quickly as he could. The addicts had their fix, but with beer this magnificent, one hit wasn't enough. Glasses slammed down and the patrons demanded more. A vampire's bloodlust couldn't compare.

Any other barman in the world would've been daunted by the ferocity of The Miner's Arms' patrons, but not Kevin. He'd made them. He was the shepherd and they were his flock. He pulled another round. This was a good day. He couldn't wait to put the prices up.

"Where's Rathbone?" asked Kev.

"He won't be out till it gets dark," replied Brian.

"Eh? I thought he'd be here at opening for the free beers, the greasy, horrible, little bastard."

"Oh, he would've been, Kev, but he's one of them vampires now."

"Really?" said Kev, taking it in his stride. "What did he go and do that for?"

"He hasn't said; we haven't asked. Who cares what he does, anyway? He'll be here soon enough, and I guess that prick, Rich, will be here, as well."

Kevin rubbed his hands together in glee. "Champion! He was spending a fooking fortune in here before them vampire bastards shut us down."

"But he's a reet twat."

"He seems decent enough to me, Brian." Kev wagged a finger. "Don't you go a starting something. I've only just got the place back."

"You only like him because he spends his fooking wedge in here. But, don't worry about me. It's Rathbone you wanna be watching. Rich shot him in the head a few days back."

"Eh? Oh, he's a vampire. I don't want any gunfights, not yet, anyroad. It's hard work running a fooking pub at the best of times, but when fookers start shooting each other and stuff..." Kevin let out a sorry sigh. "It makes landlording difficult." He was called away; the banging down of a pint glass meant he had a job to do.

Satisfied that they had sufficiently oiled themselves, the three heroes, Arthur, Brian, and Sid each took a couple of pints to a table to chew the fat.

Arthur held his pint of ale and put it up to the light, marvelling at the glorious clarity. He then enjoyed the majestic smell of the fine beverage, unaware that it contained over 650 aromatic compounds, but he knew it smelled good, tasted good, and it got him pissed. He downed half and it hit the spot. "Drinking with the boys, man. I need this after all that nagging."

"We can go on the pull together, Arthur," said Sid. "I won't need to keep using the fooking Internet to try and get a shag, then."

"Give it a chance, our Sid, it will come through," Brian soothed. "But you're reet about one thing. Arthur should dump the baggage, like."

Arthur shook his head. "I ain't going through this again. I know what you think, but it ain't gonna happen. I'm gonna do my duty and raise that kid, right. I may even name him after his granddaddy."

"That'll be a nice touch, Arthur." Brian gave him a slap on the back. "Your daddy would've liked that, unless it's a girl. That's by-the-by. What's the old bat been giving you grief for this time?"

"What hasn't she been giving me grief for, is more the question. It doesn't matter what it is, she just has to find something, and this time, it's the laundry. You know I'm a karate master, but what you probably don't know is that to keep my devastating kicks at major league level. I have to maintain my flexibility and strength. So, I'm training, and I've just ate some fucking bean casserole she made me. It fucks my guts, man! It fucks my guts! I'm in a deep squat and I pass a bit of gas. Big deal. Nothing would've happened if it weren't for that bean casserole. Who the fuck eats a bean casserole, anyhow? She starts calling me a 'dirty bastard' and going off on one. Then, I tell her I'm taking a day off to celebrate the opening of The Miner's, and she really goes to town!"

"You don't need that," said Brian. "Deep squats and bean casseroles? What does she expect? And as for not allowing a man to celebrate the reopening of the best pub in the world, that's ridiculous." Brian was about to moan some more but Reece arrived. "And *that's* the end of another good session!" announced Brian.

Arriving at the table, Reece noticed Sid was wearing a lot of bandages. "What happened to you?"

"Big scrap—*gulp*—vampire twat—*gulp*—drinking today—*gulp*—don't be a wanker." Sid got to the end of the pint before pointing to the bar. He was on free booze all day, but if he didn't have to get up, apart from saying goodbye to the extra-large chicken parmo he had the night previous, it was going to be all the better.

Reece bit the inside of his cheek hard but obliged and came back with a tray full of drinks.

Kev never missed an opportunity and made sure he charged the cash-heavy vampire hunter extra for the free beers.

"There you go, you drunken bums. Sid, tell me everything while I have a look at those wounds."

Sid tucked into the new batch of beer and, at first, didn't notice his wounds were being tended. Once the ale was down and his senses returned, the interference wasn't welcomed. "What the fook you playing at?" he said, pulling his arm away.

"I'm checking for infections."

"Gerroff!" he cried with a scowl. "There's nowt wrong with me except that I'm sober."

"OK, calm down," said Reece, secretly slipping one of the blood-soaked bandages into his coat pocket. He didn't need to be too secretive as the lads were already too drunk to notice. "Now, what happened the other night?"

"It was a fooking nightmare, mon. The night went from one of the best I've had in ages to one of the fooking worst. I was that far"—he indicated a span of millimetres with his fingers—"that fooking far from shagging a red-hot divorcée. Then her son came home, and he was, you know, very close to his mother. Next thing, I'm arrested for attempted murder."

Reece would've loved to ask him why he'd been arrested for indecent exposure and lewd behaviour in a men's toilets, but knew it would only end in pain.

"Like last time, all the charges were dropped if I knocked out some vampire fella from Nottingham. Tough fella. I didn't even finish him off. Anyroad, they said, for me services, they'd open The Miner's again. The rest is history." Sid downed a pint of history.

Reece nodded. "So what do you have planned for the rest of the day, or do I need to ask?"

"I'm gonna get pissed, and you ain't gonna even try and stop me," he warned. "I have me Bolton back, and we need some alone time."

Brian was sober enough to realise something was fishy. "Hang on a second. When Sid normally gets involved in any sort of shenanigans with them vampire bastards, you won't leave him alone. You fooking knew, didn't you?"

Reece's eyes narrowed for a split second. "I have my sources on the inside. I'm just sorry I wasn't there to help."

It was Brian's turn to narrow his eyes.

"Anyway, I have something for you, Brian." Reece took something out of his coat and placed it on the table. "Something that will come in useful if you ever find yourself confronted with the lamia."

"What's that, man?" asked Arthur. "Is it some sort of gun?"

"It is." Reece took a packet of balloons out of his pocket and unclipped a cartridge from the gun. "You can load ten at a time. Observe." He showed Brian how a balloon could be stretched across the clip, and then another balloon could be placed over the top, just like a magazine. "Click it back into place." He placed the clip in the handle and slapped the bottom with the palm of his hand. "You're ready to go." He offered the handle to Brian.

Brian hesitated for a second and then took it. He suspected the weapon would come in handy. He pointed the gun at one of Kevin's flying ducks on the wall. The balloon's velocity was incredible. Decoration in The Miner's Arms was reduced by thirty-three per cent.

The Cumapult was born.

"What the fook was that?" screamed the landlord.

"Nowt! Pour the beers," said Brian.

The landlord seethed, knowing the lads had him over a barrel but pulled the pints.

"That's impressive, like. How long can I store 'em? You know, me stuff burnt through the other ones you gave me."

"You have a week if you use these." Reece took out of his coat a small package containing balloons made of the same rubber used to make the gloves for cleaning up toxic waste. He gave them to Brian. "On impact, they explode. This is a lethal weapon."

Brian nodded.

"What the fook do you want a balloon gun, for?" asked Sid. "You ain't becoming a fooking clown are you? I fooking hate clowns," he said through gritted teeth. "I hate clowns worse than fooking ice-cream men."

"No, Sid. I'm gonna fill the balloons with a chemical toxic to vampires," said Brian, keeping secret the recipe for his special sauce.

"Champion."

"Man, it ain't fair," moaned Arthur. "You can both kill vampires, and what can I do? I get one of the ball-busting bitches up the duff."

"At least you got a shag out of it, Arthur," said Sid, lighting a tab. "Since them vampire bastards turned up, I haven't even got fingers and tops." He drew in deeply on the Lambert and Butler, a gift for a tasty left hook eaten by Ade Claudistine, a vampire who would never drive irresponsibly past horses ever again.

Arthur gave Sid a double point. "I'll get some beers, baby. That will cheer us up."

A few hours later, the boys were hammered and, with the wane of daylight, came the vampire. Rathbone burst into the pub, smoking.

"Get me a beer, quick, Ackroyd!"

Every muscle in Kev's body tensed as he pulled a pint. Serving the greasy, horrible, little bastard was the worst part of this awful deal. "What you smoking for?"

"I always fooking smoke, ya twat," said the rudest vampire in all the land, lighting up a tab.

"No, *you're* smoking. As in: you."

Rathbone wafted his crimson cape and smoke rose to the already-yellow ceiling. "Oh, reet. It weren't fully dark when I left, but I was fooking dying for a pint."

"You missed the best beer in the 'boro?" asked Kevin, proudly.

"No," Rathbone lied, slamming his glass down. It was his first pint of Bolton Bitter in months, and boy, had he missed it. For the first time since becoming a vampire, he felt content.

24

SANDERSON LAUGHED. "This is all he wants?" He stood outside The Miner's Arms, acknowledging the depravity of the area. Tillsley was from a humble background, just like Sanderson. If it hadn't been for the army, would he be drinking somewhere like this, right now? Probably not. He'd almost certainly be dead.

The army had saved him. His sergeant major saw the potential in him, even as a sixteen-year-old. Sanderson was beaten to a pulp on a nightly basis to make him into the man he was now. Sergeant Major Atkins knew what he was doing and had pushed Sanderson through to the Special Forces division as soon as he was eligible. He shined. A decorated veteran of the Gulf Wars, he was handpicked for his role on the Coalition.

He remembered being told the truth about the world. He'd known that if he didn't accept a place on the Coalition, he would've been killed, and sometimes he wondered if it would've been a better option. The Coalition was a shambles. It wasn't what he'd signed up for. He took the job to do what was best for mankind. Saving Tillsley wasn't the best of ideas for his career, but Tillsley was what mankind needed.

Sanderson recognised the smell as soon as he entered The Miner's Arms. He remembered it from every Friday and Saturday night as a fifteen-year-old boy, smashed out of his brain and about to smash in someone else's. It was the smell of the dregs of society. The smell of men with nothing in their lives but the next pint of beer. He approached the table where Sid sat.

"And that's why I stopped doing that bird with the conjoined twin..." Brian trailed off. "Who's this twat?"

Sanderson knew the face of Brian Garforth, Tillsley's best friend. He recognised Arthur Peasley too. He really did look like his father. Reece Chambers, now that was someone Sanderson had always wanted to meet. If the man wasn't such an arrogant fool, he could've used him to rid the world of some of the nastier bloodsuckers. One more sat with them, Peter Rathbone, who promptly received a bullet between the eyes.

"Do you know him?" Brian casually asked Sanderson.

"I know what he is."

"A reet wanker?"

"Eh'up!" said Sid, with a grin on his face. "This is the lad who reopened The Miner's, everyone!"

A half-arsed cheer arose from the pub's patrons.

"Hello, Sid." Sanderson was still looking down the barrel of his gun. He moved smoothly around the table to take aim at Rathbone. From the corner of his eye, Sanderson saw Chambers bend over the vampire, mop the blood from around the bullet wound with a handkerchief, and slip it back into his pocket. *What are you up to?* wondered Sanderson.

"I'm astonished to find you cavorting with a vampire, Chambers." said Sanderson.

"These gentlemen convinced me killing him was a bad idea."

"Yeah, don't kill Rathbone. He's not always a complete wanker," said Sid.

"I'm watching him like a hawk," said Chambers. "He's harmed no one, so far. I hope to learn more about them, through him. If he harms a hair on a human's head, he'll be dead. Sooner, if Sid lets me."

Rathbone came to and sat bolt upright. "What the fook did you shoot me for!"

Sanderson didn't acknowledge him. He went to the bar instead. "Anyone want a beer?"

"YEAH!" shouted three humans and a vampire.

"You work for that vampire-council thingy?" asked Kevin after Sanderson ordered his round.

Sanderson laughed. If they truly were to cover up the vampire activity in Middlesbrough, they'd have to kill everybody in it. "Yes, you could say that."

"Ah, reet. Do you reckon they'd be interested in a vampire night, like? I do a regular ladies' night, you see, and it's a huge success. Them vampires seem to get a hard time, with Sid always smackin' 'em, and even they must need to unwind with a few beers after a day's work."

"I'll see what I can do," said Sanderson, keeping his hysterics on the inside.

"Champion."

Sanderson took the beers back to the table and drew up a chair. He brought two beers for everyone, even Rathbone. Everyone tucked in apart from Chambers. "To Sid and The Miner's," Sanderson toasted.

No one replied. They were all lusting after ale. Sanderson laughed before finishing his beer, like the lads, in a single draught. He banged the glass back down. "You don't drink?" he asked Chambers.

"I never let my guard down," he replied, coolly.

Sanderson nodded. Just like the intelligence reports suggested: an arrogant arsehole. He turned and looked the ridiculously dressed vampire up and down. "When did you become a vampire?"

Rathbone ignored the agent.

"He doesn't talk about it," said Brian. "He just turned up one day like it."

"I see." Sanderson really didn't.

"And my ji—" Garforth checked himself. "Sid, look! A parrot!"

"Where?" The big man started looking around the pub.

"Me jizz kills vampires too," Brian whispered to Sanderson. "Look. Rich made us this gun, the Cumapult." Brian handed it to him.

Sanderson sensed nervousness from the vampire hunter. He could tell from the look on Chambers' blanched face that Garforth told the truth. Could it be that Chambers was trying to hide all of this? Something crazy, something special was materialising on this rundown council estate in, of all places, Middlesbrough. Coalition scientists would have a field day here. Sanderson took the gun and looked down the makeshift sights.

"Good work," he said to Chambers, before handing it back. Unfortunately, the Coalition would take off the streets the weapon they needed right now: the right hand of Sid. If his friends could back him up, all the better. Haemo would give them support in the long run, and after Sid saved Sanderson's life, he wasn't going to subject him and his friends to a life of a lab rat. "And you, Arthur? Do you have any special powers?"

"None worth bragging about," he said and the other lads laughed at him.

Sanderson smiled. "I don't know what you lot are, but your secret is safe with me."

The lads didn't breathe a sigh of relief on the grounds that they didn't appear to give a shit.

"So why have you come in person?" asked Chambers. "Why not send a minion to do your duty?"

"Sid saved my life."

"Where are the fooking parrots, Brian!"

Sanderson choked on his beer. Chambers wasn't laughing though. He said, "I thought your valuable time would be better spent protecting the vampires you're paid to babysit."

Sanderson, raising a fresh pint of ale to his lips, simultaneously drew his gun, and pointed it at Chambers' head. A bitter flash of annoyance crossed Chambers' face, who hadn't come close to drawing his weapon.

"Never let your guard down, huh?" Sanderson took a long draw of ale, and as quick as the gun had appeared, it disappeared.

"That was like fooking John Wayne, mon," said Sid, who'd stopped hunting for parrots. "That was brilliant. 'Ere, Rich, how come you can't do that?"

Sanderson would remember the look on Chambers' wounded face for as long as he lived. "Chambers, I've seen humans do far worse to each other than vampires have ever done. Still, there's a reason I'm here."

"Ah, fook, what now?" Sid groaned.

"We need you, Sid. We need you to finish what you started."

"Look, I flushed that bastard, several fooking times. I'm not going back to Nottingham to take a coat hanger to it, reet?"

Sanderson began, but Sid's tirade was in mid-flow.

"The problem with you fooking Southerners is that you're all fooking vegetarians and don't know how to lay a good turd."

"Sid, I don't give a fuck if you blocked the gents. Why would I drive up from London for the sake of a toilet? Don't answer that. Listen, I need the use of them fists of yours. Gunnar Ivansey, Sid, it's time you finished him, once and for all."

Chambers looked on, not saying a word.

"Who?"

"The vampire you fought two nights back. Remember? You were blown off a toilet by a grenade? He inflicted the wounds covering your arms, remember?"

Sid looked at his arms and then at the seven empty pint glasses in front of him.

Sanderson understood. "You'll have one vampire to kill, Sid. That'll be it. I have secured this pub. It will never be shut. You have my word. Do this one thing for me."

"Come on, lad," said Sid, "with this pub, I have everything I need. If I keep making a habit of knocking those fairies out, then you're gonna start expecting it, regular, like. He keeps me in tabs, booze, and dollar." He nodded at Chambers. "I'm a simple man of simple pleasures, pal. What's your name, again?"

"Sanderson. Sid, Chambers cannot give you this." He took a piece of paper out of his pocket and slipped it across the table.

Sid took the paper and squinted at it. His eyebrows shot up. "Fook me, mon. That's a generous offer indeed, Mr Sanderson. Rich canna offer me that."

Chambers jumped to his feet, knocking over his bar stool before screaming, "It's fucking REECE! *Reece!* You get his fucking name right and it has three times as many syllables!"

"Think you better calm yourself down, ya wanker," warned Brian.

Sanderson was taken aback by Chambers' mentally instability.

"What do you need? What can't I give you that he can?" Chambers sounded like a wounded lover.

"My old life back." Sid slid the paper over to Chambers.

"Sixty quid a week! Is that all? I'll fucking double it— triple it!"

Sid ignored Chambers and quickly grabbed the cheque from him. "Can I work? Will the Benefit Bastards be after me?"

"Complete immunity. That weekly benefit cheque is yours, for life, no matter what, and you will never be investigated by the Benefit Fraud Agency ever again." Sanderson threw a smug look at a seething Chambers.

"That's pretty amazing," said Arthur.

"You could retire, Sid," said Brian, slapping him on the back. "With the odd job, here and there, like."

"Aye."

"Retire?" said Chambers incredulously. "He never *started* work in the first place!"

Sid nodded. "I know, mon. It's all I want. That and a shag, like."

"I need some fresh air." Chambers got up and left the pub. Sanderson watched him all the way, his hand close to his gun.

"I'll fooking do it," said Sid. "I'll do it for me benefit cheque. Get the beers in to celebrate."

Sanderson went to the bar, and the door to the pub opened.

"ACKROYD, GET THE BAILEYS FLOWING!"

The shout was accompanied by a cacophony of offensive sounds: the jangling of jewellery, the rolling of pushchair wheels, the screaming of children, the rustling of McDonald's wrappers, and use of the word "fook."

"Ah, shit. It's Maggie and her lot," said Brian.

They piled into the bar, pushchairs and all. Even the harshest of Northern winters couldn't force these modern-day warrior women, Middlesbrough's answer to Boudicca, to cover up. In the Northeast, flesh, gold, and tattoos were all part of the brutal courtship display that made the world go round.

"Eh'up, lads," said Maggie, the biggest and strongest of the pack. "Haven't seen you in a long time. How you all keeping?"

Maggie and her clan of teenage, obese, mothers-of-five were the only regulars who were technically the female of the species. They were feared all over the estate, just like Sid. It was they who destroyed The Miner's Arms six months ago when Kev hired the smallest pecker in the Northeast for a striptease. Everyone ignored them, except...

"Did you just wave, Rathbone?" asked Brian. "Did you actually *wave* at 'em?"

Rathbone looked the other way. "Don't know what you're on about."

"You did, didn't ya? I know your drought is even worse than our Sid's— since birth, ain't it? But, shit, mon, you can't think of going near Maggie's lot. Has turning into a vampire made you desperate or 'owt?"

"Fook off!" Rathbone helped himself to several of the ales that had just reached the table, courtesy of the Coalition, before taking another peek...and then another.

NIGHT RETURNED, AND NONE TOO SOON FOR GUNNAR IVANSEY. He didn't know how long he'd been asleep. He needed blood, desperately, but he'd no idea where to find it. There was no regeneration this time. Sunlight was absolute, and it had burnt past his testes and deep into his body. The wound wasn't healing and would be fatal if he didn't find blood fast.

He couldn't remember how he'd ended up at the manor house and had no idea where it was. With all his will, he made it to his feet and limped from the outhouse and towards the main building. He was in tremendous pain, but it was ecstasy compared to what his torturous testes had inflicted.

Finally, he made it through the front doors. It wasn't worth the time searching through the bodies on the floor, as the blood would have congealed. He needed to find out where he was, and there would likely be a computer upstairs where he could access the Internet. A child's bedroom would also offer the opportunity of pets. Any fresh blood would help.

Slowly, Gunnar crawled up the stairs of the manor house. He was slowing down, but his renewed lust for life stopped him giving up. He pulled himself up on the banister and opened a door off the landing. He fell through the door's opening and his bones shook as he hit the ground. He looked around from the comfort of the floor. No blood had been spilled in this home office, but it had a computer.

He pulled himself up onto the leather armchair. Luckily, the PC was logged on. Gunnar despised computers, but Ricard had told him of a trick if he ever found himself in trouble. His friend had probably foreseen it. How Gunnar missed the old fool.

He browsed the history until he found a well-known shopping website. He was lucky. The household's details were saved in the memory. He was in the Peak District National Park, a few miles away from Abney. He'd travelled forty miles from Nottingham Police Station to get here. How had he managed that and murdered all these people before the sun rose?

It didn't matter now. He typed the information he required into the search engine and picked up the office phone. He needed to feed.

"Is that Mario's Pizzas?"

25

THE ALL-DAYER WAS NOW TEN HOURS OLD. Sanderson had continued to drink with the boys and was embraced as one of their own. Reece still sulked outside after the lads got Sanderson's name right. Maggie and her clutch of hens were a drunken mess. Of the five who'd started the evening, only four remained as one had left to give birth. She swore blind that she'd be back for last orders and threatened the pub with gratuitous violence if anyone touched her Malibu and Coke.

The only person who wasn't there just for the drinking was Rathbone. He had his eyes on the brood despite Brian's constant ridicule. He just couldn't help himself. Sex had never really bothered him until now. He'd developed...urges. And besides, he was a vampire whom he assumed were out shagging every night. Not only was he the only person from Middlesbrough who was a virgin, he believed he was the only vampire in Middlesbrough who was a virgin, and he wanted to put that right. No one noticed him leave.

"So when was the last time you got some, Arthur?" asked Brian.

"Hell, man, don't start that bullshit, again. The last thing I wanna talk about is women." Arthur hid behind a pint of ale, and when it disappeared, he hid behind another.

"You had it this week, like?"

"Nah, last week," conceded the beautiful man.

Brian jeered. "I knew it. I told you it would all dry up. I fooking told you. Was it a proper, shite, Friday-night-run-through too?"

Arthur put his head in his hands. "Ah, man, it weren't with Lucia. It was with that chick who takes the charity tin round the working men's clubs in the 'boro."

"Three-Tits Tracey?"

Arthur nodded.

"Has she really got three tits?" asked Sid.

"I don't know, man. I don't know what the fuck that third thing is, but I haven't seen anything like it before." Arthur shook his head. "I can't believe I cheated on my chick—with that." Arthur turned the attention from him. "Sid, how's your luck with the ladies, or are you still stuck in Heartbreak Hotel?"

"Luckily, I ain't on an attempted murder charge anymore, but the lass hasn't called back."

"Oh, yeah, I forgot...you...had an incident. Nice of you to sort that out,

Mr Sanderson," said Arthur, raising his glass.

"It was the least I could do." He chinked glasses with Arthur just in time for Reece to come back and witness the newly formed friendship, but that wasn't the only thing Reece noticed. He also noticed Rathbone enter the gents with one of Maggie's lot. He uncocked his pistol.

Sanderson followed suit. These men were trained to notice anything untoward, and it wasn't difficult when there was a vampire in the room dressed like a kid trick-or-treating.

Only Reece and Sanderson heard the pub toilet door unlock. Reece raised his pistol, as did Sanderson. They both pointed their weapons directly at the vampire leaving the toilets.

"You slipped up, vamp," said Sanderson.

"I told you you'd never be able to quench the thirst," added Reece. "Now you pay for the life you've taken."

Peter Rathbone, vampire, stood outside the bogs, blood covering his jaw and dripping from his fangs, a sign of his guilt, a sign of his weakness, a sign of his kind.

Justice was swift.

Rathbone fell back into the toilets with a spray of blood, two bullets embedded deep in his brain. The smoke from the pistols trailed to the ceiling, mingling with the considerable levels that were already being breathed into the room. Sanderson and Reece rose as one. There was nothing the 'boro boys could do to save their drinking buddy now.

"That will teach the little twat a lesson!" One of Maggie's clan stormed out of the toilet where Rathbone nursed yet another bullet wound. A vampire is a horror of the night, but a tanked-up, Middlesbrough maiden who's had a half-job done on her is something far more terrifying. "That was the sorriest excuse for a fook I've ever had."

"Are you OK?" asked Reece. "Did he harm you?"

"Harm me?" She let out a shrieked laugh. "With that little maggot in his pants? Don't be fooking stupid. He could've stuck it in sideways and I wouldn't have known."

All the Middlesbrough residents were in hysterics.

"Where did all that blood come from?" asked Reece.

"Oh, aye, cheers for reminding me. Ackroyd! You got a fooking jonny machine in there, so when are you gonna get yourself a tampon machine, you sexist pig?"

Sid, Arthur, and Brian paled. The *woman's curse* was never discussed in the North. Never. The only exception to this was when a woman, for any reason, any reason at all, was a little irritable, and then the Northern man would tell her what her problem was until his throat was sore. It was in his genes. However, a worse crime had been committed this day.

Rathbone had got to his feet and stood in the doorway of the toilets, now covered in his own blood after sustaining double gunshot wounds. "What the fook are you all looking at?"

"That's disgusting, mon," said Sid.

"Yeah, well when was the last time you got some?" defended Rathbone.

Brian held his mouth as sickness rose.

"Has your thirst been quenched?" asked Reece.

"Yeah, I shot me bolt. What's it to you?"

Reece shuddered, trying to rid himself of the thought. "No, no, that's not what I mean. Has your unquenchable thirst been satisfied? I told you only blood would satisfy it."

Rathbone weighed it up. "Yeah, now you come to mention it, it has."

"That's the only way that you will feel any sort of satisfaction."

Rathbone looked uneasy. "Really?"

"Yes. You are a vampire, and you need it."

"She made me do it!" said the red-winged vampire. "I don't wanna do it again!"

"You're fooking not doing that again, Rathbone!" Brian spat on the floor. "For fook's sake, mon, have some fooking dignity! Every lass in the 'boro will know what you did by end of the week. You'll be a fooking target for each of 'em, one week a month. The only thing that'll save you is that tiny pecker of yours."

"It's average for a vampire."

Arthur shook his head. "I thought that my encounter with Three-Tits Tracey was a low point." He shivered.

"It looks like it has given you a fright, Arthur. Look, a grey hair!" Reece pulled a hair from the beautiful head to show him.

Arthur flinched. Not because he was a pussy, but because his roots were as strong as an oak's. "What do you think you're doing, man? You touch the 'do one more time and you're gonna force me to take care of business." He emphasised the full stop with a mid-air roundhouse kick.

"Sorry, no offence meant," said Reece placing the hair safely into a compartment in his pocket.

Sanderson looked at his watch. "Well, I must be leaving. Sid, I will be in touch about reinstating your benefit money and the mission."

"Right you are, Mr Sanderson. Just let us know when you want me to smack someone."

Reece burnt with anger when Sanderson showed him absolute disregard by turning his back on him and leaving the pub. Reece's trigger finger itched, but he stayed it. Once Sanderson was away, Reece also said his goodbyes, not that anyone cared, and nor did he. Now, he had everything he needed to get to work.

GUNNAR PULLED HIMSELF ACROSS THE GRAVEL. He needed every ounce of strength to hold his groin off the ground. Every now and then, his abdominal muscles would give way and he'd fall onto the stones, and each time he'd scream when the gravel entered his open wound.

The deliveryman would bring him the sustenance he needed. He couldn't call the police or the paramedics. His face would be plastered all over the most wanted lists after his little stunt, but he was in no fit state to fight. It would be the end of him.

That's why he waited for the deliveryman. It was often said that you can't put a price on human life. Gunnar disagreed. It was £14.99, with a free bottle of Coke.

"Are you all right, dude?"

The delivery boy was eighteen at most and had arrived bang on time. He rushed over to Gunnar, who was barely alive, lying on his back, and twitching on the ground.

Gunnar had to be cautious, if he missed his target, the kid could easily escape and bring the police and the Coalition. He beckoned the boy closer, as if to whisper into his ear. The boy leaned forward.

Gunnar lunged, clawing desperately to get hold of anything. He finally grabbed his victim's sleeve.

"What are you doing!" the delivery boy screamed, pulling away.

Gunnar let go of the boy's sleeve and grabbed his leg instead, bringing the boy crashing down onto his behind. Pulling him closer, Gunnar sank his teeth deep into the top of the boy's ankle, finding the artery. Blood gushed down his throat and spread life throughout his body. The boy screamed, and he kicked at the vampire's face, but it was too late. Gunnar could feel the cuts from the gravel heal and skin graft over the burns caused by the sun. He drunk until the boy's heart had nothing more to give. He reached down to where his knackers had once been.

Nothing.

Gunnar Ivansey was born again.

REECE SLAMMED HIS FOOT DOWN on the accelerator and overtook another car on a blind bend. He was on his way back to his hideout, and he wasn't sparing the horses. He hated the Coalition and everything it stood for, but now, he, too, was one of their puppets. Not long after Sid became his right-hand man, Reece had received a note left for him at one of his regular haunts. It was from his future Coalition partner.

With the Coalition leak and Sid's right hand, Reece had performed feats unparalleled by his forebears. The attack on the Occursus was the most audacious vampire hunt in history. He was a hero of mankind, but there was no homecoming, no celebration. He was a hero...and no one knew it.

He didn't know which member of the Coalition he worked for. He didn't even know whether it was a human or a vampire who ordered him around like a dog. He didn't know what the councillor's master plan was, but he did know they wanted to hit the vampire nation hard, and he was happy to oblige. Especially when he had such gifts bestowed upon him, gifts that could unlock untold powers and give him everything he'd always wanted.

Sanderson, the arrogant bastard, could control Sid for the time being. He'd probably be safer with him and with the Coalition's support. But now, it was time to work. Reece's toys were here, and he had samples from each of the freaks: blood from Sid and Rathbone, a hair from Peasley, and Garforth's putrid semen. These four items would yield the ultimate weapon. *His* ultimate weapon.

26

GUNNAR RAN LIKE THE WIND through the Peak District National Park, leaping from mountains, jumping streams and swinging from trees. His body was strong and powerful, but now, his head was clear as the winter night's sky, his senses heightened. He could hear the beating of an owl's wings as it hovered almost silently over an unsuspecting shrew crawling through the grass. He felt the turning of the wind and the odours that it brought; the town, ten miles away; the couple camping on the hillside making love; the fox, hunting at the bottom of the valley.

Only a dull ache reminded him of his curse. His testes had brought him nothing but sorrow and drove him to kill his only friend Richmond, whose undignified and violent death would haunt Gunnar to the end. A tear traced its way down his cheek. It was the first tear he'd shed since the loss of Gabriel, and there was nothing he could do to stop the waterfall that followed.

He stopped in his tracks, and tears flowed for Richmond, for Ricard, and for Gabriel. He wept for the loss of Michael Vitrago. He wept for the old days. He wept because it felt good and he no longer had anything to hide.

He was free.

Free! He hadn't been free for centuries! Free from the Agreement, free from his Coalition puppeteer, free from his testes-induced rage. He cared not that his life had been turned upside down, for right now, he was in perfect balance, and he would savour every moment.

The scent of the couple making love drifted past him once more. Another feeding would, hopefully, make all pain from his groin subside. He had a mile to cover, but there was no rush and it was such a beautiful night.

From the top of the mountain, Gunnar admired the beautiful scenery. Peaks stretched as far as the eye could see. He could see the tent pitched on some sheltered grassland on the adjacent hillside. In his mind, he worked out the path. A fifty-foot jump to the ledge below and then a long leap to reach a small waterfall that bisected the two hills. The dive into the ice-cold pool below the waterfall would be invigorating, as would the blood when he reached the tent at the end of the stream meandering its way down the hill.

He jumped and the wind whistled through his hair. He coiled as he hit the ground and allowed his powerful thighs to absorb all the plyometric energy that catapulted him across the ravine. But, much to his amazement, his fingers missed the cliff ledge.

SANDERSON WAS LATE TO YET ANOTHER MEETING. Bwogi called a meeting if he ran out of toilet paper. Sanderson walked through the extensive security, which was invisible to any unsuspecting intruders. He knew the system inside out, because he'd redesigned the whole building due to his predecessor being an imbecile.

"Stevens, Peterson," he nodded as he walked past the last two guards before he reached the Great Hall.

"Sir, hold on."

"What is it, Peterson?" Sanderson liked the young agent. He was gritty; he had potential. He was a soldier, too, and he looked it, even though he wore a suit. He was growing his mousy brown hair to soften his appearance, but it didn't work. He was average size, just like Sanderson, but that meant he had to fight harder, and Sanderson could see it in his eyes.

"There's a new guy in there, scary piece of work, sir. Not really sure what's going on but thought you should know."

"Good work, soldier. I best go find out."

"And, sir, Sebastian hasn't shown up."

"So?"

"Apparently, no one has heard from him for a couple of days."

Sanderson gave him a nod before passing. *Scary, hey?* Peterson didn't use the word lightly. Who could it be? And where was Sebastian? He didn't trust that son of a bitch for a reason.

GUNNAR OPENED HIS EYES. His head throbbed. His scalp was knitting together...slowly. His regenerative abilities were always strong, and the increased testosterone had made him indestructible, but not now. Lying on his back, Gunnar could no longer feel his feet. His back must be broken. Judging by how long it was taking his head to heal, he was going to be here a long time. Backs were complicated things.

He hadn't made the jump. Why? Was he losing his power too? He'd put every ounce of strength into the leap. Maybe his power had waned, but at this moment in time, all he cared about was freedom. Gunnar mapped the stars and waited until the feeling returned to his legs. The blood would be needed for a full recovery. With his heightened senses, the taste would be even more exquisite.

"WHERE'S MY DAUGHTER!"

Borg Hemsman. Sanderson had to stop himself reaching for his pistol.

Peterson's instincts were right. This was one dangerous son of a bitch, and he was real pissed too.

Hemsman stood above Bwogi, screaming, his eyes almost glowing with resentment. The African counsellor saw Sanderson as a handy distraction. "Where have you been, Sanderson?"

"I've been busy trying to save the world." He sat down, nonchalantly relaxing into his chair. It had taken effort. "Where's Sebastian?" he said looking at the empty seat.

"No one's heard from him since the last meeting a few days ago. Perhaps your friend Tillsley might know?" said Bwogi.

Tillsley's employment by the Coalition was now common knowledge, and Sanderson would bet his house on Sebastian's disappearance having everything to do with it. "Tillsley's been with me. I thought we kept Coalition business within the Coalition." Sanderson nodded at the interloper.

"You dare address me?" Borg stalked around the table towards Sanderson who subtly moved to a position where his pistol was handy and exposed.

"My yard, pal." It took all his training to sound cocky.

"Enough!" cried Caroline. "I've had it up to here with this macho bullshit." Hemsman gave her a look of daggers. "Sanderson, you're right. Coalition business is kept within the Coalition, and that's why we're keen to get hold of Sebastian as it seems that Coalition business is well known by others." She nodded towards Borg. "The use of Tillsley is now common knowledge as is our inability to hold on to our own councillors."

"You better find my daughter quickly," said Hemsman, "otherwise I'll contact Ivansey to see if he can aid me, and then, who knows? The vampire nation is simmering and is ready to boil over. First, the Occursus and now the use of Tillsley. This is a pathetic excuse for a united power. If anything happens to Lucia, I'll destroy everything. I promise you." He glared around the room, finishing with Sanderson. "Everything."

Sanderson stared him out. There was no way the old warlord could have known about Haemo. It would be game over if he did. Sebastian was the leak. Sanderson's gut was right, and these stupid fucks hadn't seen it. If the bastard wanted war, then leaking Haemo would've been the quickest way. What was his game?

Hemsman stormed out of the Great Hall and everyone breathed a sigh of relief.

"Rempstone, what happened?" Sanderson asked when the elder had gone.

"We've found incriminating emails on Sebastian's computer," he replied.

"He's a computing genius. He could've covered his tracks with his eyes closed," said Sanderson.

"Unless he didn't care," said Caroline.

"You're probably right," said Sanderson. "I bet he's following Ivansey. With his computer skills, he can still access anything on our systems."

"We know," said Caroline. "That's why you must bring Ivansey down, and Sebastian, if he's with him."

"Make sure you triple the guard on the new Haemo plant," Sanderson added. "You're going to need the army on this one."

"It's already done," said Charles. "This whole thing needs sweeping under the carpet as quickly as possible. Use any force necessary."

"That I will." Now, he had the right hand of Tillsley at his disposal, not to mention the skills and attributes of his drinking companions.

"We're running out of time, Sanderson," said Caroline.

He got to his feet to leave. "I know. A telephone call would do, you know."

"We like to make sure you're behaving yourself," said Charles.

Sanderson looked straight at Charles. "Every hour costs lives and brings war one step closer. Save your politics for your yearly appraisal, you fat prick!"

The stunned faces were a picture.

GUNNAR SNEAKED INTO THE TENT, SILENT AS A MOUSE. The couple didn't notice. They were passionately entwined, and Gunnar watched the young man's pert buttocks rise and fall with powerful thrusts. He was captivated. He'd never watched two humans make love before. He closed the tent flaps behind him.

The show was ruined when the girl caught sight of him and screamed. She was young, pretty, but her make-up didn't suit her. Gunnar felt a twinge in his back and remembered why he was here. He leapt forward and swatted the girl unconscious with a backhand, leaving her startled, naked boyfriend to deal with. Gunnar feasted on the young man's meat.

His injured back found the energy and nourishment it required, and all strength returned. Blood tasted so much better now. He savoured it all and then turned to the girl. She really should've done something different to her hair. He pushed aside her mate and crawled on top of her. A little running would do her good. Her thighs could be more toned. Gunnar brushed her hair back to reveal her neck but did not bite...She'd benefit from a better conditioner.

He was going through some rather strange changes. He considered leaving her alive, the male had filled him up, but the awful hair convinced him otherwise, so he snapped her neck before leaving the tent. He took in the cold air and stretched his back, basking in the wonder of healing. He'd taken it for granted for so long. All violent, barbaric males take things for granted.

He strolled through the woodlands of the Peak District and reflected on his new self. In all his years, blood never tasted so good, and he'd revelled in savouring every last inch of the young man. Suddenly, he began to sprint through the trees, leaping low branches. His initial thoughts were correct; he wasn't as strong now he'd lost the testosterone boost.

He was still a wanted vampire, but he was no longer invincible. Times were going to be tough, but so many other positive feelings were coursing through his body, drowning the sadness and the worry. He was reborn. He was free. There were three hours until sunlight and it was sixty miles to his Yorkshire home. He owned other residences closer, but he loved the comfort of the bed in his grand bedroom. Tomorrow, he would wake in the finest of surroundings and remember everything from this fabulous night.

27

TONIGHT, LIKE MOST NIGHTS, LUCIA WAS AT THE SINK. Until she met Arthur, she'd never washed a plate in her life. She hated it. Every night, stood by the sink, scrubbing, soaking, scouring. It was taking its toll on her mental state. She once made decisions that affected the entire world, and now, the most important decision she made was what dish would negate the need to soak Arthur's pants in bleach come wash day. This reminded her that she hadn't done the laundry yet. The washing machine was broken, which meant she had to traipse down to the all-night laundrette, pregnant.

Things shouldn't be this way, but at least she'd get out of the house. Arthur didn't take her anywhere anymore. They used to go for long walks under the moonlight and make love under the stars. They used to sit and talk for hours. Not now. Now he came home from work and she was lucky to be grunted at before he took himself off to that shithole of a pub before coming back home, watching the American football and then passing out, drunk.

She was so lonely. Things would be better when the child came but that wouldn't be for another eighteen months. Eighteen months of this! Could she take it? Yes. For the child, she could. The birth would present other challenges. A vampire birth required the blood of the father. Would this hybrid be any different? She prayed to the Maker it would be; otherwise, it could spell the end of her or her man. There was good in Arthur. She just needed to find it again. He would make a fine father. She had faith.

She picked up the laundry basket and her heightened sense of smell told her Arthur had been performing his deep squat exercises again. She put the basket down and took the bottle of bleach out of a kitchen cabinet. It was empty, which meant a trip to the corner shop. Two trips! She was being spoiled.

REECE WAS EN ROUTE TO HIS SECRET LABORATORY situated in a warehouse in an industrial estate in Leeds. He'd struggled with Sanderson's company. How could Sanderson hold his head high when his hands were covered in the blood of the victims he disposed of? That was of no consequence now. Reece had skulked in the shadows too long. When war was declared, he was going to be the hero.

Satisfied that he hadn't been followed, he parked up and began the rigorous task of disabling the many alarms and unlocking his facility. He knew he was paranoid, but paranoia kept him alive.

He turned on the lights and marvelled at the state-of-the-art equipment filling the laboratory. These toys were his prize for his attack on the Occursus. He had everything he needed and, more importantly, the samples he needed. There was no way he could've sourced this equipment secretly without the help of someone with immense power and cash. He wondered who it was. They were careful, and they were damn good.

Reece had all the pieces, and now, he needed to put the puzzle together. He had the DNA of the four anomalies displaying incredible yet completely different attributes when interacting with vampires. These four men had the power to destroy the vampire, and he was determined to tap into it.

LUCIA ENJOYED THE SHORT, EARLY-EVENING WALK to the corner shop. The moon was out, which was rare here in the Smithson Estate. It was usually hidden by a thick layer of smog.

She'd popped the washing in the machine at the laundrette and would collect it after buying some bleach from the corner shop. She'd binned Arthur's offending undergarments. She knew there'd be trouble, but there was no way she was leaving them in the house, and it was a waste of time putting them in the washing machine.

"How you doing, our pet?" said Gladys as soon as Lucia entered the small, but well-stocked, shop.

"Hey, Gladys," said Lucia, smiling at the old shopkeeper.

"The bump is growing, my dear. You're glowing."

Lucia looked at the shop window where she could see her reflection with the bright lights of the shop, and the black night behind. She looked far from glowing. She looked haggard, worn, and tired. Still, she smiled at Gladys for the compliment. She was glowing in comparison to Gladys who looked like she'd endured a hard life.

"I need some bleach, Gladys."

Gladys looked concerned. "What's wrong, pet?"

"I've run out."

"That's not what I mean and you know it. What's wrong?"

"Oh, nothing. I'm fine," she lied.

"No, you're not. That Arthur Peasley is being a bad boy again, isn't he?"

"What do you mean?"

"Oh, pet, I'll make a cuppa." Gladys shuffled from behind the counter in her slippers and locked the shop door. She was dwarfed by Lucia but grabbed the vampire's hand and led her through to the back room and put the kettle on.

"He's a good lad at heart, you know," started Gladys. "Oh, take a seat, dear. No formalities here."

Lucia perched on a small stool. The stock room was cramped and filled wall-to-wall with various produce. There was just enough room for a small table and two chairs, one of which Gladys sat her fragile frame on. She rolled up the sleeves of her tatty, pink cardigan and poured boiling water into two mugs that'd been stained black through years of nonsensical nattering.

"As I said, Arthur is a good lad at heart. You could do a lot worse than him, you know." Gladys took some milk out of a small fridge under the table and finished making the tea. "There you go, dear."

"Thank you." No one had taken care of her in months. She choked back a tear.

Gladys offered her a pat on the knee. "I've known that lad, man and boy. Oh aye, he used to run in here as a nipper for his sweets." She chuckled to herself. "I knew all of them as young'n's, you know. Sid and Brian were lovely bairns. I know they both enjoy a drink, but they've always respected their elders. Although, I must say, I never took to that Rathbone lad."

"I don't know any of his friends." Lucia blinked a couple of times, aware that tears were trying to force themselves out again. "He never takes me anywhere."

"That's terrible," said Gladys, placing a soothing, wrinkled hand on Lucia's arm. "I'll have a word with him, next time he's in."

"Please, don't!"

"He was raised better than that. I guess it's difficult with you being a vampire, and all."

Lucia dropped her mug of tea, but her vampire instincts enabled her to catch it again before it reached the floor. She didn't spill a drop. "How...how do you know that?"

"Oh, dearie, everyone knows. Don't you worry. Your secret is safe with Middlesbrough." Gladys gave her a motherly smile. "We look after our own."

Lucia put the mug to her mouth and took a sip of the best cup of tea she'd ever tasted. She allowed herself to relax, and it felt good. "He doesn't want to spend any time with me at all."

Gladys nodded. "Aye, he was always a bit of a lone wolf, a wild stallion, was our Arthur. I guess that's one of the things that attracted you to him?"

Lucia nodded.

"Aye, and the thing about Arthur is that he's always loved fanny."

"Sorry?"

REECE HAD DNA SEQUENCERS, BIOLOGICAL PURIFIERS, and analytical instruments at his disposal. The Coalition member he'd dealt with knew he had a scientific background and would've known he had grand designs.

He took Sid's blood sample and noted in his lab book that he'd never tested blood that smelled of chips before. Cholesterol levels above 5 mMol/L are considered dangerous in humans, and Sid's was off the scale. It was higher than a pork scratching. He should be dead. So the question Reece needed to answer, before he went on to Sid's vampire-killing ability, was how come the man was still breathing?

A monumental task confronted him.

"SORRY, GLADYS," Lucia said. "I don't think I heard you right."

Gladys smiled. "Arthur, he loves the fanny, doesn't he?"

Lucia didn't like hearing someone talk about her man like that, and it was worse coming from an old, motherly woman.

"Aye, I thought that was what was getting to you. You won't change him, pet, no matter how beautiful you are. It's in the blood."

"He is not cheating on me. I'm carrying his baby."

"Oh, he'll love you. He'll love you more than anything in the world, but the fanny calls. As for me, I love a big, hard cock."

Lucia was horrified as Gladys held out a fist, grabbed the crook of her elbow with her other hand and pumped her arm suggestively.

"Weyheyy!...I still do. Even when our Burt was alive, I still had to go looking for more. Couldn't get enough, like."

Gladys's hungry eyes gave Lucia no reason to doubt. The vampire clambered to her feet, desperately seeking freedom. "I need to go, Gladys."

"Finish your tea, first. Aye, poor old Burt. I loved him dear, but he couldn't fill up a chicken with the little thing of his. I had to go into town for real meat."

Lucia poured the near-boiling tea down her throat and waited for it to heal. It was the longest five seconds of her life. "Well, I best be on my way." She made her way out of the storeroom.

"Right you are, lovey. You'll just have to forgive our Arthur. A leopard can't change its spots, and he's a good lad at heart."

Lucia couldn't get out of the door quick enough.

REECE RUBBED HIS EYES. For six hours he'd sat at the microscope. What enabled these men to exhibit such extraordinary abilities attuned to their personalities: Sid and his strength; Arthur and his ability to seduce; Brian and his diseased genitals; and Rathbone's annoying habit of not going away, even when murdered?

Reece had spent time amplifying the DNA, which was necessary with the small samples available. It was now time to start the laborious task of DNA sequencing in order to understand what building blocks made up the DNA itself. It could take days, weeks, months, maybe years, but this was the only way to discover the secret behind these four drunks, what connected them, and what made them unique.

He took a sip of strong coffee. It was late. Staring through the microscope was slow, boring work at the best of times. He took another sample and placed it under the scope. His eyes were tired and he was...seeing things.

Surely.

DNA sequencing was used to determine the sequence of four small molecules: amino acids, the building blocks of the human genome. From Arthur's single strand of hair, Reece could examine the genes that made up his entire body. He sat back from the microscope, took a moment, and went back for a second look. His eyes were not deceiving him. Something else was in there. Something had smeared down the plate. He repeated the experiment, and replicated the results exactly. This wasn't just a mutation; this was something different. He held the plate in his hand. Could this sample hold the key?

Reece placed the sample in an analyser. In minutes, the instrument would identity the smear and the chemical that made Arthur Peasley's DNA unique.

LUCIA RETURNED TO THE LAUNDRETTE to pick up the clothes. *Everyone knows I'm a vampire?* she thought. She used to think she was paranoid when she went out, thinking everyone was talking about her and her predicament. It turned out she was right.

A couple of women in the laundrette threw her filthy looks. She let it go. They were only in their late teens and it was best not to cause a scene. She unloaded the wet washing before transporting it to the drier.

"Right up her own arse, Tracey."

"You're right, Stace. Just 'cos she's a fooking vampire, she thinks her shit smells of fooking roses."

Lucia didn't need heightened senses to hear the girls. They were practically shouting. When she didn't bite, they upped the ante.

"I don't know what that stud Peasley sees in the skinny, pale bitch," said one of the sunbed-shrivelled women.

"Aye, you can see why he's been putting it about even more than usual."

The metal drier door crumpled in Lucia's hand. She would've ignored them, but Gladys had gone into detail about Arthur's love of women.

"I know, Trace. Fancy doubling up on him this weekend?"

The clothes drier flew across the laundrette, past the two gossipers, and into the washing machines behind them.

"I should rip your face off!" screamed Lucia

"Just fooking try it, ya skinny bitch!" The one called Tracey rolled up her sleeves and hitched her bra over what looked like a third breast. Women of Middlesbrough were not easily scared, and it shocked Lucia.

"I could kill you in the blink of the eye. Why do you goad me?"

"Eh? Ya posh bitch! I ain't gotta clue what you're talking about, but if any more of your kind come around stealing our men, there'll be a fooking mob!"

"Well, I might as well set an exam—" Lucia grabbed at her stomach, mid-sentence. Pain. A second later, she doubled over, her insides burning.

"Not so fooking tough now, are ya?"

She stumbled to the doorway, ignoring the jeering of the women. Once in the cold, evening air, the pain completely disappeared. She feared for the baby. She feared for her own life. Things couldn't get any worse.

REECE SCANNED THE RESULTS of the chemical structure responsible for the mysterious band on the DNA sequence. It couldn't be right. He ran the search again, and it heeded an identical result.

He looked at his watch. Too much to do. He needed another sample. The results had to be wrong. The sample had to be contaminated.

He ran out of the lab.

28

GUNNAR AWOKE...IN PEACE. No pain. No rage. No bollocks. He hadn't slept in his own bed in weeks. He stretched out and caressed the fine fabric. The delicate sense of touch was something he hadn't the pleasure of experiencing since his testicles had held him hostage.

He recalled the previous evening and smiled. He could remember absolutely everything. Still, he'd struggled to cover the sixty miles in three hours. He was weaker now without his sack.

He got out of bed and decided to change the sheets. He'd spent too long living in squalor. It was time to regain a sense of order, and the feeling of crisp, clean sheets was difficult to beat.

He entered his massive bathroom. He hadn't washed in weeks and looked nothing better than a tramp. The repugnant stench of his armpits sickened him. It was time to wash away the dirt, the grime, and the memories of a hellacious six months.

Gunnar had kept his head shaved head for the past thirty years, and it was time for a change. His hair had grown with his insanity, and now, he sported naturally straight, dark hair, and a short, yet thick, beard. The beard had to go. Gunnar used an electric razor to make quick work of the facial hair, but as he removed most of the hair from his cheeks and throat, it dawned on him that a moustache might suit him. A cutthroat razor proved the point, and he removed all the stubble to leave a thick, impressive, black moustache. He twiddled the ends, and the result was quite spiffing.

"Yes, *magnifico*, but what about the hair?"

Gunnar pushed his hair back with his hand and looked instantly ravishing. He strutted out of the bathroom before picking out a casual designer suit and a comfy, yet smart, pair of shoes. He gave himself another once over in the mirror.

"*Perfecto!*"

GUNNAR DROVE SENSIBLY THROUGH THE WINTER NIGHT. Soft, beautiful music washed over him. He was in no rush. Every mile he drove, he slowed down, ever so slightly. The excess testosterone was leaving his body, bringing him closer to peace.

It was time to unwind. He wouldn't forget what Tillsley had done to him. That hadn't changed, but he had. Tillsley would most likely come to him if the Coalition has anything to do with it. War was coming, but at this moment in time, he didn't care. He basked in tranquillity.

What would the Coalition think of the new him? What would his former puppet master say, whoever they were? They expected him to bring war, and now, they were going to get...him. Just him.

Gunnar turned onto the motorway. He'd no idea where he was going, he was just driving. There was, surprisingly, hardly a car on the road. *Manchester*, he read from a junction sign. Maybe, it was time to get reacquainted with society. Actually, it was time to introduce himself to society. Would his hate of the human race dissipate along with his insatiable bloodlust? It was time to find out.

Gunnar indicated for the first time in his driving career and entered the slow lane. He'd been driving in the middle lane for the past five miles even though there wasn't another car on the road. Strange.

As he turned off, he noticed how much fuel his beast, his classic Ferrari GTO, guzzled. A classic, maybe, but it was certainly not good for the environment, and the handling was a little heavy. Time for a little cabriolet, perhaps?

He drove into the city, and the concrete jungle closed in with every passing yard. Before, it had oppressed him. The stink of mankind's taint on the world was impossible to ignore, but no longer did it fill him with hate. Hate was gone. What would Ricard and Richmond say if they saw him now?

Richmond.

The pain and the guilt hit him harder than Sid Tillsley ever did.

I'm so sorry, my—

Gunnar's train of thought was thrown as he crashed into the back of the car in front. "Oh, blast!"

He got out and surveyed the damage. He hadn't seen the traffic lights, and he'd totalled the front of his beautiful treasure.

"You fucking idiot!" said a youngster who jumped out of the wrecked car in front, although it looked like his car was probably wrecked before Gunnar collided with it. "You stupid prick! Didn't you see me?"

Gunnar's mouth gaped open but not at the words—but at the boy himself. A baseball cap, greasy hair gelled over his forehead, acne, a repulsive tracksuit with a hood pulled over his cap, socks rolled over his trousers, and a hideously garish pair of trainers did not impress him. "My god, what on earth do you look like?"

"I look the dogs, innit!"

"What?" Gunnar moved his ear closer to try and understand the youngster.

"I look the bollocks."

"You look like whose bollocks? And why are you dressed like that?"

The youngster gesticulated in a bizarre fashion by throwing his hands around. "My clothes are fucking reem, man. What about you!" he said aggressively. "Dressed up like a faggot!"

Gunnar lashed out. His right hand slashed across the pond-life's face, and he felt his nails dig into the flesh, gouging out spots, puss, and blood. It all collected under his fingernails. With the momentum, Gunnar dug deeper, ripping through the yob's cheek until his nails emerged from out of the youth's mouth.

Screams echoed around the concrete jungle. One from the disfigured, hideous youth and one from Gunnar, who examined his fingernails and despaired. It was grotesque.

The wounded youth ran off, clutching at his face, but Gunnar didn't hunt him down. He'd no intention of touching such a vile, disgusting, uneducated organism ever again. This would need a trip to the manicurist, for sure. He abandoned his car before entering a public house to clean up the abomination that was his nails and left as quickly as possible.

He walked free through the streets of the bustling city, like a tourist on holiday. In the past, his disdain for humans made him run across city rooftops in case he couldn't resist the urge to rip out a throat. Not now. The lack of testosterone placed him at one with his inner Zen. He'd have to read a book on feng shui.

Gunnar noticed the number of CCTV cameras scanning the streets. He never had to deal with them when he ran across the rooftops. The sensible thing would be to hide, but why should he? Why should he hide in the closet? Where was the pride? Gunnar strutted with his head held high.

His new outlook on life did not improve his opinion of the human race. City centres attracted drunks, and this place had more than most. Football hooligans were the worst specimens in Gunnar's opinion, and Manchester had plenty. They wore their football shirts like tribal colours and invested in distasteful artwork in which to scar their bodies. It was just after 11 p.m. and many of them spilled out of pubs, cheering and leering at the women, like packs of wild animals but with less manners.

"You fucking queer!" The shout was loud enough for the entire street to hear. It came from a pub beer garden and struck an offensive chord with Gunnar, not just because of the pathetic nature of the language but of the terrible enunciation. The vulgarity came from a skinhead looking over a tall fence at the back of a pub

The Neanderthal wasn't shouting at him but at a man a little farther up the road who pretended not to hear. Gunnar shook his head. The young man was extremely well dressed. Fantastically so! What had he done to deserve such a derogatory, embarrassing, and hate-filled heckle?

From behind, it was obvious that the young man took care of himself. Tight white trousers hugged pert buttocks, and the young man hadn't committed the faux pas of showing any panty line. The coat he wore looked like fur, but as Gunnar approached, he was relieved to see it was imitation. He didn't really know why he was relieved.

"Hold up a minute," called Gunnar over the jeering cries of the skinhead, who had been joined by an equally hideous and offensive companion.

The beautiful man carried on regardless until Gunnar's massive hand came down on his shoulder. The man tried to shrug it off, but there was no way that was going to happen. "Just leave me alone!" he yelled.

Gunnar spun him round. He was a wonder to behold. "Why did you let them yobs get away with that?"

"You get used to it," said the young man, pushing his long blonde locks behind his ear.

Gunnar frowned. "Someone as handsome as you shouldn't have to get 'used to it.' You're stunning. Your eyes are like those of an immortal. Why don't you put that scum in their place?"

"Found a boyfriend, have you, darling?" yelled the skinhead from the beer garden.

The young man shook his head, weary of the world. "It's OK. They're just idiots. They don't know any better. In truth, I feel sorry for them."

"Don't. They're disgusting."

"Well, there's nothing we can do about it."

"Well, they're going to learn, my friend. It just so happens that I speak their language." Gunnar grabbed the man's hand, and this received more jeers from the skinheads.

"What are you doing?" said the man, concerned for his welfare, as Gunnar dragged him across the busy road.

"Playing with the traffic is all that's good for your sort!" yelled the skinhead, encouraged by his drunken friends.

"Watch out!" screamed Gunnar's new friend.

Gunnar turned. A small hatchback approached at a speed that would've ended the beautiful boy's life. Gunnar thrust his foot out and into the car's grill. The car crumpled around his foot until the hard engine block brought forth the full momentum of the half-tonne car, Gunnar's foot stopping it dead.

Gunnar wasn't the vampire he used to be, but he was still one tough bitch.

That shut the ruffians up.

Gunnar led the awestruck young man safely across the road and took position in front of the skinheads. They looked down at him from above the fence and must have been standing on a pub bench. After witnessing Gunnar's superhuman strength, their macho posturing no longer offended the neighbourhood.

"I'd ask you to repeat what you said, but your kind are cowards. You hunt in packs and are scared of anything different from your culturally retarded circle of friends. You attack others to make yourselves feel better about your own pitiful existences. You are the lowest of the low, and it's time you were taught a lesson."

Gunnar stood in front of the mouthiest of the gang, clenched his fists, and drove them through the fence. The sound of splintering wood was disguised by the screams of a man with splintering kneecaps.

Gunnar vaulted the fence to find more of the gang, hanging around outside smoking and drinking. It was time to teach them all the error of their ways. He wasn't angry, but he had a point to prove, and it wasn't just that beer bellies and football tops were quite ghastly. He wanted them to educate the rest of the sheep that followed them. So, he taught them a lesson in the language they understood, one they were happy to speak, but not very happy to listen to: He beat them all to within an inch of their worthless lives.

He leapt back over the fence before the shocked young man really knew what had happened. Gunnar dusted off his hands. "They won't bother you again."

"Who are you?"

"I'm Gunnar Ivansey."

The young man offered his hand and a winning smile. "I'm Tim. Fancy a drink?"

Gunnar considered it. He was...curious. He'd seen skinheads all over the country, and he knew the sort of establishment they frequented. This young man, however, was articulated, beautiful, and well groomed. Were there others like him?

"OK then." The two walked casually through the streets of Manchester. This was the most time Gunnar had spent with a human without gutting it. Deeper into the city, the clientele changed for the better. Many of the humans were actually good looking. Gunnar was pleased to notice many moustaches like his own, although he wasn't a fan of leather, especially leather chaps. It wasn't long before Tim ushered him into a nightclub.

The club was small, but oh-so-grand, and Gunnar was pleased when he saw the patrons.

"Is this where all the beautiful people come?"

"By the end of the night, yes," joked Tim. "Have you never been to a gay bar before?"

"This is a gay bar?" said Gunnar, stunned with disbelief.

"Of course it is? You're not gay?" asked Tim, grinning from ear to beautiful ear.

"I...I don't really know."

"Listen."

"At what?"

"The music. Do you like it?"

Gunnar took in the music, and before he knew it, his foot tapped along, and then, remarkably, he began to dance. "What is this heavenly sound?"

"'Dancing Queen,' by ABBA, and yes, you are most definitely gay."

29

"Haymaker?"

"SIR!"

"Karate?"

"SIR!"

"Balloons?

"SIR!"

"Dracula?"

"SIR!"

"This is ridiculous."

"Heroes need codenames, Chambers. Aren't you coming along for the ride?" Sanderson's cigar was adding significantly to global warming. He held it in his teeth as he always did before a mission. He took it out and tapped it with his finger, the ash drifting towards the pavement.

The lads stood outside The Miner's, well oiled and ready to kick vampire ass (not Rathbone's).

"Yeah," said Balloons, aka Brian Garforth. "You can be 'Wanker.'"

"Nah, he looks more like a 'Prick,'" said Karate, aka Arthur Peasley.

"Come on, Rich, you're normally always up for this sort of thing," said Haymaker aka Sid Tillsley.

"I'm not doing the Coalition's dirty laundry, an organisation that watches its own people being slaughtered every day."

"Yeah, but you get your own codename," said an excited Sid.

The time had come for the mission. This was where Sid earned a lifetime's worth of benefit money in one night's work just to knock a vampire out. It was a week since Sanderson had offered Sid the life-changing proposition, and Sid spent the week training—well, drinking—it had been thirsty work. He'd only had one pain-in-the-arse duty, and that was to get fitted for a suit for the evening, but then, Sanderson had come up trumps. The others had agreed to help for a few beers and a suit just like Sid's.

"You ought to get involved, Rich. These uniforms are amazing, man. How cool do I look?" asked Arthur, who did indeed look very cool.

Reece pointed aggressively at the big man. "Every time I tried to kit you out with battle armour, Sid, you turned it down."

"I know, mon, but all your stuff was a bit, you know...shite."

"I see." Reece folded his arms defensively. He looked Rathbone, aka Dracula, up and down. He, too, wore a suit, and Sanderson had equipped him with a black cloak with a deep red inner lining. "How'd he get you to go along?"

"This cape is fooking mint. I look like a sexy Batman."

Reece shook his head. "So what's the plan, then?"

"Top secret," said Balloons. "On a need-to-know basis, pal, and you don't need to know."

Only the briefest of snarls crossed Reece's face. "Are you going into a mission sober, Sid?"

Sid gave Sanderson a knowing smile and then gave the boys a nod. As one, they crossed arms, before firing out a punch in front of them. A whirring noise accompanied small hip flasks shooting from the inside of their matching jackets and landing in their hands.

"HOOOOOOOOO!" They shouted in unison, before each downed a slug of twenty-year-old malt whisky.

"Cute, but now you're out of ammo."

"Nah, mon," said Sid. "There's a bottle stored throughout the outfit. It refills between scraps. Fooking brilliant, ain't it? Makes that posh car of yours look really shite, don't it?"

Reece ignored him. "You're still using the weapon I gave you, Brian. That wasn't too bad an invention, was it?"

"You did well, Rich," said Brian, unholstering the Cumapult, spinning it round his finger and holstering it. "Gold star for you. It even goes with these cool uniforms. I got sucked off on my way here, 'cos of this outfit."

The lads looked like something out of a futuristic sci-fi film, but not in a shit way. They'd all met in The Miner's and had certainly kicked up a stir in the 'boro. No one in the pub could give a monkey's, though.

"You lads not having a few beers to calm the nerves?" asked Reece, trying to put a spanner in the works.

"No, Rich...well, we've already had a few, like, but this is a serious mission," said Sid the professional.

"Well, fuck the lot of you." Reece stormed away from the pub. There was no chance of him getting another sample while Sanderson stood there. At least Reece had not wasted the last week. He'd been very busy indeed. He knew the nature of what was waiting for them in Manchester, and it would not go according to their plans. Things were about to turn nasty for Tillsley and his band of scummy men.

With Reece gone, Sanderson asked the question, "Are we ready, gents?"

"HHHHHOOOOOOOOOOOOOOOOOOOOOOO!"

THE LADS TRAVELLED AT PACE TO MANCHESTER in a multi-million pound battle cruiser. They raced down the motorway with the flashing lights of a police escort making them feel even more important, if that were possible.

"This is fooking mint!" said the most impressed man in all of Teeside,

Sid Tillsley. "This is proper fooking *A-Team* shit, this."

"That it is, Sid, that it is," agreed Sanderson.

"I'd be Mr T, Arthur would be Face, Brian would be Hannibal, and Rathbone would be the annoying twat."

All the 'boro boys nodded agreement.

"I ain't shitting on no plane, fool!" said Sid.

Everyone knew what he meant. In fact, if Sid ever did make it *international*, which would be a feat in itself considering Sid's phobia of camp air stewards, then it was best that no one corrected him.

Sanderson took the opportunity to brief them. "We tracked the target to Manchester a few nights ago, and he's been coming to and fro ever since. To our knowledge, he hasn't killed a single human being. I've never heard of a vampire suffering from schizophrenia before, but his change in nature is bizarre."

The four lads looked at one another. Brian, the spokesman piped up, "We don't do all that mental bollocks, mate, it's all a load of shite. You've spent too much time watching fooking women's programmes. Let's simplify things. Who do you want Sid to hit?"

"I think you know him quite well. Sid's had a number of confrontations with Gunnar Ivansey over the past six months. When Sid first killed a vampire Gabriel, Ivansey was his accomplice. Sid had a fight with him outside The Miner's Arms at the last ladies' night. Then, last week they had their third confrontation at Nottingham Police Station."

"I remember that wanker," said Brian. "Sid, didn't he throw knives in your arse? And weren't he helping that doris whose tit you grabbed? They were trying to get you done for benefit fraud. Remember? You smacked him in the bollocks," said Brian.

Sid's face was blank. "You don't mean Rathbone, do ya?"

"Rathbone is sat there, ya daft bastard. Look, don't worry, I'll show you who to smack."

"You got it." Sid unleashed whisky from his cool suit.

The police escort disappeared once the enormous vehicle carrying the lads was within a mile of its destination.

"They'll be no back-up. You're on your own in there," said Sanderson.

Sid shrugged. "I always go scrapping on me own."

"OK, Brian," said Sanderson. "Here's a picture of the target. It's not great, but it's the best we could take."

"He's grown a moustache," commented Brian, squinting at the grainy picture. "Looks pretty good, that. It'll be a shame to give a man a pasting with a 'tash as good as that, but it's all for the greater good of Sid collecting benefit money, so we'll do it."

"That's good to hear." Sanderson opened the door of the cruiser, which was receiving a great deal of attention from the Manchester locals. It was a Saturday night and town was rammed. Sanderson hadn't planned it this way, and it would lead to more bad publicity, but it was now do or die.

"He's got nearly thirty bloodsuckers—" he ignored the tut from Rathbone, "—with him. He's in that nightclub over there." Sanderson thumbed behind him.

"That ain't a club, surely? It's a shit heap," said Brian, looking at what appeared to be an abandoned building. Only flashing lights several stories up gave an indication that there was anyone inside.

"They don't advertise. It's now the most exclusive club in Manchester. Right. We're gonna back this beast off. Just send me a message through the intercom if you get into trouble." Sanderson jumped into the van and it sped away.

Five minutes later, an agent buzzed through to Sanderson on the intercom. The lads had found trouble. The van turned back towards Manchester at a dangerous speed until it reached the lad's drop-off point. They pulled up with the screech of brakes. Sanderson jumped out of the van and fought his way through the on-looking crowd, his gun drawn and ready for the worst. He pushed to the front to find the four lads scrapping—but with no vampires in sight.

Thirty to forty bodies lay sprawled out across the pavement, all with consciousness hours away. A mixture of red shirts and fluorescent yellow jackets made up the bulk of the victims. The 'boro boys were throwing punches at two parties: football fans, and a large congregation of Her Majesties' finest.

The lads were heavily outnumbered, but that wasn't a problem. Sid was used to fighting crowds. He didn't move much and took far more punches than he landed, but punches had never affected him much. When he landed a shot, however, it echoed around the built-up square. The victims collapsed as if shot, unconscious before they hit the ground. Brian had developed a strange, symbiotic fighting style with Sid. He hid behind him and darted out when he saw an opening to kick an unsuspecting victim in the bollocks.

Arthur used his karate, and Rathbone flourished his cape an awful lot without really getting into the action, but when he did land an ungainly right hand, he yielded a knockout blow.

"Stop the police!" yelled Sanderson.

Every policeman had batons and pepper spray drawn, and it was completely ineffective due to the fighting style of Sid and Brian. Whenever pepper spray was fired, Brian would leap out and absorb it because he was immune to lachrymators. And, whenever a baton was swung, he'd jump backwards and let Sid absorb the blow as if he was taking part in a pillow fight.

With the flash of their special badges, the agents had the police backing off. They weren't happy about it. About a dozen of their fellow officers and friends were all in need of hospital assistance, and now, they were ordered to let the Middlesbrough lads go.

Realising there were no more police to hit, Brian and Sid turned all their attention to the football fans, who were getting their backsides handed to them by a vampire and a karate master. When Sid waded in and knocked a few extra out, the rest decided it was best to leg it.

"What the fuck happened?" yelled Sanderson, losing his cool. "Why are you fighting the police?"

"Weren't our fault, mon," said Sid. "We were scrapping and they thought they'd get involved."

"Of course they're gonna get involved! They're the police! Why were you scrapping in the first place?"

"It weren't our fault!" said Brian. "Fooking Manchester United fans turned up."

"They attacked you?"

"Aye, they fooking did," said Brian, still bobbing around, ready for more.

"Why?"

"'Cos I smacked one of the twats," said Brian.

"What? Why?"

"He's a Manchester United fan!" justified Brian.

Sanderson shook his head. "You're a liability, the lot of you." He called to one of his agents. "Disperse the crowds, Jacobs, and get rid of the police before they make a bigger mess." The lads would've been doing five years minimum, each, for the GBH they'd unleashed in five minutes. Sanderson calmed down and even had a smile for the four lads. "Well, that's a good warm up for you boys."

"Yeah, I'm thirsty now," said Sid. "Is it time for The Miner's yet?"

"Will be soon, Sid," said Sanderson, "and I'll be buying."

"Champion!"

"Now, go and give Ivansey a right hook for me."

WALKING INTO THE NIGHTCLUB ENTRANCE, the boys wondered if they were in the right place.

"Are you sure this is a fooking nightclub?" asked Sid.

"Must be," said Brian. "Sanderson was pretty sure."

"It looks like it's about to be demolished. There's rubble and crap everywhere, Brian."

"Hey, man," said Arthur. "Ain't we meant to be using our codenames?"

"Fook that, Arthur. I got bored of that as soon as this suit gave me a reet sweaty crack." Sid tried to pull the tight, knife-proof material from the vice-like grip of his buttocks and failed. "I ain't fooking washing these when we're done. They shouldn't have made the fookers so tight. It ain't my fault if it gets soiled."

"If this is a nightclub, then where're all the people?" asked Arthur.

"There are people three floors up," said Rathbone.

"How do you know that?" asked Brian.

"Got super-hearing now I'm a vampire, like. I can see in the dark too. There's a flight of stairs over—"

"That's it," interrupted Sid. "Fook the benefit money. It ain't fooking worth it. I'm not taking another set of stairs. I had a whole fooking staircase to climb on the last trip I went on, and I've had enough of it!"

Sid started to walk back to Middlesbrough.

"— by the lifts," finished Rathbone.

"HHHHHHHHOOOOOOOOOOOOOOOOO!"

Sid unleashed the whisky-providing contraption in his suit and found disappointment rather than fine malt. "Aw, fook, I'm all out."

"Me too," replied his fellow vampire hunters and the vampire.

The boys trudged over to the lift. Missions weren't as exciting without whisky ejected from battle suits. Nothing was. The lads jostled into the cramped lift.

"Reet, what's the plan then?" asked Brian.

"Not you, too, Brian," said an angry Tillsley. "I hate fookin' plans. Just 'cos we're on a mission doesn't mean that we have to have a fooking plan. We'll get out the lift, you'll show me which twat needs a smack, I'll smack 'em, and we go home. Reet?"

"Sounds like a plan," agreed Brian.

"No, Brian, I said *no* fooking plan. Reet?"

"Sure thing, Sid."

"Champion."

DING! The doors to the nightclub opened...

"Now, this is reet swanky," said Brian, nodding his head in appreciation.

It was a masterpiece of architecture hidden inside a shabby building. High ceilings tested the eyesight while flowing fountains enchanted the ears. Brian was impressed, because he'd never been in a pub that didn't smell of piss.

"Why the fook don't they advertise this place? They'd make a fortune with all the minted Mancs," said Sid.

"Sanderson said they only want a certain clientele. I guess he means it's gonna be all vampires or summat," answered Brian. "Might be some nice-looking birds. That lass I nailed from snooker hall was top drawer."

"The last thing I need is to get another one preggers," grumbled Arthur.

"You can smack the blokes, and I'll nail the women," Brian said. "This place is massive. It can't just be the foyer. Rathbone, where are they?"

"Oh, yeah, that's right," said the vampire, his fists slamming into his hips in protest.

Brian's face screwed into a confused look. "Eh?

"Because I'm a vampire, I should know, right?"

"What the fook are you talking about?"

"You racist prick! You think that just because I'm a vampire, I'm gonna know where all the other fooking vampires are, don't you? You're all the fooking same."

"You've only been a vampire a fortnight."

"My people have been persecuted for billions of years by you white folk!"

"Eh? You're white! Anyroads, we're on a mission to kill vampires, which *you* wanted to go on because you got that cape."

"I look like a sexy Batman," Rathbone gave a quick flourish.

Brian went back to ignoring him. "If this is the foyer, the club is gonna be pretty snazzy."

"Where's the bar?" asked a thirsty Tillsley.

"Through that door over there," said Rathbone

"Let's go get hammered!" said Sid.

"HHHHHHOOOOOOOOOOOOOOOOOOOO!" cried all.

As soon as the door at the end of the hallway opened a millimetre, the room flooded with sound. Amazingly, the hallway was dull and drab compared to the main dance hall that exuded ostentation to the nth degree, as did the clientele. This was where the beautiful people came to get away from normal people. For people as special as these, only palatial surroundings would do.

"Fook me!" said one and all. Four jaws hit the floor.

"I ain't been anywhere like this before. The women are fooking amazing!" said Sid.

"I love being a vampire," Rathbone gloated.

"I need another vampire chick," said Arthur.

Brian was a swordsman, good and true, but for once, his "Swordy-sense" wasn't tingling. There would be no loving to be had in this room. There was only one reason why stunning women would come to a nightclub like this, and that was to avoid the attention of lecherous, drunken men. "We need to go."

"What you talking about, man? I have needs." pleaded Arthur, "The last jump I had was with Three-Tits Tracey!"

"Yeah! I need to meet some of my fellow vampires," Rathbone whined. "I need to find myself. You lot are suppressing the inner me. I wanna go travelling."

"Eh?" said Brian.

"I wanna see some tits!" Rathbone confessed.

Brian looked around nervously. "Look, guys, I have a bad feeling about all this."

Brian could feel the cold, hard eyes of the beautiful people burrowing in to him. It reminded him of the time he was caught peeping in the women's changing rooms at Middlesbrough swimming baths. Sid wasn't smart enough to notice, and Rathbone was used to tramps looking down on him. Only Arthur fitted in with this crowd, but his matching outfit tarred him with the same common brush of the others.

"It's a trap," Brian said. "They knew we were coming. Let's get out of here."

"Don't be so jumpy, Brian," said Sid. "You're not one to run away from a scrap. Come on. Let's get a beer. I'll stick it on me expenses."

The lads tried to saunter coolly to the ornate bar. The crowd parted as if letting a group of lepers pass. Everyone at the bar disappeared as soon as Sid placed his paw, clutching a tenner, on the smooth marble.

"Four ales, please, lad."

The barman raised a sculpted eyebrow. He wasn't like any barman Sid had seen before. He was more like a waiter at a posh-nosh restaurant, or so Sid would imagine. "*Ale*?" the barman said in a tone normally reserved for the words "*Jimmy Savile?*"

"Aye."

"*Aye*?" he repeated with the same disgusted tone.

"You got any ale? Bitter? Beer?"

"Oh, we don't serve *beer*, here."

Sid didn't like the way the posh bloke said "beer." "This is a fooking pub, ain't it?"

The barman raised his nose high in the air. "No, it most certainly is not!"

"What is it then?"

"It's a club. A club with a guest list, I might add," said the barman.

"Give us four whiskies, then. I can fooking see that on the shelf." Sid raised a threatening digit. "And don't be a tight twat with the measures, either."

The barman reluctantly prepared the drinks.

"What a wanker," said Sid loud enough for the population of Manchester to hear. The barman returned with the drinks, and then placed them on the bar. Sid looked long and hard at what was placed in front of him. "What the fook is that?"

"A coaster, *sir*."

Sid picked it up between his thumb and forefinger and examined it closely. He didn't know why, but it made him angry. "And what the fook is one of them?"

"It is part of a well-presented beverage, *sir*."

"And where the fook is the beverage?"

"In the glass, *sir*."

Sid examined the beverage or, rather, lack of. He narrowed his eyes at the barman. "You a cockney?"

The barman raised his nose a little higher.

"How much?"

"Forty pounds, *sir*."

If the barman raised his nose any higher, he would've fallen backwards. The barman hadn't dealt with a Tillsley before. Physical violence did not exist in his world where a condescending tone was the equivalent to a big, straight right. Sid's condescending tone removed the barman's bottom set of teeth.

Sid looked over the bar at the bloody mess he'd created. "Brian, was he the one I was meant to smack?"

Brian winced when he popped his head over the bar for a look. "Don't think he is, Sid."

"Shame."

The big right hand hadn't attracted too much attention. Most of the clubbers had turned their backs on the lads, and the punch and the barman's descent to the ground were so quick, no one had seen.

"Come on. Let's find the bloke we're gonna give a pasting," said Sid before his eyes were drawn upwards. "Fook me, she's tall!"

"Yeah, come on, let's hurry it up," said Brian, pushing Sid past the exceedingly tall lady with the Adam's apple.

"That fella over there has got his top off!" Sid pointed to the stage next to the dance floor. "What's that all about? They don't sell beer, yet they let fellas jump around with their tops off. What the fook is he getting so excited about dancing to Kylie Minogue for?"

"I don't know, Sid. Come on, the quicker we get this done, the quicker we get back to The Miner's for some ale." Brian pushed the big man forward as best he could.

"That lad's got lucky!" Sid pointed to where a couple were enjoying each other's company.

"Come on, Sid, let's move on."

"I've never been a fan of short hair on a woman, but these are modern times, Brian. Each to their own. He's proper getting in there too. Fook me, he's got a hand down the front of her knickers, although that is a strange action for stimulating a lady's part, that's for sure. Shame she's as flat-chested as a schoolboy."

Something caught Sid's eye. "What the fook are they?" he asked, squinting at the club's commissioned artwork, which was rather unusual.

"I don't know, Sid," lied Brian. "Keep your mind on the mission, OK?"

Sid's eyes opened wide when he identified the theme of the paintings. "Why are there pictures of cocks all over the wall?"

"There're no cocks, Sid. Come on, let's go."

After walking past several men entwined in passionate embraces, at least half a dozen transvestites, and numerous pictures of erect men, things began to dawn on Sid. His suspicions were confirmed when his gaze wandered across the dance floor and onto a lone man, dancing by himself.

"HE'S WEARING A PINK T-SHIRT!"

"Oh no...," Brian groaned.

"Brian, this is a...this is...Brian!"

Sid didn't have many epiphanies, but he couldn't remember ever having one accompanied by a spotlight being shone on him.

The music suddenly cut off mid-song and the dancers began edging their way to the corners of the floor, leaving the spotlighted Sid and his friends very alone on the dance floor.

"SID TILLSLEY!" came a booming, festive voice from over the speaker system.

"Ah, fook!" said Brian, all his fears confirmed.

Sid was in no position to talk. The camp voice echoing around the club was enough to send his Gay Defence System into a *Pink Alert* overload. His heart began to pump blood so quickly around his body that, even through his clotted arteries, he couldn't faint. The voice continued its onslaught on the world's most homophobic Northerner.

"Sid Tillsley is a name that has haunted my dreams for the past six months." The echoing voice filled Sid with a primeval fear. "No human has impacted one such as myself since time began. Your actions have changed the world, and you killed me, Tillsley. You killed me."

The crowd drew back even farther from the four lads. The spotlight suddenly turned pink, striking Sid like a laser beam. He felt the gay light probe him, trying to enter him. He clenched his buttocks tight, but he couldn't keep it out. The other lads were suffering too. Obviously, not as badly as Sid, but this was not the natural territory of the Northern man.

The spotlight left Sid and slowly crossed the dance floor and to a sweeping red carpet that continued up a magnificent staircase, past the cock-shaped plinths, until it rested on royal blue velvet curtains.

"SID TILLSLEY! I AM YOUR DESTINY."

The curtains opened...

"Sid! SID! We've gotta go!" screamed Brian over the din of "Sometimes" by Erasure. "Come on," he said again, desperately looking back up the stairs at a vision of sequins, Spandex, and splendour.

"Hey, man," said Arthur. "This is freaky shit. Let's go. That crazy son of a bitch is coming down the stairs. I haven't got a clue what the fuck he is, but I don't wanna be here when he arrives."

Rathbone hid behind his cape while Sid entered the foetal position—but with his bum planted firmly on the ground.

"Arthur, help me get him to his feet," said Brian.

Arthur complied. "It's no use, he's too heavy!"

"Shit! His Gay Defence System has completely shut him down!"

"We've gotta do something, man!" said Arthur. "That thing's gonna be here in a minute—"

"I know, I know," said Brian. "Drastic times require drastic measures."

"What do you mean?" asked Arthur.

"Remember that time when Sid laughed at that Lily Savage joke and then found out afterwards she was a bloke dressed as a woman?"

"Sid knocked out three police horses before we calmed him down."

Brian nodded before whispering into Sid's ear.

Sid's eyes opened, and Brian backed off slowly. The blue touch paper had been lit. The thing was almost here. With pupils darting and head twitching, Sid awkwardly got to his feet. His body jerked with the movements of the possessed. The inner beast had been unleashed by Brian reminding Sid of his unfortunate attendance at Middlesbrough's premiere of *Brokeback Mountain*.

Sid roared a note so deep that homosexual men everywhere couldn't hear it, but they could feel it, and it inspired fear.

"I...AM...MAAAAANNNNNNNN!"

His opponent slowed. Man's energy, or "Manergy," was what it fed on, thrived on. But the energy Sid created was more than that, it was the pure essence of Manergy, like the soul of a Black and Decker Workmate.

"I AM THE CAMPIRE, AND I AM COMING FOR YOU, SIDNEY!"

Sid's opponent stepped farther into the Circle of Man and drew upon its inner self, and the other side felt the effects. Ball sacks remained unwaxed. Shirts weren't ironed. *Mamma Mia* was only watched twice.

The two beings faced each other, opposite ends of the spectrum. Sid drew even deeper from the Well of Male, and the surrounding areas felt the effects. Dads felt no urgency to unnecessarily polish their cars. Balls remained unscratched. Farts were held in.

This mental battle threatened to destroy the fabric of the universe. The opponents were evenly matched, but...there was a chink in the armour. Sid's enemy got distracted.

The beautiful face of Arthur Peasley was something that only red-blooded males could fully resist, and even that was a struggle after a few pints.

"Hmmmmm...Who's your friend?"

"AAAAAAAAAAAAAAAARRRRRRRGGGGHHHHH!"

Sid ran like the wind (a small, easterly breeze coming off a sewage factory, but wind, nonetheless). Partygoers were thrown aside as he bulldozed his way through the dance floor.

With the momentum, Sid didn't have the angle to make it through the doorway to the foyer, but that wasn't going to stop him. He smashed through the wall as if it was paper. There wasn't a building material strong enough to keep him in the same room with that...thing.

Sid didn't even clock the stairs. Stairs were his friend right now. They led to freedom and they led to the Northeast where such things didn't exist. He took two stairs at a time before bursting through the front doors of the camouflaged building, smashing local clubbers out of his path as he went.

"Sid, calm the fook down!" Brian shouted after him. He struggled to keep up even though he was the fastest man over thirty yards in Middlesbrough.

"You saw it, Brian! You saw..." The spent adrenaline could no longer suppress the physical exhaustion, and Sid's hands crashed on to his knees. "You...saw...it!"

The screeching breaks of the battle cruiser got everyone's attention, and Sanderson jumped out. "What happened in there? Why haven't I heard anything from you?"

"Get us out of here!" Sid climbed into the car and tested the structural integrity of one of the cool swivel chairs. "This whole fooking town...He'll turn the whole fooking town! You can stick that benefit cheque right up your arse! Back to The Miner's! I...I need an ale. You're...you're buying."

"What happened, Brian?"

"I'll tell you on the way back, lad. He ain't gonna be scrapping tonight. That man needs a lot of beer after what he just went through."

Sanderson ushered them all back in the vehicle and slammed the door shut. "Goddamn it!" If Ivansey was too strong for Tillsley, there was nothing that could stop him.

BACK ON THE SMITHSON ESTATE, Lucia couldn't stop the flood of tears cascading down her cheeks. She caught a brief glimpse of herself in the bedroom mirror before smashing it with her fist. She'd turned from a beautiful vampire to a fat, worthless lump, sat at home waiting for her man to get back from the pub. A man who treated her like shit and was possibly cheating on her.

How could she have fallen for him? She knew he'd be bad for her before she moved into his flat. A vampire, a member of the Coalition, responsible for the welfare of the world, and now all she had to look after was his dinner, which he didn't appreciate, anyway. She tended the saucepan where she cooked spaghetti bolognese.

She couldn't leave him. She put herself in this predicament because of her love for Arthur, the lying, cheating, drunken scumbag!

She threw the saucepan across the room and a kitchen cupboard exploded in a shower of splinters. She wiped her wet hand with a tea towel. The spaghetti bolognese splattered everywhere, or so she'd thought. Her hand was wet with blood. She'd lacerated her knuckles when she punched the mirror...and they hadn't healed.

"This isn't right..."

Suddenly, the pain she'd experienced in the laundrette came flooding back. This time, it took her to her knees. She collapsed and writhed in agony on the floor. She doubled up and screamed, but no sound escaped her lips.

Clutching at her belly, she reached for the phone. Arthur should've been home by now, but she couldn't risk the baby, not for anything.

Arthur had left her no other choice...

30

THE ENTIRE COALITION WERE ON THE SCREEN IN FRONT OF SANDERSON. He had to explain why Ivansey was still alive. He thought he'd be explaining Tillsley's survival, not both.

"What happened?" asked Caroline.

"Tillsley couldn't fight."

"And Tillsley is still alive because...?" asked Charles.

"He's still the best chance we've got."

"God help us. How many lamia were with Ivansey?" asked Bwogi.

"Surveillance said high-twenties."

Bwogi shook his head. "Nearly thirty voices proclaiming, rightfully, that the Coalition sent a vampire hunter against them. Our failure is complete."

"Don't get melodramatic," said Sanderson, rolling his eyes. "We knew what we were getting into when we sent Tillsley. There was always going to be witnesses. There's no strength left in the whole vampire nation besides Ivansey, but if you want to secure this country, you'll need another warlord like Vitrago or a drug that will make all our problems go away."

Everyone on the screen turned to look at Garendon who was more interested in the piece of paper he scribbled on.

"How are you progressing, Garendon?" asked Caroline.

"Yes...erm...there has been a slight complication," he said, as he rubbed out a chemical formula.

"*Slight complication?*" shrieked Bwogi, standing up from his chair.

Garendon kept his head buried in the chemistry. "I've lost one of my synthetic chemists, a brilliant vampire whose name escapes me."

"Lost?" Caroline readjusted her position in her chair. It was as close to agitated as she got.

"Yes. Hasn't turned up for a couple of days, and he'd locked his supplies cupboard. I could really use the spare test tubes he keeps in there."

"Don't you think losing a scientist is more important than test tubes?" said Augustus.

"Most of his work was complete. I don't need him anymore," replied Garendon matter-of-factly.

"And why haven't you told us?"

"I found some more test tubes in another drawer."

"I despair!" cried Bwogi, visibly shaking. "Rempstone, track down the scientist. He could've been killed, kidnapped, or he could be the leak for all we know." Bwogi sighed heavily and turned back to the screen where Sanderson was biting his lip, trying not to laugh at the shit they were all in. "So yes, even though Haemo is on track, despite the complications, the Agreement could be broken tomorrow."

"The Coalition is weak," said Caroline, "but so is the vampire nation. Recent reports note the deaths of Vlastisluv Branko, Elias Cai, Farai Killato, Basilio Gorka, and the infamous Daedlus Karnus." Before the questions rained down, Caroline explained as much as she knew. "I only found out this morning. It was Ivansey. He ripped them all apart at Richmond's nightclub in Newcastle. I'm afraid to say that Richmond was also killed."

Bwogi struggled to speak. "Richmond? Oh, this will devastate the nation as much as the loss of Pontius. Ivansey was...his friend."

"He's descended into madness, but he's rid us of our biggest threats," said Augustus.

"Ivansey seeks world domination," said Bwogi. "Sanderson's intel said there were nearly thirty vampires at the Manchester club. Nearly thirty! With the state of the nation, he will quickly rally more to him."

"There's more," said Rempstone. "He attacked a house in Abney, Derbyshire a week ago. I received the reports this morning. Luckily, there were no eye-witnesses, and only a single body was discovered by the public."

"Is such a small incident worth bringing to the table," asked Charles.

"It wasn't a small house. We believe there was a party and nearly a hundred were killed."

"A hundred!" said Pervis in a high-pitched squeal.

"He just wants chaos!" wailed Bwogi. "He's unstoppable."

"Before you all run out into the sunlight," Sanderson interrupted, "let's calm the fuck down. He's been in Manchester for a few days and hasn't brought the reign of terror we feared."

"What do you mean?" asked Bwogi.

"Tillsley wasn't able to fight because Ivansey didn't take the fight to him. Tillsley can still finish this. In Manchester, he didn't get the chance." Sanderson didn't need to divulge all the information and tell them how dramatic and strange Ivansey's change had been. He remained convinced Tillsley was the key.

"You're right." Caroline sighed. "We're too far down the path to turn back now."

"Yes, but unsanctioned kills have skyrocketed," said Rempstone. "We're more stretched now than when Sparle was decimating the Northeast."

"We shouldn't just simply plan for upholding the Agreement," she said. "We should plan for its inevitable downfall."

Her words carried no subtlety, no cushion. She spoke the truth. A truth the other councillors had feared since Sparle's appearance.

Sanderson broke the silence, "War isn't easy. Next time you hear from me, you'll have one less thing to worry about. Find out where that scientist has gone, Rempstone. This whole organisation is a fucking joke."

Sanderson hung up the video call.

ARTHUR OPENED THE DOOR OF HIS FLAT AND WAS STUNNED. He couldn't smell cooking. "Where's my supper!" he hollered through the house.

Arthur stormed through to the bedroom to find Lucia thrashing around on the bed, two women by her side, trying to calm her down. He knew it was wrong, but he couldn't help noticing how hot they were; they had to be vampires.

He couldn't believe it. Lucia was giving birth. The old dude giving him a look of thunder had to be her daddy. Arthur didn't care, only Lucia and his baby mattered.

Arthur rushed to the bedside. "Baby!" he said with genuine concern. "Is she OK?" he asked one of the chick vampires (the hot blonde one).

"YOU!" Lucia's daddy started towards him. Arthur tensed, ready to use his karate.

"No, Father," said Lucia, weakly. "I love him." She reached from her bed and grabbed his arm.

"Hey, man," said the cool cat. "I love your daughter, and I wanna marry her. I was gonna ask your permission, but she didn't want you to know she had a bun in the oven."

"I'll deal with you later," said her father, turning back to Lucia.

"You want me to boil some water or something?" asked the modern-aged man, but he was ignored. "Just shout if you need anything."

"You need his blood, Lucia!" said her father.

"No! He'll die. He's not a vampire. He'll die..." She looked at Arthur. "He's my life."

"But if you don't, *you* will die!" He turned a cold eye towards Arthur.

"No, Father...please!"

Borg caught Arthur unawares, grabbing him by the scruff of the neck. He thrust Arthur towards her. The sight of Lucia in such pain distracted Arthur from taking care of business with his karate.

"Father! Let him go!" she screamed.

He released his grip on Arthur before sobbing. "I can't even save the only thing I care for."

Arthur watched helplessly as Lucia grew weaker. Tears streamed down his face. "Take my blood. I'll die for you, Lucia." He meant it too.

"No. This baby, this pregnancy, is unlike any other. Nothing will save me. I'd forfeit my life a thousand times to know you and the baby are safe. But, please, tell me one thing...Do you love me?"

Arthur looked her in the eye and told her, truthfully, "With all my heart."

An agonising hour passed. Lucia's screams ripped through the block of flats. No one came to investigate. The neighbours were used to ladies in Arthur's flat screaming the house down. Most screamed a lot louder and lot longer than Lucia did now.

Arthur wasn't a squeamish man, but seeing the amount of blood Lucia lost made him sick. Finally, when he thought that things couldn't get any worse, he heard the screams of a baby.

"It's a boy!" said the blonde vampire. She wiped the baby down and gave it to Lucia.

"Arthur...where's Arthur?" said Lucia, on the edge of consciousness.

Arthur's heart melted. He had a son. A son! A tear dropped from his cheek. "He...he's perfect. He looks just like my daddy."

And that he did. The baby was the spitting image of Arthur's daddy, right down to the perfect hair and trademarked half-lip sneer. How the baby had managed to endure birth while maintaining hair that fucking cool was a mystery. But, this baby wasn't born under normal circumstances.

What had Arthur done? All those months of neglect, drinking down the pub with his buddies, and Three-Tits Tracey...oh momma. How could he do that to the mother of his child? She'd given him this gift and stood by his side after all he'd put her through. He pulled her hand to his face, smothering it with soft kisses. "Baby, I'm the luckiest man in the world. I'll never leave your side again. You're my queen, Lucia."

"Oh, Arthur! I love—" Lucia clutched at her stomach before she gasped for air. A cry escaped her lips and the other vampires rushed to her side. One took the baby from him, and Lucia's father swept Arthur aside with the back of his hand. "Don't hurt him!" Lucia managed, reaching for Arthur with an outstretched hand.

Arthur saw stars, but he didn't care. His woman and his baby were all that mattered. He shook his head, trying to clear it. "Lucia!"

"Arthur!" she whispered weakly. "Let me see him."

Arthur pushed his way through to her bedside. She was incredibly pale, even for a vampire. "Arthur, take care of him. I...I...am not going to..."

"Don't say that! You're gonna be fine."

Somehow, Lucia managed a smile through the pain. "I will...love...you...always." The smile faded along with her life.

"Lucia!" Arthur shook her gently, refusing to believe what he already knew. "LUCIA!"

"Get away from her, human!" Again, Arthur flew across the room as her father stuck his boot into his ribs.

"Lu...Luc...," Arthur murmured, trying to speak.

"Do not say her name again." Lucia's father left her bedside and picked

Arthur off the floor by his throat, holding him with a vice-like grip. "I would tear you limb from limb, but I have a crueller fate in store for you. You will see your son again, but only after I have driven in a hatred for the human race so deep, he will despise every molecule of your worthless body. He will be your doom, human, but not just yours. He will be the doom of your species. He will know that it was *you* who killed his mother. His beautiful, precious mother."

He smashed Arthur's head into the wall, which ended the beautiful man's suffering, if only for a moment.

SANDERSON WAS DRIVING BACK TOWARDS MIDDLESBROUGH from yet another trip to Manchester. He'd been driving too much lately. The radio was interrupted as his telephone rang. "Sanderson."

"Sir, we have a Code 7."

"Phone Rempstone. "

Code 7 was commonplace these days. It was a 999 call suggesting vampire activity. The Coalition monitored all emergency lines electronically for certain words and phrases. When the computer system detected them, it alerted an agent who would verify and contact a field officer if necessary. Sanderson was only called personally when the Agreement was threatened. But that was now Rempstone's responsibility.

"We would, sir, but we think you should deal with this one."

He sighed. "Give me the coordinates."

An hour later, Sanderson pulled up to the farmhouse in the middle of nowhere in the Yorkshire countryside. The Coalition were already present, and, thankfully, no police, which meant no more unnecessary deaths. As day waned and the cold night closed in, Sanderson surveyed the farmhouse, the only building for miles in any direction. Why would they call him out for this?

"Harry Dean, long time, no see."

A middle-aged, portly man approached him and warmly shook Sanderson's hand. The two men went back years and had been in more scrapes than most.

"Rempstone keeping you on your toes, Harry?"

Harry took off his flat cap, revealing a heavily receded hairline, and spat on the ground. "Jumped-up twat." Harry pointed at the farmhouse and changed the subject. "Weird shit in there, kidda."

"Yeah?"

Harry nodded. It must've been really bad to have this man spooked. Harry was hard as nails, and his portly exterior made people, and vampires, misjudge him at their peril.

"Witnesses?"

"Oh no. This was called in by a vamp."

Sanderson couldn't believe his ears.

Harry read his old friend's mind and laughed. "Just come have a look."

Sanderson followed Dean into the rundown farmhouse and into the dilapidated kitchen. If he'd closed his eyes, he would've sworn he was walking into a butcher's. He took in the scene. "Who are they?"

"The farmer who owned this land was a well-known supporter of the British National Party, and some of his friends are hard-line Nazis. That's the farmer over there."

The farmer's frozen, silent scream spoke of the torture he'd suffered. His naked body hadn't left a dignified corpse with a mass of cuts and what looked like bites. Lipstick had been applied messily to his lips. Blusher tinted the cheeks and mascara covered the lashes and even his eyeballs.

"I take it he didn't apply the make-up himself."

Harry laughed. "I don't think so." He walked through the copious amounts of dried blood on the floor to stand over the mutilated body.

"This is strange, Harry. Why so much blood?"

"This attack had nothing to do with drinking it. This was about spilling it. It looks more like an animal attack. A lot of damage was caused with blades, which ain't usual for a vamp attack. This whole shebang was a grand display for us to find."

"No shit." said Sanderson. The other victims all were decorated with the same, bizarre facial artwork, and all of them had been worked over as badly as the farmer. "So why call me?"

"Let us retire to the lounge, sir," said Harry, putting on a voice of aristocracy.

If the sights of the kitchen were strange, the sights of the lounge were truly freakish. Sanderson unwittingly took a sharp intake of breath.

On the wall next to the fireplace, a body had been suspended with chains to the wall. He'd been dead for more than a day; no blood dripped from where his legs had once been. It was just a torso. The arms and legs were suspended from the ceiling in the corners of the room. The head and the genitals were missing, courtesy of a sharp blade and a saw.

"Where's the rest of him?" asked Sanderson

Harry gestured behind Sanderson. "You haven't noticed the unusual centrepiece."

Sanderson turned around.

Sebastian from the Coalition stared him straight in the eye with an unfaltering gaze. He, like the farmers, was covered in make-up, but this wasn't a Picasso masterpiece like the others, great care had been taken in the application. His severed genitals sat on top of his head like a crown.

"This dickhead sat on the Coalition."

"I didn't know." Harry turned to face Sanderson with a wry grin. "You're still shit at jokes, by the way."

"Point taken. Any idea of cause of death?"

Harry nodded. "We think that most of the injuries were caused after his death. We reckon he was killed by gunfire."

"You sure? There were enough humans here to feed on, and dying 'cos of a bullet is rare for a vamp."

"We won't know for sure until the autopsy, but look. He's riddled with bullet holes in his torso."

Sanderson scanned the room continuously. "Why is his make-up perfect and the farmer's grotesque?"

"I have no idea, at all." Harry lifted his cap to scratch his head.

"This one has everyone stumped. That's why we phoned you."

Sanderson shook his head, and then he thought back to what the lads from Middlesbrough had said about Ivansey and his newfound femininity. It dawned on him. "This is a shrine."

"A shrine?"

"Ivansey did this."

"Ivansey? I thought he was in Manchester."

"That's where he's based, but we know he's been moving around. He's gathering vampires to take down the Agreement, and Sebastian was leaking him information."

"You sure?"

"'Course I'm sure. That's what this display is for. Sebastian and Ivansey were toying with these Nazi fucks and Sebastian bit off more than he could chew. This is a tribute to that traitorous bastard Sebastian. At least the leak has been plugged." *Now we've just got to find the damned lost scientist*, he thought.

Harry rubbed his considerable jawline. "You've got yourself into shit before, kidda. At least wait for the forensics report, yeah?"

"I haven't got time for that shit, Harry." Sanderson turned on his heel.

"Cool it! Think about things. We've got the mobile lab working on it. They'll have the results soon."

Sanderson looked at his watch. "You better be quick."

An hour later, waiting in the mobile lab parked outside the farmhouse, Sanderson's foot tapped irritably behind the young Coalition scientist at the computer.

"Got it!" The scientist tapped a button and up popped a list of names. Sanderson read through several names before tapping the screen with excitement.

"I fucking told you, Harry. I knew it. Ivansey!"

Without a goodbye, Sanderson rushed out of the lab.

31

"SO, WHAT HAPPENED?" asked Kevin.

It was the day after Sid's confrontation. He'd gone straight to bed after returning from Manchester and couldn't even face the pub. Today was a day of healing, and there was only one magical drug that could take away the pain.

Sid, Brian, and Rathbone were in The Miner's licking their war wounds. Sid was busy drinking and smoking. Five empty pint glasses surrounded him. Poor bar keeping wasn't why so many glasses had been left out to stud, it was because Sid had demolished ten pints in twenty minutes, and two glasses had collected some of Sid's used ale. Kevin wouldn't be happy when he found out, but Sid couldn't waste time walking to the toilet. It was drinking time.

"He ain't gonna be able to talk for another few pints at least," said Brian, "and then he ain't gonna be able to talk because of the previous few pints."

Reece entered The Miner's Arms.

"Ah, fook, not you again." Reece didn't bat an eyelid. It was the usual greeting he got from Brian, who continued, "You look knackered, mon. What you been up to, then?"

"Always on the move, you know me."

"Not really," said Brian snidely.

Reece ignored the rudeness. "What happened, Brian?"

"It was a gay bar."

Sid's pint glass shattered in his hand, and without a word, he pointed at the Bolton Bitter pump demanding more painkillers.

"What do you mean?"

"That vampire who Sid had to smack has set up headquarters in a *them lot* bar." Brian saved Kev another pint glass by not using the G-word.

Reece relaxed against the bar. "And that's it?"

"Well, no. There was something there...something unlike I have ever seen before, even on *Eurotrash*. I could've sworn there was a pink glow around it. You should've seen him...I think it was a him. Mincing is a word that doesn't do it justice. Sid had no chance, you know, with his ways."

"Who was it?"

"I think it was that same bloke that Sid gave a hiding to at ladies' night all those months ago."

"Gunnar Ivansey?"

"Aye, but he called himself the Campire." Brian struggled to get his tongue around the word.

Reece opened a bottle of water that Kev had pushed his way and took a sip. "Did they fight?"

"Nah, the big man legged it. That's the first fight Sid has run away from since Graham Norton stole his parking space in the ASDA. If Sid's the only hope for them posh, Southern, council bastards, then they're up shit creek."

"I ain't going anywhere near—*hic!*—fooking Manchester, ever again. I ain't—*hic!*—fooking going anywhere outside of the 'boro, ever again!" Sid was past the ten-pint barrier which meant he could talk. "They're fooking everywhere!"

"I never asked you to fight him, Sid. You made those deals with the Coalition," said Reece with a shrug.

"Fook 'em!"

"Tell me more about Ivansey."

"He..." Sid paused, gathering the mental strength, "you know, me. I'm...a liberal fooker—*hic!*—but I tell thee, he was reet, fooking, you know, *them...lot.*"

"Really?"

"I could see him with me—*hic!*—ears closed, mon! He was after me, Rich. He was after me—*hic!*—man bits."

"What did he say to you?"

"It was what—*hic!*—he didn't say."

"And what didn't he say, Sid?"

"Exactly!"

Reece decided to question the brain cell behind the operation and leave Sid out of it. "What did he look like, Brian?"

"That's a difficult one, mon. I've never seen 'owt like it before. He dressed like Liberace but reminded me of Kenneth Williams, Boy George, and Rock Hudson, all at the same time. On top of that, he had Freddie Mercury's 'tash. It was a fooking good 'tash, like."

Sid took solace in his ale. He'd lost a hard fight. It wasn't a physical battle, but it had been a mental one. He needed to replenish his masculinity levels. The Northern man could do this in several ways: watching sport, playing darts, walking dogs, eating dripping on toast, and boozing. Sid invested heavily in the latter.

"Did he say anything to you?"

"Not much, like. In fact, apart from telling Sid that he was coming for him," another pint glass shattered, "he didn't say much at all. He was giving Arthur the look, though, if you know what I mean. "

"Where is Arthur?"

"Dunno, but he'll be here soon enough. His woman will drive him to the boozer."

"So, does he still want to kill you, Sid?" Reece asked.

"I think that was the last thing on his—*hic!*—mind, pal," said Sid. "That's it. I'm out of this fooking vampire-hunting lark. I knew most of 'em were *them lot*, but I didn't know there were any like that!"

"You can't quit, Sid." Reece shook his head slowly. "You work for the Coalition now. Your only chance to get rid of them is to follow me." He said matter-of-factly.

"You, and those Southern bastards, can fook off. Put me in jail, try an' take me on, whatever. I ain't getting pushed around anymore, and I certainly ain't having any dealings with *them lot*, again. In fact, prison will be reet. It will just be blokes, and them lads won't stand for any of that nonsense, not in—*hic!*—prison."

There was a commotion at the door. Arthur stumbled in before falling to his knees, Hollywood style, and collapsing on the floor.

"Arthur!" yelled Brian and rushed from his chair to his friend. "Sid, come and help me!"

Sid lumbered over and lifted Arthur onto his shoulder with one arm. "Get this man an ale!"

"I think he's had enough, like. He's steamin'!" said Brian.

"So am I. We both need ale!" cried Sid.

Arthur's hair was a mess. Stubble on his manly jaw normally looked stylish, but not today. His clothes were dishevelled and not one part of him looked up to his normal standard.

Brian took Arthur's head in his hands in order to stop it flopping drunkenly from side to side. "What's happened, mate? What's wrong?"

"She's gone..."

"Your missus? She's left you?"

Arthur didn't say anything.

"She'll be back," reassured Brian. "She won't be able to stay away."

"She...she's dead."

"Fook!" said Sid, and in all fairness to the lad, that was sympathetic for him.

"What? How?" asked Brian.

"She died during childbirth. I'm a father."

"Howay the lads! Time to wet the baby's head!" Sid got half way to the bar before realising this wasn't the time for celebration. "Sorry—*hic!*—mate."

"That's OK, man. I know you mean well. That drink will be appreciated, though," said Arthur.

"Reet, mon, mourning starts and ends tonight." Sid ordered double beers and chasers.

"Lucia's dead, man. She died in my arms after giving birth to my son." Arthur didn't hide his tears; never before had a Northern man cried in a Northern pub without being punched in the face. "And then, Lucia's daddy knocked me out and took my boy, vowing that he'd turn my own blood against me. Lucia...she's gone. She's gone."

The only one thing Brian could do to make Arthur feel better, was to get as drunk as his pal. Misery loves company. Rathbone didn't go in rounds with the lads, but he put an extra effort into getting drunk. He was enjoying the ale a lot more now his annoying thirst had been satisfied, although he wasn't looking forward to quenching it again...not after what happened in the toilets.

Reece sat back and took everything in. Studying a human/vampire hybrid with the new toys in his lab was an opportunity he couldn't pass by. What sort of genetic mutations allowed conception between two different species? What would this child turn into?

He walked around the bar table to where Arthur Peasley sat, hanging his head. "You're bleeding, Arthur, let me help you."

Before Arthur had a chance to acknowledge him, Reece had a handkerchief on the back of his head, dabbing the wound he'd received when Borg Hemsman rammed his skull into the wall. The handkerchief absorbed some blood, and Reece had his fresh sample.

"Get that shit off me, man!" said Arthur, shooing him away. "I need beer, not TLC, baby!"

"As you wish. Lucia's father is a powerful vampire. He will be back, Arthur."

"Like I care, man. Just get me an ale."

Kevin brought the beers over. No one was ordering, so he'd decided to take the initiative. This was going to be a good day for his takings as long as Sid stopped breaking glasses. This was the first day he could charge them for ale after they caught him shagging his doll. Shame Arthur's missus died. Kev would be devastated if he lost one of his dolls. If Mrs Ackroyd died...well, worse things happen at sea.

An hour of drinking passed.

"We'll get you a new woman, mon, and not one of them vampire fookers!" reassured Sid.

Moral support in the 'boro was different from what you'd get if you phoned the Samaritans. Sid and Brian had forgotten Arthur's grief, but they were all getting pissed, so nothing else mattered to these Northern men of stone.

"Thanks, man," said Arthur, placing a thankful hand on both the shoulder of Brian and Sid. "That means a lot. But, Sid, she was the most wonderful thing in the world. She loved me so much, and I treated her bad, man."

"I went through this with that bitch from Benefit Office," recollected Sid. "I thought she fooking loved me and she fooked me right over. I could've lost my fooking benefit money 'cos of her! You don't need that shit, lad!"

"You guys are the fucking best!" said Arthur with a tear in his eye. It wasn't a tear of sadness; it was a tear of happiness. "What are you drinking?"

"You ain't putting your hand in your pocket," said Sid. "Not tonight."

"Pint of bitter," said Rathbone.

"Fook off, Rathbone," said Sid before heading to the bar.

Reece smiled at not having to buy the—

"Didn't see you there, Rich. Get 'em in while I go for a piss."

Reece sighed. Once his lab work was finished, things would be different. Kev gave Reece a hand bringing the drinks over. Never a man to look a gift horse in the mouth, Kev asked, "You on for a proper good sesh, like?"

Sid, coming back from the toilets, answered the question by downing a perfect pint of Bolton, and Brian took up the mantle.

"We sure are, Kev. This man needs fixing, and that's what mates are for. Arthur, do you know the best way to get over a woman?"

Arthur didn't. This was the closest he'd ever been to getting dumped. He shrugged his manly shoulders.

"You get in the next one."

"No way, man. I can't disrespect Lucia or my child."

"Just come along for the ride! Come on, boys, we are hitting the town!"

Kev looked mournfully at his till. "Bastards!"

32

THE LADS DIDN'T GO INTO TOWN MUCH ANYMORE. The beer was shit and the music too loud. Truth be told, they were getting old. Brian and Sid were in their mid-forties, and Arthur a touch older, which shocked everyone since he looked early thirties, didn't have a grey hair, and sported a six-pack. Then, there was Rathbone, who was now immortal but still looked shit.

Town was for youngsters and was jam-packed with sixteen- and seventeen-year-old kids who got smashed off their tits at home and then went out late for a fight or a fumble. Saying that, there were a lot of punters in their fifties doing the same thing. More regular stints into town would be good for Sid and would probably end his drought with the ladies, but he couldn't part from the Bolton, not for too long.

The boys strutted through the town centre with Arthur moping behind them. The lads caused a mixed reaction from the Middlesbrough residents. Everyone knew who they were and what they were capable of. They were legends, but then again, Vlad the Impaler was classed as legendary.

Sid's hulking figure parted the crowds like Moses parted the seas. His fame throughout the 'boro got the respect it deserved or, rather, the fear it deserved. Brian was also a well-known face, and a lot of the younger lads had more than a passing resemblance to the swordsman. Brian recognised them. He knew his own bloodline. He gave them all a filthy look that said, "Don't even think of talking to me." If he was a lion, he would've eaten the scrounging little bastards.

All the girls swooned when Arthur, the local heartthrob, walked by, but he stood behind his friends, protected by their repellent personalities. Then there was Rathbone. Everyone knew he was a vampire, and everyone still thought he was a prick.

Reece walked behind the group, taking in the surroundings. He didn't like the attention. He didn't like walking through the middle of a town. He was a man of the shadows. But, he was forced to follow as he still wanted more samples, plus Ivansey was out there, and to Reece, he was more dangerous now than ever. Vampires were drawing to Ivansey, and Sid was his target. But why didn't he try to kill Sid in Manchester?

"Reet, lads, what do we all fancy?" asked Brian, rubbing his hands. "The streets are paved with fanny!"

"Bolton!" demanded Sid.

Brian sought reason. "Sid, come on, mon, you can survive one night without it. You already had twelve pints before we hit town."

"I want Lucia and my child, man." Arthur had sobered up enough to feel the pain.

"I want some more action!" said Rathbone, ignoring his depressed drinking companion.

"Not what you did last time, surely?" said Brian.

Rathbone would love to tell Brian where to go, but he was literally caught red-handed. "No," he muttered.

"I should think fooking not!" chastised the swordsman. "Reet, we need somewhere heaving with titties and good beer that ain't a sausage fest."

"Sounds good to me, Brian," said Sid, "but does such a place exist?"

"Probably not, but we can at least try." The boys continued their quest until they reached a pub with music spilling out on to the street. "Reet, what about this one? The Spaniel's Ears. There was karaoke on earlier. Lasses love karaoke."

"Aye," said Sid, "and the sign outside says they serve the best ale in all of the 'boro."

"Every pub says that, Sid."

"You know how I feel about false advertising, Brian," said Sid, cracking his knuckles.

"I know, mate. Reet, The Spaniel's Ears, it is."

Reece's gaze darted from the street to the rooftops and back again. His gut told him something was wrong. "I'll take a look around. Be back soon." He disappeared into an alleyway, not that anyone cared.

The lads moved single-file through the dilapidated front door. The doormen turned white as a sheet when they saw the big man roll up, and who could blame them? If it kicked off, there was nothing they could do except run.

"It don't look too bad in here, Brian," said Sid, admiring the decor. "Pretty snazzy."

Pretty snazzy to Sid meant no flies. Plaster crumbled off the walls, and the door to the toilets hung by only one hinge. There was even a dried bloodstain on the dance floor. It was a shithole, and most good and honest folk wouldn't set foot in a pub like it.

"There's even some lasses in!" said Sid excitedly.

"Aye, mon," said Brian, rubbing his hands together seeing middle-aged housewives drowning their sorrows at the bar. "And some of them ain't bad at all. Arthur, any take your fancy?"

"Just get me a drink."

"Miserable bastard, ruining everyone's night," mumbled Rathbone, who fancied his chances with a granny passed out in the corner.

"Stop being a prick, Rathbone," said Brian. "I'll get the beers in." He pushed himself to the front of the busy bar, upsetting people on the way. It was a good venue for a piss-up. "Four pints of your cheapest, best ale, please, barman," he asked semi-politely.

The barman, who was changing an optic, turned to his customer and dropped the bottle of gin he was holding.

"Jimmy!" Brian smiled. "What a surprise this is."

The young barman looked worse now than when he'd run The Badger. He was only young, but he looked worse than a pit pony, and his clothes hung off his gaunt frame. Jimmy tapped manically at a button that was hidden under the bar. Brian almost felt sorry for him. Almost.

"I asked for four pints of ale, you stupid twat. I didn't ask you to press a button under the bar over and over again," he said.

"You arsehole, Garforth. I lost fooking everything 'cos of you. I lost The Badger, I lost my home and my livelihood. I was fooking sectioned for a week. I'm now owned—fooking *owned*—by some bad people all because of you. Well, you're gonna get yours. The fooking lot of you will!"

Brian sighed. "Can you at least pour the beer first?"

"HAHAHAHAHAHAHA! You're in for it now."

Brian followed Jimmy's line of sight to where a large, solitary figure entered the bar from a back door. He was big, most likely a handful, but something wasn't right, and he walked over almost robotically.

Jimmy stopped his manic laughter in a heartbeat. "Where are the others?"

"Out...out back," said the heavy nervously.

Brian was bored. "Sid, strike this ruffian."

The sight of an advancing Tillsley rolling up his sleeve triggered a survival instinct in the hired heavy. "Wait! They've got your mate Reece round the back."

Sid let the tension drain out of his fist. "Eh? Who the fook is Reece?"

"Your mate. He was with you, tonight."

"We don't know anyone called Reece," said Brian. "Sid, strike this ruffian. Twice."

Sid rolled up his other sleeve.

The heavy quickly added, "He's wearing all black with a trench coat on. He's got long grey hair."

The four lads looked perplexed.

"He's a bit of a wanker," offered the heavy.

"You must mean, Rich!" the penny dropped for Brian, while Sid dropped the muscle for hire with a short, sharp jab.

"It's fooking rude getting someone's name wrong!" Sid admonished to the unconscious heavy.

Jimmy's shoulders sagged. He was on his own. All the patrons and the bouncers on the door had legged it. No one wanted to be around Sid, especially when he was hitting people. Yet another pub ruined.

"I was wondering where Rich had disappeared to," said Brian. "Jimmy, you shouldn't play silly buggers. Four pints of..." Brian scanned the pumps. "Bolton! Jimmy, I can't believe you've had another crack at it! You better have learned your lesson."

Jimmy stared at the floor. "You...you...shagged my mum," he said weakly. "I...I've done nowt wrong."

"Four pints of ale!" Brian banged his palm on the bar. "NOW!"

Jimmy got to it and proceeded to line the ale up in front of the toughest of critics. All—except Rathbone who only drunk Bolton in The Miner's—picked up their pints. All closed their eyes and placed the glass against their wrists, making sure it was served at the correct temperature. Next, they examined the beer by holding it to the light. Then, as a unit, they put the beer to their noses, taking in the aromatic pleasures. Suddenly, all hammered the beer down their throats as quickly as possible. Sid, being an exceptionally quick drinker, finished Rathbone's pint as well.

Four glasses slammed down, breaking the tense silence that filled the eerily empty pub.

Jimmy looked on hopefully. They'd finished their beers in record time, and he really had been taking better care of his ale since his release from the mental hospital. He held Brian's gaze, whose eyes gave away nothing. Brian relinquished the stare first. He slowly turned to the ultimate consumer of beer in the North, and therefore the universe—including parallel ones where beer is 5p a pint cheaper.

Sid's face was unreadable, even by the finest of poker players. Jimmy was close to losing control of his bladder. "I'll have another one of them, lad."

Jimmy let a little bit of wee go.

"Make that two more," said Brian.

"I'll have one too," said Rathbone.

Jimmy hated these men more than any other, but these were the toughest ale connoisseurs in the whole of the 'boro, and if they liked his ale, it was damn good. Jimmy beamed and strutted to the pumps with professional pride.

"Aye, good work, lad," said Brian. "Proper good drop, th—"

He was interrupted by another heavy coming through the back door. This guy was bigger than the last, but this one had been worked over badly and struggled to stand up straight.

"I've been sent...to remind you that...they've got your mate...Reece," said the heavy, wheezing due to broken ribs.

"Eh? Who the fook is Reece?" said Brian.

"Your mate. He was with you tonight."

"We don't know anyone called Reece," said Brian. "Sid, strike this ruffian. Thrice."

Sid, realising that both sleeves were rolled up, rolled up his trouser leg.

"He's wearing all black. Got a trench coat. Long grey hair. Bit of a wanker."

"You must mean, Rich!" the penny dropped for Brian, while Sid dropped the muscle for hire.

"It's fooking rude getting someone's name wrong!" said Sid to the unconscious heavy.

"Four pints of ale!" Brian banged his palm on the bar.

The door opened again, and in limped another ten hefty men, sporting a plethora of tattoos and symptoms of steroid-abuse. All of them had been on the end of a nasty beating. They took seats around the pub and nursed their wounds. Reece flew through the door after them, skidding across the floor, burning his face on the cheap nylon carpet. He slowly got to his feet.

The door opened again, and in walked the tiniest of men. He stood only five feet on tiptoes and was as slight as a schoolboy. Sid's eyes widened, he was convinced his eyes were deceiving him. He didn't understand whether the things the midget wore were actually clothes or not. He'd never seen anything like them before, and they certainly weren't available in Greenwoods.

He's wearing a fooking skirt! thought the big man.

"Good evening, Mr Tillsley. It's my pleasure to finally meet you in person."

The impossibly camp lisp caused Sid's eyes to widen some more.

"My name is Peaches Slackring."

"Your parents were cunts," said Brian.

Peaches ignored him and adjusted his kimono before standing like a teapot. "I'm here with a gift from Gunnar Ivansey, the Campire, the vampire you freed with a swipe of your right hand." Peaches dabbed at the corner of his eye with a handkerchief, trying not to smudge his mascara. This was all rather emotional for him.

"You can take that gift and stick it up your arse, lad!" said Brian.

"Later," said Peaches fleetingly. He addressed Brian as he could tell that "Sidney," as Peaches called him, wasn't capable of making decisions. He reasoned that his cute, Emo haircut put Sid off. "My master and Sidney have been at war for so long. They are yin and yang. The prophecy of the Firmamentum describes balance, but this is the *real* Firmamentum. To celebrate this, my master is offering Sidney a gift...a choice.

"These brutish men were hiding out the back of this pub, and the manager of this quite filthy establishment hired them to perform fisticuffs on poor Sidney, here. Some of my friends cottoned on to this and had words, as you can see. My friends are waiting out the back. Would you like to meet them?"

"No!" shouted the four lads, including Sid whose senses were back.

"We also found Mr Chambers skulking in the gutters. My master has had dealings with him before. My master knows some secrets about Mr Chambers that he's willing to share with you. In fact, Mr Chambers is busy trying to find out that little secret of yours, you know, how you kill vampires, Sidney."

"That's a lie!" cried Reece.

"Quite," said Peaches, examining his manicure.

Reece considered the little man, Peaches. He didn't have a clue where Ivansey had found him, but what was more disconcerting was that Ivansey was privy to Reece's dealings. He wanted to kick himself. He should have never followed the lads into town.

"Sidney, my master's gift to you is the punishment of your enemies, and he gives you a choice. Do you wish to punish Jimmy the barman; the man who was going to attack you and incur physical violence on yourself for ruining his livelihood and because Brian shagged his mum?" Jimmy flinched, his left eye twitching uncontrollably. "Or do you pick Reece Chambers; the man who is using you for his own needs; the man who is a puppet of the Coalition; the man who is scientifically studying your DNA to uncover your secrets?"

Reece stood defiant, staring at Peaches with an unblinking stare.

"Why are you helping us?" asked Brian.

"My master wants peace. Sid is no longer his enemy."

"We will discuss," Brian answered and turned to confer with his crew.

Reece was in trouble. The vampires out the back of the pub would tear him to shreds, if he was lucky. Apparently, his puppet master pulled more than one set of strings. There would be no chance for revenge.

The lads weren't too subtle in their discussions.

"I always told you that Rich is a wanker," said Brian.

"Aye, but he did always get the ales in," said Sid.

"I can't believe he's been experimenting on us like that."

"What do you mean, Brian?" asked Sid, startled. He didn't like the sound of the word "experimenting."

"You know, big fella."

"I don't like that, Brian."

"I know you don't, Sid. Tell you what, if he's that untrustworthy, he may work for the Benefit Bastards, after all."

"Fook me...never thought about that."

Reece could hear every word from his judge and jury. "They're telling lies! I saved your li—" He shut up when Peaches uncocked a pistol.

"What do you think, Arthur?" asked Brian.

"My life has turned to shit since I met these vampire bastards," he said glumly.

"Rathbone?"

"Rich shot me in the head, and Jimmy has sorted his beer out, like."

The four lads turned to Peaches and Brian took the lead. "What is the punishment?"

"Let's just say that your chosen target won't be able to sit down for a long, long, long time."

"Why is that?" said Sid.

"Dead leg, Sid," said Brian, not wanting Sid to hear the real reason. Brian confronted Reece. "Rich, I've never trusted you."

"Fuck you!" Reece shouted, shoulders back, head held high, defiant to the last.

Brian stroked his chin, carefully. "But...We cannot forgive Jimmy for the beer he kept in The Badger all them months when The Miner's was shut."

"*What?*" said Reece and Jimmy in unison.

"Jim, we gave you enough warnings. You didn't clean the pipes as often as you should, and you charged too much for the ale."

"W...what?" Jimmy's mouth evaporated to dryness and his pulse quickened.

"Now then, you've started serving good ale in here, and hopefully, once you get over your little encounter with Peaches and his mates, you'll continue to serve good ale."

"But..." Jimmy's bottom lip wobbled. "You shagged my mum. That bastard down there's using you and—"

"Aye, he's a wanker, but you didn't keep your ale the way you should've done. Let this be a lesson to you." Brian turned to his mates. "Come on lads, let's go."

"We will be in touch, gentlemen," said Peaches, performing a few stretches, warming up for the forthcoming events.

The lads started to leave the pub with Reece and the rest of the heavies. Behind them, they could hear the commotion, and it made Brian wince.

"Thank you, so much," said Reece once they were down the street. His tough-guy persona was gone along with the bravado. His eyes shone with unshed tears.

"Well, you would've been in for it, but that lad committed a far worse sin," said Brian. "We can call it quits after this. He keeps a good pint now, but Peaches should hammer the lesson home. All's well that ends well."

"Peaches was lying, you know," said Reece.

"Yeah, well. We'll discuss this back at The Miner's, between the four of us," said Brian.

Reece nodded, taking the hint, and headed in the opposite direction.

"We ain't really gonna discuss it, are we, Brian?"

"'Course not, Sid, but at least we can have an ale in peace."

"Good," said Sid, relieved.

"But I'm wondering why that *them lot* fella has changed his tune. He wanted to rip your head off a week ago."

"I don't wanna talk about it," warned Sid.

"Best keep an eye out. Reckon summat big is gonna go down. Come on. Maybe we can make it to The Miner's before closing time."

FUCKING IDIOTS. THAT SHOULD'VE BEEN THE END OF ME. Reece smiled as he got in his car. The Miner's was a no-go area now. He'd hoped for more samples, but at least he obtained some of Arthur Peasley's DNA. He could now repeat the tests and see if the remarkable results he'd obtained were truly possible.

If his research was successful, it would mean he'd never have to go into that pit The Miner's Arms ever again, unless he fancied taking a flamethrower to it. Once his research was finished, he could spend time investigating who on the Coalition left him for dead at the hands of Ivansey and his flock.

33

DRINKING WASN'T AS FUN LATELY. Sid had his pub and, more importantly, his beer back, but he was in a constant state of unease and had never experienced anything quite like it. When he was working while on the benefits, he used to look over his shoulder for the Benefit Bastards, but that was something he'd learned to live with.

Them lot, though...He was always caught short when they turned up. They were multiplying out of Manchester, and it was scary. It was all because of the biggest *them lot* Sid had ever seen, the one with the 'tash. He was the ringleader. If he came to the Smithson Estate...

"You OK, our Sid?" asked Brian.

"What? Yeah, I'll be reet."

Sid lit up a Regal. Teo Bertrand, a vampire who had influenced the Renaissance, had taken a headbutt, a knee to the groin, and a big right hook for not thinking that pictures of dogs playing pool were art. The cigarettes were a bonus.

The lads had started drinking late on. Sid, Brian, Arthur, and Rathbone were all there to get drunk, but the rate of ale suppage was down because the pacesetter, Sid, was moping. "What the fook was that thing that turned up in The Spaniel's Ears?"

"Peaches Slackring?" asked Brian.

"Yeah."

"Don't worry about it, fella. It was probably a dream."

Arthur helped Brian's switcheroo. "You should be happy, big man. Haven't you got a hot date at the end of the week?"

"Aye, suppose so."

"How did you meet her?"

The big man stared into his pint in between looking up at the front door. Brian could read the big man like a book. It was best to take his mind off it. "Reet cracker this one, lads. Sid met her over the Internet, like."

"Did you ever hear back from that one whose kid you nearly killed?" asked Arthur.

"Nah, miserable bitch," said Sid, mournfully. "Sue was well up for a shagging and *them lot* ruined that for us too. Why have they got a problem with me? What have I ever done to them?"

No one stated the obvious.

Rathbone didn't talk much, but when he did, he shouldn't. "Well, you do give the wrong signals, like."

Arthur and Brian both put their heads in their hands.

Sid sat up straight. "What d'ya mean?"

"You know, with your tight jeans and your wiggling hips, and all."

"Finish your beer, Sid. It's Rathbone's round."

"No, it ain't."

"Get the fookers in, ya worthless twat!" said Brian, throwing a tenner at Rathbone, who gladly took it to the bar.

"Tight jeans...?" Sid pulled at the waistband.

"Ignore him. He's just trying to wind you up," said Brian.

"Yeah, man. Tell us about the chick you're taking out." urged Arthur.

Sid sighed but conceded. "Raunchy Rita she's called. She's a forty-six-year-old divorcee with no kids. Thank fook."

"She sounds nice."

"What's wrong with her, like?" Rathbone returned from the bar. He was just as much an arsehole as a vampire as he was as a human.

"Fook off, Rathbone," said Brian, "or we'll let Rich and Sanderson cut your head off. We were close to letting them last time, you know?"

"Yeah, that's right. Just 'cos I'm a vampire, you want me dead, you racist prick."

"No, because you're a greasy, horrible, little bastard is the reason I want you dead."

But Rathbone continued, "Look, if she's on the Internet, then there's something wrong with her, ain't there?"

Brian stepped in. "Things are different now. Loads of people are meeting online. Where else can you meet lasses? Pubs are fooking dying. Government's attacking pubs for the binge drinking 'cos some sixteen-year-old drinks a bottle of five-quid vodka, goes out, bottles another sixteen-year-old before nailing a fifteen-year-old down an alley and getting her preggers. It's the pubs which pay for it, and look what's happening: No fooker in them. Once you're settled and start moving in the same circles, you've gotta use the Internet; otherwise, you'll never meet anyone."

"You manage it," said Rathbone.

"I am Brian Garforth. I am a swordsman." To which Sid downed his pint in salute. "Look, I ain't saying it ain't possible, but it's hard, and the Internet is the answer. It may fook everything else in the long term, but Sid is still gonna be shaggin' come Saturday night."

"Yeah!"

"Great to have you back, Sid," Arthur said. "Now, tell me about the girl of my best friend."

"As I said, no kids, which is a big thing for me now. And, you should see the size of her jubblies, mon. And, at forty-six years old, they're gonna be nearly in the right place too."

"She ticks all the boxes, doesn't she, Sid?" Brian laughed, giving him a hearty slap on the back.

"She sure fooking does, like."

"What are her likes and dislikes?" asked Arthur.

Sid shrugged, "No idea. As I said, cracking norks. Ticked all the boxes."

"Reet good norks, actually," said Brian. "Think I have her profile picture on me phone." He rummaged in his pocket until he noticed an air of hostility fall upon the pub and assumed a vampire had come in from the cold winter's evening, but there were none to be seen. No. The whole pub was looking at him and the technology in his hand.

"What...the *fook*...is that?" asked an aggressive landlord.

"Eh? Oh, Raunchy Rita."

"It looks like a phone to me."

"Yeah, but the picture of the lass is Raunchy Rita. She's the lass that Sid is taking out next week."

"Brian, you're making a scene," whispered Sid.

"What are you on—" It hit home. Brian quickly hid the phone back in his pocket.

"You don't bring phones into pubs, man," said Arthur.

"You always manage to get on everyone's nerves," said Rathbone.

Sid couldn't look him in the eye.

"That ain't good enough, lad," said the landlord reaching under the bar for his shotgun. Since his musket signed by Sharpe had blown up in his face, he decided to rely on more advanced technology. Touching the cold metal reminded him that he owed Lieutenant Colonel Sharpe a visit.

"Sorry." Brian went to turn off the offending contraption, but it decided to ring instead, causing the pub to resemble a room of ligyrophobes clutching their ears at the din. Brian struggled as "There's No Limit" by 2 Unlimited failed to entertain The Miner's patrons. He wrestled with the phone and finally silenced it.

He lowered his head in shame.

Normally, Brian would've fought back and used his intelligence to get out of this sticky situation, but he couldn't. They were right. After he put the world to rights about the spiralling demise of British pubs, he'd gone and contributed. What a hypocrite he was. What a tosser.

Kev stood over him with his shotgun. "You know what you have to do, lad."

Brian nodded. The phone was new, and last week he'd added the numbers of some red-hot sluts from Hartlepool whom he hadn't ran through with his sword, but it didn't matter.

He took the gun from Kevin and took the offending beast with him. The phone was going the same way as Old Yeller.

Everyone in the pub gave a nod of satisfaction when they heard the gunshot. Brian traipsed back into the pub and morosely gave Kevin his gun back.

Now, there were no distractions, and the lads could get back to drinking again. Brian's faux pas was forgotten; Sid's Gay Defence System had taken away the memory of Peaches Slackring and Jimmy's mystery punishment; Arthur could mourn his loss by getting hammered; and then there was Rathbone, quite content that he didn't have that weird thirst thing urging him to go down on menstruating women.

This all came to a swift end with the opening of The Miner's front door. Kev smiled and rubbed his hands together greedily. The lads who had come in from the cold were all at least 6 feet 6 inches tall, which meant vampires, which meant lots and lots of money. They were all wearing hooded overcoats, but Kev didn't need to see their gleaming eyes to know what they were. "What can I get you fine gentlemen?"

"Four pints of lager."

It was if they had all answered their mobile phones at once. Even Kev was taken aback. "Lager, you say?"

"Yes," said the lead vampire.

"You do realise this is a pub," said the landlord slowly.

"Yes," said the vampire, somewhat confused.

Brian reached inside his red woollen suit and eased towards the handle of his Cumapault. He expected trouble as soon as they saw the state of Kev's lager.

Kev gambled and put a glass under the lager tap, pulled the pump, and marvelled as a family of baby mice ran out of the lines. "Barrel needs changing."

All the vampires stepped back. Before they had a chance to ask for something else, Kev opened the cellar trapdoor and ran down to change the barrel. Only Southerners drank larger, and the lads usually set upon Southerners before they could finish asking for a "lager, innit."

The four Middlesbrough heroes had their sights trained on the vampires. Sid wouldn't have batted an eyelid usually, but since his confrontation, he kept an eye on every man, bird, and beast. He knocked out a robin on the way to the pub for looking too festive. Arthur was also unsure. He had his son's grandfather to worry about. He wanted to see the old vamp to get access to his son, but sparks were guaranteed to fly. Brian was there as back-up, dying to try out the new weapon. Rathbone was keen to chill with his homies.

Kevin rushed back upstairs from the cellar and pulled some more lager. The pipes spluttered and kicked out some foul-smelling, brown liquid that was a combination of twenty-year-old lager and five years' worth of mouse droppings. "Don't worry, lads, it will come through in a minute." The punters didn't make an effort to grab the four glasses of opaque, muddy liquid. Stuck in The Miner's cellar for a couple of decades, the "fresh" barrel hadn't aged like a fine wine. "That will be fourteen pounds, please."

"I think the beer is off," said one of the vampires.

Kevin picked up one of the glasses and put it up to the light. The beer absorbed every wavelength the tungsten filament could throw at it. "Nah. Nowt wrong with that, like."

"Can we have four white wines, instead?" The vampire paused. He could've sworn something flew past his ear.

Brian quickly hid the Cumapault. After a few beers, he wasn't as accurate as when he was practising in his back yard earlier. He'd messed up the neighbour's cat pretty badly. "Fooking white wine!" he said. "These vampires knew how to get themselves smacked."

"Lager?...Wine?...Not more of *them lot!*" Sid covered his eyes.

"Easy, Sid," said Brian, "That don't mean 'owt. They could just as easily be Southerners."

"So, the best I can hope for is a bunch of fooking cockneys ruining me night? Fook me!"

"Hey, man," said Arthur, "it might not be all bad. The vampires who used to come here before you hit that big vampire-monster fella used to buy us beers. Why not ask them?"

Brian went to shout over to the vampires, but Sid stopped him. "Don't be fooking daft, mon. Thought you were bright."

"Free beer sounds clever to me. If not, you can just smack 'em instead and earn some free tabs. Well, that depends if that wanker Rich is selling us out to some other bastards. Gotta watch him, lads."

"You're reet, like, but that's by-the-by," said Sid. "If I ask one of them for a beer, then they may think that I am, you know...interested."

"In what?"

"Shut up, Brian, you know. Say if he's like *them lot* from the other night. If he buys me a drink, then I'm as good as..." Sid didn't like the train of thought.

"Bummed?" offered Rathbone.

Sid went pale.

Brian and Arthur sighed. Rathbone, satisfied that his work was done, announced, "I'm gonna hang out with my posse. I've had enough of your discrimination."

"What are you talking about, man?" asked Arthur.

"Yeah, you're the fooking worst," replied the nonsensical vampire, before making his way to his brothers in blood.

"Is he more of a horrible, little twat now he's a vampire?" asked Brian.

"I don't think so, man," Arthur mused. "I prefer him now. I think he's still fired up after losing his virginity the other day. Hey, Sid, you alright there, big papa?" Arthur gave Sid a hearty slap on the back, which brought him out of his trance.

"Eh? Your round, like." Sid's Gay Defence System had wiped "bummed" from his memory.

"Wine, eh? Is that what us vampires drink, is it?" asked Rathbone, approaching the four immortals.

All four saw him coming over and edged a little closer together, turning their backs on the horrible, greasy, little bastard. Four pairs of shoulders sank with relief as it detoured to the bar.

"Kev, mon, get us a wine, will ya?"

Kev pulled a face. "You don't drink wine."

"I fooking do. I'm a vampire, me. That's what we drink. Now, get us a wine."

"Wasn't it *red* wine you were drinking when you were in the bogs with one of Maggie's lot the other night?"

"Shurrup, mon," Rathbone looked around, hoping the vampires hadn't picked up on Kev's euphemism. They hadn't. They'd moved as far away from the world's greasiest vampire as they could.

Kev handed over the goods. "That'll be ten pounds, please."

"You fooking joking?"

"No."

"Ten fooking quid for a wine?"

"It's a large one, like."

"I ain't fooking paying it."

"Well don't then."

Rathbone looked over to the vampires sipping their wines and grimacing at a substance too acidic to clean drains. "You robbing, little, fat, doll-shagging twat!" he said throwing over a note.

Kev smiled to himself. It was a good day.

Rathbone intruded on the vampires' night out. The vampires waited for him to say something, but Rathbone was never bothered about talking. He took a sip of his wine, which was as disgusting as it was expensive. The four vampires exchanged looks before turning their attention back to Rathbone. Most people would've been compelled to break the silence with all eyes on them, but not Rathbone. He leeched off all other life forms even before he was a vampire. He was toxic to cancer.

It was too much for one of the seven-hundred-year-old immortals to cope with. Centuries teach patience, but it doesn't teach you how to deal with Peter Rathbone.

"*What* are you?"

"Vampire." Rathbone flourished his cape to prove the point.

"Oh." One line in and already the vampire was lost for conversation. "Do you know Sid Tillsley?"

Rathbone lit up a cigarette, trying to look cool. He had his ticket in. "Oh, aye."

SANDERSON DROVE BACK TO MIDDLESBROUGH to make sure Sid didn't get into any more trouble. Once he was safe, Sanderson could report back to the Coalition, personally, about Sebastian's unusual demise and give them the comforting news of the plugged leak. Sanderson deduced that Haemo pushed Sebastian over the edge, and he sent information to both Ivansey and Chambers so they could bombard the Coalition with precision attacks. The question was: if Ivansey knew about Haemo, what was he going to do about it, and why hadn't he done anything yet? Ivansey was unpredictable before, but now, he'd taken his...turn, who knew what he'd do?

Haemo could not be compromised. It would bring order, and any vampire making an unsanctioned kill would be hunted down like a common criminal. Killing vampires is what he should be paid for. He didn't want a war. Too many good men and too many innocent women and children would die. Garendon would be the world's saviour, and he hoped the Coalition would be able to defend the new plant when the inevitable attack came.

His phone rang. It was one of his operatives staking out The Miner's Arms. "Talk to me."

"Four vampires just entered The Miner's Arms. I don't think Ivansey was one of them, but Sid, Arthur, Rathbone, and Brian are in the pub."

"What've you got ready?"

"Six armed agents."

"That ain't enough if Ivansey turns up. Is Chambers there?"

"No."

What's the piece of shit up to? he wondered. "I'll get a police escort and be there in thirty-five minutes. Keep me informed. Don't go in till I get there."

"HOW'S RATHBONE GETTING ON?" asked Sid.

"The vampires are a bit confused, I think," whispered Brian. "They made the mistake of talking to him."

"What they gonna talk to him about, like?"

"No idea. He'll piss 'em off sooner or later."

Rathbone was enjoying himself. He didn't often get the chance to meet new people, and he felt at home with his own kind, even though they did not reciprocate the feeling.

"How old are you?" asked an immortal.

"Forty-five."

"You don't look like a vampire."

"Nor do you," said Rathbone defensively.

The vampire looked at his friends for support. They shrugged their shoulders but refused to make eye contact. He was on his own. "Why are you wearing a cape?"

"Why aren't you wearing one? Call yourself a fooking vampire. You're a fooking disgrace is what you are."

The vampire narrowed his eyes, unconvinced. "How many other vampires do you actually know?"

"Fooking hundreds."

"Of whom wear capes?"

"Fooking hundreds."

The vampire wasn't enjoying this. He looked, once again, for support from his friends, but they'd broken off into a separate group, turning their backs on him.

"...Erm...Sid Tillsley is a vampire hunter. How come he hasn't killed you, yet?"

"'Cos I'm fooking rock, me. Beat Gary Barlow in an arm-wrestle, once." Rathbone downed his horrible wine. "You getting a round in?"

The vampire looked down at his drain cleaner. "No, definitely not."

"Wanker," Rathbone shook his head and walked back over to the lads.

"Do you reckon they're gonna do anything, Rathbone?" asked Brian. "They're just standing there drinking wine. It's fooked up."

"Bunch of tossers, if you ask me. You ought to go smack 'em, Sid."

"Nah, they ain't done 'owt so far, like. Look, one of them's going over to Kev. What the fook d'ya reckon he wants?"

"I don't like it, Sid," Brian whispered. "Look, that greedy, little, fat bastard is grinning from ear-to-ear."

"HOW FAR AWAY ARE YOU?"

"Why?" asked Sanderson. "What's happening?"

"I don't know, but music has started blaring from inside of the pub."

"I'm fifteen minutes away. Has it kicked off?"

"Not yet, but a limousine just pulled up, and I'm pretty sure Ivansey's going to be sat in the back of it."

"I'll be there in ten."

THE LADS SAT SPEECHLESS. This was a nefarious attack of unbelievable cunning. As one, the vampire group ripped off their clothes, which were fastened with Velcro, *a la* Bucks Fizz's Eurovision Song Contest 1981, to reveal hot pants so tight that only a vampire could survive the lack of circulation. Music hit them from every direction and "Gimme! Gimme! Gimme! (A Man After Midnight)" by ABBA was the audio atrocity. The choreography was magnificent; the audience, however, was unappreciative. Sid, Brian, Arthur, and Rathbone's jaws hit the table.

Only Kev clapped along to the music. He was the reason this impossibly camp act was taking place in the impossibly masculine pub. He was a traitor. He was a greedy bastard. The vampires had come to him the day before offering to install a music system free of charge. He knew the vampire dollar was where the money was. Who was he to turn it down?

The lads, on the other hand, were in trouble. They didn't really know what type, but they were about to find out.

"IT'S IVANSEY! HE'S GOING IN!" came the call over the phone.

"Almost there!" said Sanderson, driving like a lunatic.

"Shall we send in a squad?"

"No, wait for me. We go in as one, unless Tillsley's in trouble. He's all that matters."

34

THE ENTRANCE WAS GRAND. The door opened, and the Campire swept into The Miner's Arms with a gait exuberating grace and elegance, the clicking of his walking cane rhythmically accompanying every other step. He was a dandy of the highest order. His coat of faux chinchilla was left open as there were many layers of equal extravagance to show off. A leather three-piece suit, cut to perfection, was as luxurious as it was ridiculous, and only someone as fine as the Campire could pull it off, especially in royal blue. His ruffled silk shirt was a masterpiece but still didn't compare to his grooming. Not a hair on the thick black moustache was out of place, and it glistened in the caress of the pub lights. His hair was swept back over his head and was so dark that it reflected blue to match his suit.

If Sid looked scared before, he looked positively petrified now. His nemesis was here. Only the Campire could have such an effect on the hardest man in the North. The Campire was the anti-Sid, the physical manifestation of the zenith of homophobic nightmare.

The music came to an end, and the four all-but-naked vampires turned and bowed to face their master who glided past them. The Campire allowed one of his assistants to remove his coat and another to place a chair, dusted and polished, behind him. He sat with a creak of trouser leather.

The lads were pleased Peaches Slackring wasn't with him, but another vampire worked as the Campire's aide, and he didn't look the kind of fella who'd subscribe to *Tits*.

"One Cosmopolitan, barkeep," asked the aide.

Kev's brow furrowed. "I haven't got a clue what you're talking about, lad."

"You were told to buy provisions for our arrival," said the aide.

That snapped Brian out of his hot-pants-induced coma. "You knew about this?"

Kevin ignored him. "Aye, I got some stuff," he said, lifting up a jumbo bag of cocktail umbrellas.

"Imbecile," chastised the aide and then to Ivansey, "Sire, I will have to make one in the limousine."

"What's a Cosmopolitan? So, I know for next time," asked the barman who was always willing to help, at the right price.

That was enough for Brian. He'd been double-crossed and vengeance was called for. In dramatic fashion, he rose to his feet and looked down the sights of his Cumapault at the Campire's aide before unleashing filthy justice.

Kevin hit the deck as soon as he saw the weapon, but his merchandise had taken the brunt of the sum of Brian's more wayward assaults. His cocktail umbrellas were ruined.

Brian emptied the clip. The time spent practising was well worth it. The Campire's aide writhed on the floor in tormented agony. The burns inflicted on his face and arms where he'd tried to protect himself sunk deeper into his flesh, and gradually his movement slowed before all his body crumpled into ash.

"You dirty bastard!" roared the barman before reaching for his shotgun. He'd seen the foul, lethal liquid many a time when cleaning up in the toilets post-ladies' night, and it cost him a fortune in mop-heads.

"Hold your fire, barman," demanded the Campire.

Kev, who knew where his bread was buttered, obliged.

"Sit down," the Campire ordered Brian.

"Why the fook should I do as you say, you big pansy?"

"If you don't, Paul here will remove his hot pants."

Brian sat down.

"Juan was a beautiful boy. I will mourn his loss, but I forgive you as you do not yet understand."

"What the fook are you talking about?" said the swordsman.

Sanderson and his team ploughed into the bar, weapons drawn. The Campire didn't move and a muscled, oiled shield surrounded him before the agents could take position.

"Relax," said the Campire.

Kev obliged.

"No, not the song, you idiot!"

Kev turned off *The Best of Frankie Goes to Hollywood.*

"Actually..." the Campire thought a moment. "Leave it on."

"Turn it off, Kev!" shouted Brian.

"It's a *them lot* anthem," managed Sid, forgetting about his fashion statement at the Occursus. "Turn it off, Kev!"

Kev shrugged, reached down to his top-of-the-range amplifier and turned up the juice. He couldn't hear what the lads were calling him, but he had a good idea.

"TURN IT DOWN!" shouted the Campire. "WE CAN'T HEAR ANYTHING NOW!"

"WHAT?" replied the barman, "I CAN'T HEAR YOU! THE MUSIC IS TOO LOUD!"

One of the dancers left the Campire's protective shield and turned the music down to a level where conversation could be heard but could still instil fear into Northerners.

All weapons pointed at the Campire. He merely laughed like he didn't have a care in the world. He ordered his minions away and sat, bold as brass with a confident grin. It made Sanderson nervous.

"Sanderson! What a lovely surprise. You look tired. The lines on your face deepen every time I see you. A good moisturiser would help, you know?" he said with mock concern. "One of my boys could give you a facial."

Sid passed out.

"What the fuck happened to you?" Sanderson hardly recognised the vampire. The lads from 'boro were right. Everything had changed: his look, demeanour, mannerisms. Normally, even looking at a photo of this sadistic vampire saturated him with carnal fear, but now, he looked at Ivansey—and he almost laughed. Nothing in the nature of the vampire appeared as if it could cause harm. His trigger finger itched.

"I wouldn't do that if I were you."

Sanderson's fear returned. *Vampires can't read fucking minds!* he thought.

"Why can't I?" The Campire rose from his chair, placed his foot on it, and rested his elbow on his knee and his chin upon his fist. "I'm not the vampire you chased a month ago. I have changed, and so will the world. Sid Tillsley is the reason for this." He gestured down to his impressive threads. "Sid Tillsley took everything from me, and then, he gave me a gift. He gave me my freedom. He turned me into—the Campire!"

He pulled down his pants and showed the pub...nothing. No balls. No cock.

"He's a fooking woman!" screamed Brian.

Sid woke up with the shout of "woman."

"Eh'up, flower," said Rathbone cheerily. He'd only done it once but had done worse.

"I'm not a woman. I'm a man."

Sid passed out again. Rathbone shrugged.

The Campire continued, "Last year, I tried to have Sid imprisoned for benefit fraud and wasn't successful, so I attempted to kill him. Again, I was thwarted, and, for my efforts, I received a blow to the penis."

Brian giggled.

"A *punch*, you imbecile. I wouldn't let that horrible, wreck of a man near my love truncheon. His hand finished my penis off."

Brian giggled.

"Shut up! That's not what I meant, and you know it. I was left with my testicles, and they brought me nothing but misery. Not releasing semen resulted in a huge testosterone build up. I would black-out, and when I finally came to, the carnage left in my wake was beautiful." His smile was as close to orgasmic as a vampire with no genitals could achieve. "But I couldn't restrain it. Still, I could've ruled like a king. I became more powerful than Vitrago ever was. The testosterone caused my body to regenerate at remarkable speeds, yet, I couldn't live with the lack of control. I placed my balls in the sunlight and they burnt."

Everyone, man and vampire, winced.

"My knackers were hanging out the side of me Speedos when I was sunbathing in the Costa Del Sol, once. Fooking hurts that does, mon," agreed Brian.

The Campire pinched the bridge of his nose in an attempt to push the image from his mind before continuing. "Now, I'm free. Having no testosterone in my bloodstream has brought me other gifts. I'm in touch with my feminine side. I can't read minds, Sanderson, but I know what you're thinking." He winked. "I know what all you one-dimensional imbeciles are thinking."

"Bollocks, mon," announced Brian. "Women never know what men are thinking. Same way they never notice when you look down their tops."

"Oh, they do. They know a man's every thought, and I have developed the skill. You, Garforth, are thinking about punching me in the face. So is your beautiful friend."

"That's obvious," Brian dismissed. "We're Northerners. It's what we do."

"Sanderson is wondering whether a bullet will finish me. You can see it in his eyes. He wants to pull the trigger. He's desperate to. He can see my powers have waned and wants to kill me, so, so badly." The Campire laughed and turned his back on the agent, but a greasy, horrible, little bastard caught his eye.

"Rathbone, isn't it?"

Rathbone looked everywhere except into the Campire's brilliant blue eyes.

"Curious?"

Rathbone shrugged.

The Campire laughed before continuing his monologue. "So yes, Tillsley took everything from me but gave me this new life. He's the reason I am reborn."

"What the fuck do you want?"

"Oh, Sanderson, always the tough guy. Even though I'm so different now, I'm still the same. Before, when I roamed the earth as a brutish thug, I didn't understand what drove me towards acts of mindless, desperate barbarism. I wasn't in touch with my feminine side. How could I possibly understand the intricate nature of the psyche when the only thing I lusted for was blood and war...or so I thought."

He sat back on the chair and crossed his legs at an angle that only women, or men without knackers could. "Now, I come to realise that I was simply lonely, and I blamed everyone and everything. I blamed the Lamian Consilium for the Agreement. I blamed Tillsley for taking Gabriel, and then, he took away my penis and made me a freak.

"It was only after I placed my testes in the sun that I found true freedom, and the gay community accepted me with open arms. It only took one night of unparalleled joy and sexual energy to know that I finally belonged. I discovered that all I ever wanted was *to belong*. And now, I am enlightened...and I want others to join me! I want others to experience the immeasurable pleasure. Other vampires have sensed this and have come to me to find it."

Brian wasn't having any of it and pointed aggressively at the Campire. "If you've come for any of that nonsense, you've come to the wrong place, pal!"

"You pathetic little man. You have no idea what I'm talking about, do you? You're just the same as all the other ignorant monkeys. I hated you when I was Gunnar Ivansey, but now, as the Campire...I forgive you."

"The killing is over?" asked Sanderson.

"Yes. Unless, someone...anyone, gets in my way."

"So, why are you here?"

"Him," said the Campire, pointing where Sid lay passed out on his back, snoring gently, and dribbling heavily.

"For fook's sake, haven't you given him enough hassle?" moaned Brian.

"He killed my best friend and punched my cock off!"

"Fair play."

"What do you want Sid for?" asked Sanderson.

The Campire smiled. "My aide Peaches Slackring and his friends saved Sid's life and gave him a gift. I wanted to show him that he has nothing to fear from me. Look at these beautiful boys beside me." The Campire gestured at the vampires behind him, tall, muscular, and oiled. "They're imprisoned by their testes. They need to be freed. They don't have the courage to face the sun as I did. I cannot force them into the sunlight, but Tillsley can take their pain away, and Tillsley will give me the companionship I desire. These boys will prove their loyalty to me by taking his fist."

Brian giggled.

"I don't think he will, man," said Arthur.

"If he wants his pub back, he'll have to. We're not going anywhere. Consider this the closure of The Miner's Arms and the grand opening of..." The Campire threw his arms theatrically above his head, and then announced for all to hear. "THE FIRST SWALLOW OF SUMMER!"

Kevin unleashed a single party popper.

Brian's mouth tried to form words, but it was unable to.

The fire in Arthur's eyes extinguished completely, his shoulders sagged, and his head dropped, a defeated man.

Rathbone couldn't give a shit.

"You know we'll just blow this place to kingdom come," said Sanderson.

"You homophobic bastard!" shouted Kevin Ackroyd, purveyor of fine, sparkling wines and Diet Cokes.

"How can you do this to us, Kev?" said Brian, feeling betrayed. Now, he knew how all the husbands of the housewives he'd banged had felt.

"You managed when I weren't here," the barman said with a shrug, "and none of you came to visit me, so you can all fook off."

The Campire continued, "Sid can find another pub, and we'll turn it. Every pub in Middlesbrough will fall. Every landlord in this town will turn for the right price. They're a greedy breed." He reached into the top pocket of his waistcoat and pulled out a money clip so thick, it would've bought all the pubs in Middlesbrough twice over.

Kev didn't object. It was a fair comment.

Sanderson didn't know what to do. How was he going to explain this to the Coalition? Which reminded him, "How long was Sebastian slipping you information about the Coalition's movements?"

The Campire looked blank for a second, and then, realisation dawned upon him. "Oh, my dear Sanderson. So much heart, yet so little between the ears. They should've kept you on the ground rather than sitting you on the grand Coalition with mighty politicians."

Sanderson never played games. "What are you talking about?"

"I couldn't possibly make it that easy for you."

"We have your DNA all over the farmhouse where we found Sebastian's body. We know he was leaking you information. That's why you attacked our chemical plant in the Northeast."

"Oh, right, because there's no chance my DNA could have been planted, is there? Everything in this world is always exactly as it seems, isn't it?" said the Campire patronisingly.

"You...don't know about Sebastian? He wasn't the leak?"

"I didn't even know the poor fellow was dead. Not that I'll miss him." The Campire pouted. "Rather ghastly hair."

Fuck, then who is it? Sanderson thought. "Why attack the chemical plant?"

The Campire smiled. "I don't care what you and your little council have in store. Edward Limkin, your personal physician, was an urologist, and I destroyed that special plant of yours to get his name. He tried to remove my testicles and failed. Such a shame it wasn't possible, if it was, I wouldn't need Tillsley, and I could give him the send off he truly deserves." His gaze intensified as he cast it upon the prone, flabby figure.

Sanderson kept a poker face, thinking Ivansey couldn't know about the Haemo project. "I thought you forgave him?"

"Hell hath no fury like a woman scorned," The Campire chuckled to himself. "I wanted to rip the Agreement apart, and my puppet master, I assume, wants the same thing, albeit, in a more discreet manner. They gave me the targets to hit, and I obliged. In hindsight, it was awfully uncivilised of me."

"Who was it?" demanded Sanderson.

"When I served them, I had no idea, but I pieced it all together with a little feminine intuition."

"Who helped you?

"As I said, I can't make it that easy for such a fine soldier like you. Why don't you go find out?" he said condescendingly and clapped his hands as if to hurry Sanderson along.

Sanderson gritted his teeth but nodded. "They're coming with me." He pointed at the lads and the unconscious Sid.

"Very well." The Campire nodded. "They'll be back. And even though we'd never think of touching that disgusting ale, Kevin is going to keep it at its very best. It will call them. Sid has nothing to fear anymore. We need him. Just like you do."

Sanderson gathered the lads and headed to the door. Brian, Arthur, and Rathbone's vampire strength struggled to follow while carrying the hefty frame of the unconscious Sid. Sanderson didn't take his eyes off the Campire as he left The First Swallow of Summer.

"Hurry along, Sanderson!" The Campire called after him. "You have much to discuss with your fellow councillors." He turned his attention to more pressing matters and raised a hand. "Barkeep, champagne all round!"

Kev snapped to attention. "Will a Blue Nun and a soda stream do?"

35

BRIAN CHALKED HIS CUE AND JAWED ANOTHER RED. None of the colours were on the spots and eighteen was the highest-scoring break of the two-hour session in which he'd only racked up a 2-0 lead over his undead opponent. This was some shit snooker.

The lads had spent a fair few nights down the snooker hall, of late. With the closing of The Miner's (it hadn't shut, but that's what Sid told everyone; he couldn't bear anyone to know the truth), they hadn't found anywhere that served decent ale. Brian regretted his choice of letting Jimmy take the brunt of Peaches Slackring's love-wrath, as they could be drinking decent Bolton down The Spaniel's Ears, but it was a lesson that Jimmy needed hammering home. Repeatedly. Snooker was good at taking the mind off the beer they were drinking. It was difficult to think of anything except suicide when struggling at the hardest sport in the world.

Rathbone missed a straight red by a good foot. Even though he was now a vampire, his snooker skills hadn't improved.

Sid and Arthur sat in silence watching the match-up.

Sid moped into his pint of Darlington Warrior. Every mighty draught was accompanied with a mighty sigh of disappointment.

Arthur looked worse. He tried to spend as much time out of his flat as he could. The flat reminded him of Lucia, and it cut him to the bone. He tried not to think of his son out there alone with those bloodsucking sons-of-bitches, filling his head with lies about the mistreatment of his mother.

Sid finished his pint, put his hand in his pocket, and came out with nothing but shrapnel. "Fook me, I'm skint!" He lit up a tab. Times were tough. He only had a few packs of Sovereigns left at home, which he earned for the pasting he gave Magnus Zarathustra. Sid was happy justice had been served knowing that the vampire wouldn't be taking eleven items into the ten items or less aisle at the Tesco ever again.

"You can't be skint, mon. You've earned loads smackin' vampires," said Brian.

"Most of it's tucked away for a rainy day, mate. How're you boys doing for wedge?"

"I've got sixteen quid," said Arthur.

"Twelve, here," said Brian.

Rathbone didn't respond and no one expected him to.

"Rich hasn't been around as much lately, has he?"

"Good point," said Brian. "I remember when you couldn't have a piss without him looking over your shoulder."

"He was looking at my todger!" asked Sid, forming a fist.

"What? No. Figure of speech."

Sid calmed down but still kept his eye on the pink ball on the snooker table, just in case. "Aye, he was always getting the beers in. That other fella, Sanderson, he was a good lad and got 'em in. Ah well, I guess since the...you know....closed...they've found another boozer."

"I don't think they were there for the ambience, mate," Brian said. "That Sanderson was a good bloke, but I reckon that Rich wanker is up to summat."

"Aye, you're probably reet." Sid turned his attention to his glum friend and then said merrily, "Hey, Arthur, cheer up. Things ain't that bad."

"I appreciate your thoughts, old buddy, but they kind of are. It goes in cycles, you know, and this is one of the bad days. I need something to take my mind off things."

"Fancy a frame of snooker?" asked Sid, trying to help.

Arthur shook his head. "We need to get out of here. I'm ready for somewhere a bit livelier. I weren't up for it when we went partying the other night, but I am now."

"We've got no money, though," said Sid.

"You can set up a tab somewhere, our Sid," suggested Brian.

"No one will give me a tab, mate, you know that." The topic reminded him to light up again.

"That was before your vampire-slaying days," he ignored Rathbone's exaggerated tut. "Everyone knows you're flush nowadays."

"Maybe you're right," said Sid. "We'll go out after you finish your frame."

The snooker continued to impress no one, and the game continued well into the evening, only because the male half of the species could not let a sporting challenge lie. Brian missed his position on the yellow by a good two feet and decided that a dirty snooker was the order of the day. "There you go, Rathbone."

Rathbone seethed on the inside. Laying snookers was nigh on cheating at this level. He played and missed the ball he was aiming at and, with the power of the immortal, fired the white around the table, seventeen times, making a considerable din.

"Oi! What ya fooking doing!" screamed Derek, the owner of Merlin's Snooker Hall. "You'll break the fooking cushions down hitting it that hard! You lot can play by our rules in here!"

"What the fook is that meant to mean?"

"Just 'cos you're a fooking vampire, don't expect to be bringing your own fooking customs in here!"

"You racist bastard!"

Derek gave an accusing point of his finger before tending to some cues.

Rathbone shook his head. He'd been treated like shit since becoming a vampire. He'd been shot, several times; people had been rude to him; he'd got piss and shit on his cape, but this was the last fooking straw. It was time to put his vampire strength into action.

Rathbone smashed his cue over his own head in a display of power.

"You're gonna pay for that, you greasy, horrible, little bastard!" yelled Derek, unscrewing a couple of cues to make some instruments whose sole purpose were to bludgeon.

"We'll see about that." Rathbone's fangs extended in reply.

Derek waddled out from behind the bar. He was a fat lad, but he knew how to handle himself. All owners of snooker clubs in the North did.

"Calm it down, Rathbone," scolded Brian. "We haven't got many places left to drink." He wasn't bothered about the outcome of the fight. Rathbone was...well, Rathbone, and Derek charged too much for the lights on the snooker table. The other locals, however, were intrigued. They knew Sid knocked out vampires regular and were interested to see how Derek would get on, as he'd never lost a scrap with his cues in his hands.

"Fook this," said Brian. "Come on, lads. Let's go somewhere with a pulse. Rathbone, it ain't worth it, son."

Rathbone conceded. "You're lucky, Derek. I would've beaten the shit out of ya!"

"A likely fooking story!"

Rathbone turned his back on the angry manager. There were women out there demanding the loving of a vampire, and he didn't need to waste his time with pitiful humans. He flourished his cape as he turned on a sixpence and followed his mates, taking the righteous path of peace.

"Your cape is fooking shite!"

Rathbone stopped in his tracks. Yeah, he'd been shot. Yeah, he'd been covered in piss. But no one—*no one*—fucked with the cape. "What did you say?"

Brian shook his head in annoyance and headed for the door. Arthur and Sid followed. "Rathbone, we'll be in The Phoenix. There's a ladies' night on."

Rathbone wasn't backing down from this fight. He confronted Derek, the fat snooker hall manager.

"I said, 'Your cape is fooking shite.'"

Derek spun his cues like batons, but with Rathbone's enhanced senses, he could follow their path as if Derek was swinging them through treacle. Derek came out of his display swinging a cue towards the temple of the riled vampire, who caught it out of the air and seamlessly began his own twirling display, mirroring that of Derek's. He blocked every attack with ease, bringing marvelled gasps from the patrons. Bored, he rapped Derek on the knees and brought him tumbling at his feet.

"Say it again, I dare you." Rathbone was cool. Vampire cool.

Derek hands were clasped in prayer, begging for mercy. "I'm...I'm sorry, Peter. I'm...sorry."

Rathbone looked around. There were a few snooker slags in, and he could sense their lust for him after his heroic display. He'd never won a fight in a cool, manly fashion before. The only way he used to win one-on-ones was by setting paper bags full of dog shit on fire, leaving them on his adversary's doorstep, and ringing the doorbell. But now, he felt the vampire within him and called on the power. Yeah, this was proper mint.

He felt the gaze of the snooker slags follow his pert vampire buttocks towards the door. He noticed there was a straight red left on one of the tables. Should he call on the vampire powers again? He grabbed a cue, lined up the pot, and jawed the red.

"FOOKING STUPID GAME!" he screamed as he turned over the table.

36

"HARRY, WHERE ARE YOU?" said Sanderson.

"Back at bleedin' Ardvreck Castle!" yelled Harry Dean down the phone.

If Sanderson hadn't been driving, he would've closed his eyes in frustration. "Why've they sent you back there?"

"Rempstone is sending me everywhere. He's making sure he's at every goddamn meeting and leaves all the fieldwork to me. Why? What's wrong?"

As Sanderson approached Coalition headquarters, he told Harry about his evening with the Campire and how the strange display at the farmhouse was an elaborate set-up designed to point the finger at Sebastian and Ivansey.

"I must say," said Harry. "I preferred the world of blissful ignorance rather than the world of shit I'm about to enter. What are you going to do?"

"Take a gamble. What else can I do?"

"Sanderson, it could be a trick. Anyone could be the leak! Don't start getting yourself in trouble again. Mate, you're paranoid at the best of times. Don't make matters worse for all of us."

"And you wouldn't be such a fat bastard if you didn't sit on your arse so much, but we are who we are. Look, the leak ain't Sebastian, and I have a gut feeling who it is. Get to Tillsley and make sure he stays alive. You're gonna need him come the end."

"You're talking like you're dead already?"

Sanderson took a moment. "Chances are I ain't gonna get through this, but I have to warn the Coalition, and that's going to stick me in the firing line." Sanderson knew the call was traceable. He had to be careful. "Harry, Tillsley is special. Trust me on that. He needs his friends around him." It was cryptic, but it was the best he could do. Harry was a good man, and a clever one. He'd work it out and do the right thing.

Sanderson hung up without saying goodbye and punched the inside roof of his car. "Fucking Ivansey. Talking to me like I'm a fucking idiot. FUCK!"

Who was leaking information and why had it stopped? Who had made such a freaky mess of Sebastian if it wasn't Ivansey? Ivansey was turning vampires to his cause, fast, and he wasn't hiding. At least he didn't know about the Haemo project. The Coalition's forces were weak, and all they had was the hope that the development of the airborne version of Haemo would be successful.

Back to the problem at hand: Which bastard put them in this position in the first place, and why?

Sanderson trusted no one, but he had to decide whom he trusted the most out of a group of politicians and murderous vampires. He drove through the Coalition's extensive security and parked up before storming through the underground chambers, noting which guards and agents were on duty and how good a shot they were.

Augustus was now his gamble as the leak. He'd been so keen to get rid of Ivansey; Sanderson suspected it was just a great alibi. Augustus didn't give a shit about the human race. He always liked to play with his food. He thought he'd kept it quiet, but Sanderson knew what he was.

"Where's Pervis?" Sanderson barked at Peterson, one of his favourite agents. He'd hoped he wasn't going to be on duty.

"He's in his office. Sir, what's wrong?"

"I'll tell you later. Be vigilant. Use your instincts."

A few minutes later, Sanderson burst into Pervis's office. Pervis was the one man who'd do anything to avoid vampire activity outside the Coalition and therefore the safest bet Sanderson had.

Pervis jumped out of his sweaty skin with Sanderson's unexpected arrival. "Don't barge in like that! You'll give me a heart attack," he said, reaching for pills in his drawer to settle his nervous disposition.

Sanderson marched up to the desk where Pervis sat, grabbed on to it, and leaned menacingly towards the shaking councillor. "Where's Augustus?"

"How should I know?" Pervis continued to push his lank, floppy, ginger hair out of his face. "What do you want?"

"I think Augustus is the leak."

"What? I thought it was Sebastian. After all that—"

"That was a set up," Sanderson interrupted, "I spoke to Ivansey. He knows nothing about it."

"How do you know...Ivansey...wasn't lying?" Pervis still couldn't say his name without grimacing. He popped another pill.

"My gut says he was telling the truth."

"Did he say who the leak was?"

Sanderson relinquished his grip on the desk. "No, he didn't."

"These are serious allegations you're making, Sanderson. You haven't been tiptoeing around your disdain for the vampire race, have you? If I were you, I'd make entirely certain of any claims you have before shouting your mouth off."

Sanderson pulled at his short greying hair. "For fuck's sake, I don't know for sure. All I know is that it wasn't Sebastian."

A knock at the door quickly hushed the discussion.

"Come in," said Pervis nervously. He wouldn't arouse suspicion. He exuded fear 24/7. The pills obviously weren't helping.

Caroline strode into the office. "Good evening, gentlemen." She shut the door behind her and crossed her arms in front of her, unnervingly calm as ever.

"Caroline, I forgot we had a meeting. Good timing, though. Sanderson has discovered that Sebastian isn't the leak," Pervis announced before Sanderson had time to regroup.

COWARD! Sanderson screamed in his head and tried his hardest not to let his feelings show, but inhuman, emotionless reactions were Caroline's specialty, not his.

"Tell me more, Sanderson." She paused to look around the small but tidy office. "Better, still, come to my office. It seems there's much to discuss."

Sanderson followed Pervis and Caroline. He wanted to involve as few of the Coalition as possible in the trickiest situation he'd ever been in. Shooting himself out of trouble was something he was far more comfortable with, but it couldn't come to that.

Caroline's office was at the top of the Coalition building. Only a few feet below ground level and hundreds of feet above the Great Hall.

In seconds, he took in his surroundings out of habit. His soldier's instincts didn't allow anything else. The office was spacious, far more so than his or Pervis's, and the quality of the furniture would've brought a tear to the taxpayer's eye. There was only one side door, which he knew was a private bathroom. The mahogany desk, straight ahead from the entrance, was substantial and could offer good cover if required. Still, the only way out was back the way he came, through narrow, easily defendable corridors. He wouldn't have the luxury of holding position as there were no windows to make his escape from. Sanderson fleetingly noticed the abstract art on the wall, but he only took in the details of strategic influences.

"Take a seat," she offered.

Sanderson took the right-hand chair and angled it so he could see the bathroom door to the left of the office, just in case. Politically, Caroline was an unknown entity. No one kept their cards closer to their chest.

"Thank you, Caroline," said Pervis.

Sickening, creeping fuck. Sanderson grimaced.

"Tell me all you know, Sanderson."

In for a penny, he thought before telling Caroline about the farmhouse and the shrine made for Sebastian's corpse. She listened intently and didn't interrupt him, which was unusual for her. He told her all about the encounter with Ivansey, the Campire in The Miner's Arms and of his strange request for Tillsley's services. Finally, he told her that Ivansey knew nothing about Sebastian's demise.

"How do you know he was telling the truth," she asked when he finished. "Do you know for certain that Sebastian wasn't the leak?"

"When I mentioned his death, he knew nothing about it. I could see it in his eyes."

"And that's what you're basing your conclusions on?" she said in a way that should've patronised him to the core.

Sanderson nodded. He noticed Pervis raise his eyes. "But Ivansey knows who the leak is."

Caroline sat forward in her chair intently. "And did he tell you who it was?"

"No."

She sat back, the tension gone from her face. "What do you suggest we do?" she asked.

"I went to see Pervis, because he's the only man I know for sure wouldn't have anything to do with Ivansey."

"Very true," said Caroline. She sighed and sat back in her chair. "These are interesting times we live in, don't you think?"

"You could say that. I'd call them pretty fucked up, but that's why I sit here and you sit there."

"Quite." She offered a brief, mirthless smile before, uncharacteristically, rubbing her face with her hands in a tired manner. "Drink?"

"No, thank you," said Pervis in a heartbeat.

Sanderson merely shook his head.

Caroline got up and made her way to the decanter sitting on a drinks cabinet in the corner of the room. "How can we go to the Coalition and point the finger? Sanderson, who do you think the leak is?"

"Personally, I think it's Augustus, but I'm sure everyone else would look at little ol' me, which is why I didn't announce it at tea break."

She turned around, holding a whisky and a gun.

"Fancied something with a kick, huh?" he said, unimpressed. He'd seen her go for the piece. He'd watched her every move. As soon as she asked if he wanted a drink, he expected as much. He could have put a bullet in her but didn't. He wanted to see her reaction and Pervis's. Sanderson had seen her at the range before. She wasn't great with a pistol. He was still in control.

"You're a good soldier, Sanderson. I've fought for your place on the Coalition as no one understands the war on the streets like you do. I knew your hate was growing. The horrors you've witnessed have caused it to spiral out of control and cloud your judgement. The Agreement is for the good of the people, Sanderson, and you lost sight of why we stand here."

Sanderson couldn't believe his ears. She thought he was the leak. She looked down the sight of the gun.

"Pervis, relieve Sanderson of his gun."

Pervis got to his feet, and confidently, arrogantly sauntered over to where Sanderson sat, legs crossed, arms folded. "Stand up," he demanded.

"Been watching *Cops* again, kid?"

"Stand up," he repeated, with only a hint of nerves showing.

Sanderson complied. He could still pull out a concealed weapon if need be, but if he shot these two, what could he do then? No one would believe him when he told them what happened.

"Hands on the desk."

"You gonna do a cavity search?" He noted Caroline putting down the whisky and now had two hands on the gun like a pro. Still, she wouldn't be good enough.

"Where's the piece?"

"Jesus Christ, Pervis, this isn't the movies."

"Where's the piece!" he said, a little more rattled.

"Inside left."

He felt Pervis reach round from behind and pick the gun out of its holster. Pervis took no precautions. The soldier in Sanderson yearned for blood, but he stayed his hand.

Pervis pointed the gun at Sanderson and retreated to the same side of the desk as Caroline. Two guns now pointed at him.

"It's time you are taken off the streets, Sanderson," said Caroline. "Give me his gun, Pervis. It may have some forensic evidence to convict him."

"I'm not the fucking leak!"

Pervis didn't relinquish the weapon.

"Pervis," repeated Caroline. "Give me the gun and call security."

Sanderson got ready to roll and fire. The gun Pervis held pointed directly at Sanderson's heart, and he could see the intent in the young man's face. Those years of snide comments at meetings weren't doing Sanderson any favours right now.

Pervis looked down the sights, his finger on the trigger, but suddenly, he relinquished his hold on the gun and placed it on the table. Caroline grabbed it. Now, she had two guns on Sanderson. Pervis went for the phone to call security. Time was running out. Sanderson had to move soon, but a hostage situation wouldn't work in such a place. *Fuck.*

Pervis reached for the phone.

"Hold on," said Caroline.

"Why?"

Her demeanour changed. She almost relaxed. "The Haemo project will bring order, Sanderson. We must utilise the airborne system in order to bring harmony to the world. We will have the best of both worlds: A safe environment for mankind and the benefits of thousands of years of knowledge. Haemo will leash the vampire, and I will let nothing stop that." Caroline walked around the table to where Sanderson stood, shell-shocked. "I've always liked you, Sanderson."

"Caroline, you—"

"Shut up, Pervis, you snivelling, little bastard." She pointed the gun at him.

"W...what?

"At last, I've finally found a use for you."

She pulled the trigger. The bullet ripped through the young man's heart and red blood clashed with the blue abstract lines that streaked the painted canvas behind him. Pervis didn't have time to look shocked as his corpse crumpled to the floor.

37

THE BEER IN THE PHOENIX WEREN'T BAD. Bolton was the flavour, but it wasn't as good as The Miner's. The landlord didn't have it quite right, and it made all the difference. The landlord was grateful he didn't keep the beer quite right, because it meant Sid Tillsley wouldn't be a regular.

Brian's sources were correct. It was ladies' night, and it was doing wonders for the morale of the downtrodden heroes. There was a bit of a disco kicking off and "Come On Eileen" entertained the punters at a level that was enjoyable and allowed conversation, all that a man in his forties could ask for.

A few heads turned when the four took their perving position at the edge of the dance floor. The reputations of these gentlemen and vampire were known all across Teesside, and this pub was no exception. "What's the plan then, Brian?" asked Sid.

"Not sure yet, mate. This place is a bit classier than 'owt on the Smithson Estate. I'm thinking that swinging the wanger on the dance floor may not go down too well in here. You see, our Sid, that's what being a swordsman is all about: knowing to use the right technique in the right place."

"I see," said Sid, who didn't. "So, what do we do?"

"Well, we're all getting the eye off that group over there."

Four lasses stood on the other side of the dance floor looking over to where the boys were looking casual and sexy, well, Arthur was. The other three managed fat, sleazy, and greasy. "Looks like you and Arthur will be shaggin' before the end of the evening, mate," said Sid, still hoping the Internet dating was going to come up trumps.

Brian could see a glimmer of hope for Sid. In fact, there was a lass for all of them in this little group. There was a stunner, an absolute stunner, who Brian himself fancied, but knew Arthur was the best candidate, and fair play to the lad as he'd just lost her indoors. Brian would woo the sluttiest one of the group, who stood out a mile; high heels, hoop earrings, short skirt, peroxide blonde, it all added up. Sure, the politically correct wankers would chastise him, but there was no such thing as a politically correct swordsman. There was even one for Rathbone in there; a skinny, greasy, wreck of a woman who stole drinks from people when they weren't looking. And last, but not least, there was a female version of Sid. She looked like Bigfoot with tits. This had to be fate.

"Come on, lads! We're going in!"

SANDERSON WASN'T SHOCKED EASILY, but he couldn't pull his eyes from Pervis's twitching corpse. He'd never felt so out of his depth in all his life. Caroline was...what? He didn't know. He didn't have a clue.

"You don't have much time. Security will be here in seconds." Caroline hurried behind the desk and angled the murder weapon so that the barrel was aimed in the same direction as from where she'd shot Pervis. She pointed the gun a micron past her own flesh, and without hesitation, pulled the trigger. She hardly winced.

"The Haemo project must be upheld, Sanderson." She rubbed her wound as if it was nothing more than a mosquito bite. "Make sure Tillsley is safe. You'll need him. It's a shame it's come to this. Here."

She threw him the gun, which he caught on autopilot.

"What's...happening?" he finally managed. He transferred his gaze from Pervis to her. Her poker face could mask murder. She was even stronger than he'd given her credit for and her voice didn't betray her pain.

"The Coalition will order Tillsley's death as soon as Ivansey is out of the way. We launch Haemo for the good of the human race. We are peas in the same pod, you and I. You're going to have to fight your way out. I'm sure that won't be a problem. I'll be in touch. Good luck."

Sanderson stood, wide-eyed, as she threw herself into a heap next to Pervis, which is why he didn't react as two guards charged into the office and bundled into him.

THE BOYS WERE DOING WELL. Sid had managed to set up a tab with the landlord and the ale was flowing. The lads entertained the girls with stories to guarantee action of the sexual nature. If there was anything to get the ladies drooling, vampire hunting had to be up there. Brian tried his luck with the slutty-looking one.

"Yep, I'm a fighter pilot."

"I thought you helped Sid out with vampire hunting."

"You calling me a fooking liar!" said Middlesbrough's answer to Maverick from *Top Gun*.

The blonde shrugged her shoulders, unperturbed, and lit up a fag. "I couldn't give a fook, love."

It was time for Brian to step it up a gear. "As I said, I'm a fighter pilot, and I...err...I..." He scratched his head, accessing the recesses of the brain devoted to silver-tongued swordsmanship. "I saved some blind...erm..." He threw up his hands. "Erm...blind, spastic kittens from a....erm paedophile...erm...Fook it! Do you fancy a shag out back?"

The blonde looked at her watch. "As long as you're done before the repeat of *X-Factor*."

"Champion," said Brian Garforth, swordsman with a tongue of solid silver.

Rathbone struggled with conversation, not surprisingly. He was only good at outdoing other people's stories, so he decided to take the tack of listening to his potential victim. Women loved all that listening shit, the daft bints. When that didn't work, he tried some of the random bollocks they like. "You met any celebrities?" he asked.

"Eh? Why would you give a fook about that?" asked his target, who was just as awkward a conversationalist as he was.

"I don't. You women love all your shite like that, don't ya? That and your shit telly programs."

"No."

"Miserable bitch," he mumbled under his breath.

"I didn't quite catch that?" she said aggressively.

"I said, 'Miserable bitch,' ya deaf twat."

"Wanker."

Rathbone walked off.

Not far away, Arthur relaxed and was in the mood for some loving, but the guilt stopped him from taking the amazing blonde over the pool table. He tried to drink the guilt away, but it wasn't helping. He just wasn't ready, and even if he were offered a blowjob later, he'd only accept out of common courtesy.

Sid was in a good place. He found it really easy to talk to his lass. Maybe it was because they shared a lot of the same interests. She'd done her fair share of debt collecting and even had a few bare-knuckle boxing matches. Aye, her looks backed up her claims, but she had a mighty set on her, which made up for the rest. Sid got on with aggressive women; they clicked. The old prison guard he used to see now and then, she was good in a ruck, and now, there was this lass. Still, it would be nice to bed a good-looking woman, but then, all those window-dressings were for show. It was the same with cars. You didn't drive a Grenada Scorpio for the electric windows; you drove it because it had a massive pair of knockers.

"I know all about you, Sid Tillsley."

"You ain't a Benefit Bastard, are ya?" Once bitten, twice shy.

"Don't be daft, mon," said Female Sid, downing a pint of Bolton. "I've heard all about you, running around at night, giving the odd vampire a fourpenny-one."

"What? No. I train dolphins, pet."

"I'd prefer to hear about the vampires, flower," Female Sid downed her second pint of Bolton. "You want a couple of pints? I'm gagging for more Bolton."

Sid was in love. This woman drank Bolton, approved of him drinking Bolton, and was now going to *buy* him Bolton.

"Aye, I could murder a pint or ten."

Sid noticed that the other girls were going on one of their infamous joint toilet breaks. He had no idea what went on in there, but women always took fooking ages. Does it really take more than one lass to unblock a khazi? Ah well, the fairer sex were a strange breed. He nudged Arthur who sat next to him. "Where's Brian?"

"He went round back with the slutty one. These are good girls, man."

"Aye," said Sid, "I really like my one."

"My one's been nailed by Michael Flatley."

"Good for you, Rathbone," said Arthur.

Brian sauntered in, still a little wobbly around the knees. "Well, I'm done. How are you lads getting on?"

"Look! My lass is buying me Bolton Bitter! Can this night get any better?"

The music ceased abruptly, and the smoke machines set about creating an atmosphere by covering the floor of the pub with a mysterious fog. Suddenly, a spotlight from the DJ stand blasted Sid in the eyes, causing him to cover them with his hand. "What the fook is going on?"

The silhouette of a figure appeared on the DJ stand. Sid's *Pink Alert* tingled, and rightly so.

A voice echoed through the pub and out onto the streets of Middlesbrough. "SID TILLSLEY IS A HOMOSEXUAL!"

"DROP THE FUCKING WEAPON!"

The air escaped Sanderson's lungs as he hit the wall of Caroline's office. One guard, Hopkiss, grabbed his gun, while the other, Jafar, held his head against the wall with a forearm against his throat.

Sanderson regained his senses. Hand-to-hand combat was his specialist subject, but these were good lads, so he'd go easy on them. He let go of the gun, and Hopkiss instinctively relaxed his hold on Sanderson's arm, who pulled it free while at the same time scraping his foot down Jafar's shin bone. The pain caused Jafar to relinquish his forearm from Sanderson's throat whose left hand sent him reeling. That left Hopkiss, who had no chance.

Hopkiss was a good fighter, just not good enough. He drove for Sanderson's legs, but Sanderson expected it from the experienced grappler and used the momentum to catapult Hopkiss, head first, into the wall behind him.

Without hesitating, Sanderson turned to deal with Jafar who, although still on the floor, had recovered from the punch and was reaching for the pistol in his jacket. Sanderson took a step and unleashed a round kick at the agent's head, who managed to get his hands up, but it wasn't enough to stop the older man's conditioned shin from smashing into his skull, knocking him out cold.

Sanderson spun with the kick, ready to deal with any further onslaught from Hopkiss, but there was no movement. He hoped he was still alive. There'd be more on the way. He picked up the gun.

This would've been fun if he wasn't maiming agents who looked up to him like a father.

"WHAT'S GOING ON? Who fooking said that?" demanded Sid. The spotlight swung round to illuminate the Campire, posing magnificently on the DJ stand after booming the slander from the PA system, which doubled up for karaoke. Dressed, as always, for the occasion, the Campire personified Disco, and his crisp, white shirt was left wide open and revealed a cut six-pack, bronzed with fake tan, and the huge collars reached all the way to his pierced nipples. His suit jacket and trousers were leopard-skin print and oh-so-tight. His slicked-back hair was no more...Disco meant afro!

"Ah, shit. Not him again," said Brian.

"People of Middlesbrough," he announced to the puzzled pubgoers. "I won't take much of your time. I'm here to make a wonderful announcement." the Campire started clapping and doing mini-jumps favoured by overly excited teenage girls. "Sid Tillsley and I are engaged to be married in a civil partnership! I am soooo happy that he will finally carry me over the threshold and I can take him as my civil partner!"

"Civil partnerships?" mumbled a Northerner in the crowd. "That's what them Southerners do."

"Please, spread the word of our love!" In camp, theatrical fashion, dry ice spewed forth once more, and the Campire disappeared.

All eyes slowly turned to Sid Tillsley.

HEAT CAME DOWN ON SANDERSON LIKE NAPALM. He wasn't taking the quickest way out, but the route of least resistance. He had to get out before any vampires turned up.

"Bitch," he whispered to himself for the umpteenth time. Caroline had wanted him to escape and escape was easiest from her offices. She knew it. She knew everything. She'd even wished him luck. It wasn't lucky that since he'd left her office, two agents were dead and two seriously injured.

He didn't have far to go, but there'd be more guards to deal with and vampires coming from deeper in the building. If he could make it to the ventilation systems, he could access the basements of other adjacent buildings.

A bullet whistled past his head. He'd expected them to hold position in the maintenance room where he could enter the vents, not here in the office areas running off the main corridors. *Clever lads,* he thought with a hint of pride. Still, the bullet was aimed at his head, which meant he was going to have to get nasty. He dived through the door of a nearby janitor's closet.

He knew there'd be two agents up ahead and more in the maintenance room. Agents would be swarming into the other buildings, but he'd shake them if he was quick. There were two offices up ahead, one to each side. Most likely with an agent in each of them. He had to act. He had to get out. This place was heaven to defend but hell to attack.

A couple of bullets placed into the doorframes of the offices hiding the agents kept them at bay and gave him a second to create a second diversion, and the janitor's closet had given him just that: cans of air freshener. He bundled them into the back of a cleaning cart and pushed it out the door and down the corridor.

The agents heard the rolling of wheels but knew not to look. They knew that if they popped their heads round the corner, they would have a 9mm present waiting for them.

Sanderson popped a bullet and gasped at the resulting fireball that vented into the two rooms hiding the agents. He charged through the corridor, with a gun in each hand, and double-tapped bullets into the doorways. Two screams. He kept running, hoping they weren't dead.

THE WORLD CLOSED IN ON SID TILLSLEY. He didn't know what paranoia meant, but he knew what it felt like. All eyes were on him, and he knew what they were thinking. They thought he was an air steward...They thought he was a fooking *air steward* who danced on the ice!

Sid looked over to where Female Sid held four pints of Bolton Bitter between her mighty paws. She didn't look happy.

"Howay, flower!"

Four pints of Bolton Bitter spilled on to the floor.

"NOOOOOOOOOOO!" Sid ran out of the door, barging aside pubgoers as he went.

NOT PETERSON.

Sanderson was close to escape and had entered the maintenance rooms that powered the immense building. It was hot, dark, and scary. Perfect for him, but not for Peterson who stood alone by the ventilation system. Peterson knew it was an escape route; Sanderson had taught him well. The young recruit hadn't noticed him, but he was on alert. He looked nervous. As well he should be.

Silently, Sanderson navigated the piping systems. He was a trained assassin. The kid didn't have a chance. Sanderson hid in the shadows with Peterson ten yards in front of him, eyes keen, pistol raised. It was a dangerous situation, but Peterson only needed to lose concentration for a second. After several minutes, Peterson checked his watch.

"Drop the gun, lad."

Peterson didn't move. His training had paid off. Sudden movements ended in death.

Stepping out into the open, Sanderson was exposed. There were too many places for back-up to hide. Boilers, pipes, and air ducts filled the room. Still, he couldn't take his eyes off the number one danger. "Drop the gun. I need to get out, and I don't want any more bloodshed."

Peterson's eyes saved Sanderson's life, which darted to his left. Sanderson whipped his head back and the bullet ricocheted around the room off various metal pipes. Sanderson whipped his right arm out and grabbed the gun of Peterson's partner, whom Sanderson had missed on his initial recon as he was hidden from view. Peterson's partner launched a punch with his free hand, a swinging, wild hook, powerful but slow. Sanderson beat him to the punch by charging forward and driving the point of his elbow into his attacker's sternum. He pushed the agent's head back and recognised the middle-aged man to be Mannings, a true company man. Sanderson enjoyed driving his head into the man's face.

With Mannings disorientated, Sanderson smashed his hand into the nearby pipework forcing the agent to relinquish the firearm. Sanderson spun him around and wrapped his forearm tight into his neck, not that he needed to since the headbutt had all but knocked the agent out. Sanderson pointed the gun at Peterson, steady as a rock.

"I was set up."

Peterson's gun didn't waver a millimetre. Sanderson again felt a touch of pride in his protégé. Slowly, Peterson's gun slowly changed angle to point past Sanderson's ear. His eyes darted at his left arm.

Clever, clever boy. Sanderson gave the briefest of nods before Peterson fired at the wall behind him, and Sanderson fired a grazing bullet at the young agent's arm, stealing Caroline's tactic with pride. He dropped Mannings from the tight chokehold and punched him in the jaw, taking away what little consciousness he held on to.

Voices came from behind. Sanderson crossed the room, and without a moment's hesitation, drove his fist into Peterson's smiling face.

38

CAROLINE LET HERSELF SINK under the hot, soothing waters of her fragranced bath. Once, she'd bathed every day, using the time to unwind from the stress, but every day quickly turned into every other day, and then once a week, if she was lucky. There was no time to relax. Not that she deserved to. She barely noticed the stinging that her self-inflicted bullet wound brought as the scented waters lapped over it. There were too many other things playing on her mind to worry about a little pain. She'd suffered a life of pain the Coalition knew nothing about. What was a little more?

Sanderson was a good man. A damn good man. She felt guilty for putting him through such an ordeal. Ivansey could still be trouble, but without him, she would never have got this far, not so quickly. She let herself float to the surface of the huge, ornate bath.

It was all for the greater good, she told herself. Everything she did was for the greater good, and hopefully, she'd be forgiven for her multitude of sins. Maybe one day, she would reap revenge for the sins that had been committed against her, and the wheels were now in motion to make it so.

Sparle was the first gift. By killing Vitrago, Sparle had turned the Coalition into a farce. Tillsley was the second and most unexpected of treasures. He'd brought destruction and anarchy to the vampire race, and idiots like Bwogi vainly tried to control them. She couldn't believe it when he'd suggested reinitiating Haemo. She thought she'd have to work years for that.

She sank deeper beneath the waters, shutting her eyes tightly and forgetting everything. She held on to the last ounce of breath, wondering whether it was worth staying beneath the warm waters and ending it all. No. What if the nightmares followed her into her eternal sleep? She surfaced...

"You really should exfoliate more."

Caroline thrashed in the bath with fright.

Ivansey laughed. He stood at the end of the bath with his foot on it, hands on hips.

Jeffrey! Caroline's thoughts flashed to her husband asleep in the bedroom.

"Don't worry, he's quite safe."

How did you—

"I have many talents," he said, answering her thoughts. "You must know I've gone through some...changes. I may not be able to tear down buildings with my bare hands, but now, I have other, more useful powers. And besides, ripping down buildings is so bad for your nails." He put out his hand for her to examine. "I'll give you the number of my manicurist. You could do with it, honey."

Caroline couldn't believe her eyes. She'd never seen the vampire in the flesh, only the many photos of him, and his transformation was baffling. Those piercing blue eyes couldn't be forgotten, though. His slick-backed hair and moustache weren't the fashion, but he still looked magnificent.

Ivansey smiled. "Enough flattery, thank you. It's good to finally meet you, my mistress."

"How did you know it was me?"

"I have acquired some friends who understand the inner workings of your all-powerful Coalition. Sanderson thought I was the one who turned Sebastian to my way of thinking. It was quite a brilliant idea, I must say. I take it that the repugnant Reece Chambers helped?"

"Yes, he did." Caroline had no idea where this was going, but she was sure it wouldn't end well.

"He doesn't know you're the contact, does he?"

"What makes you say that?"

"My boys bumped into him recently. The look on his face when the nature of his research was discussed in front of Tillsley was a picture, apparently."

"You...you didn't kill him?" she asked, surprised.

"Where would the fun be in that? I like staring into his eyes. I can see the pain of his father's murder every time I look into them. It's exquisite. And, besides, I thought it would be fun to see you squirm now he knows you've been gossiping like a schoolgirl about his extracurricular activities."

"How can you possibly know about them?"

Ivansey's grin didn't waver. Her skin crawled and was compelled to break the silence. "What do you want?"

"Isn't that a question for the ages?" he said, twiddling his moustache. "To belong is what I want. I have been in exile for far too long."

"You want to be pardoned by the Coalition?"

He laughed out loud. "I'd rather die than beg forgiveness from the Coalition, such bad dress sense, don't you think? No, I'm building an army, Caroline. An army of vampires just like me. Vampires who no longer wish to be imprisoned by loneliness. We won't wage war, but we will not hide in the closet."

"So what do you want from me?"

"You're in charge, my dear."

"We are a council."

"Oh, I'm sure you are," he scoffed. He examined some of her bathing products before picking one out. "May I borrow this?"

"What do you want?"

"'Greater depth and shine,'" he said, reading the bottle.

Caroline bit her tongue. This comical facade didn't hide the animal hiding beneath.

He laughed once more. "Things are much simpler now we know each other. We're both influential people, Caroline. I have you and the Coalition to thank for the vampires turning to me. The Agreement stifles the essence of what it is to be a vampire. I was the loneliest spirit, traversing this sick and cruel world, but losing these gave me freedom." He dropped his pants.

Caroline's eyes bulged when she saw his naked groin.

"Beautiful, isn't it?" he said, buttoning up his PVC slacks. "I experienced tenderness and passion in a gay club in Manchester. I was embraced. I have never felt so much *love*." He wrapped his arms around his body and gave himself a quick squeeze. "And love is what I can give to the vampire nation. That's why they flock to me. It's not about sex. Not at all. It's amazing how many vampires simply want to belong, to be part of a family. To be loved. I can give them that. I am a beacon, Caroline. I am a lighthouse guiding my children to safety."

"So what do you need me for?"

"I want nothing more than the same *agreement* we had to begin with. You scratch my back, I scratch yours."

"And what can you give me?"

Ivansey laughed. He took his foot off the bath and admired himself in the full-length mirror. "Steam-free. Very nice." He adjusted a strand of hair. "Obviously, your husband's life, for one, but he probably isn't the most important thing in your life, now...is he?"

His cold blue stare penetrated her skull. She tried to keep her mind blank. She couldn't let him into her most guarded thoughts.

"Didn't think so." He chuckled. "You're as dangerous as Vitrago ever was. What can I give someone so devious? Hmmm." He tapped his chin. "How about I keep the little secret you hold so close to your heart?"

"Which is?" she was becoming tired of the games.

"Why, Haemo, of course."

Her heart skipped a beat. *How do you know—*

"I told you, I've acquired some friends from your little club. One of Garendon's scientists has joined my ranks. It's amazing that weeks ago, I destroyed the Haemo plant in the Northeast without even knowing what treasures lied within...but I do now. I must say, you're very clever."

Caroline shivered.

"The hunt was once everything to me. Ricard, a wise and dear friend, whom your beloved Coalition executed, once told me, 'Love is a more powerful entity than all our race combined.' The brutal Gunnar Ivansey told him to 'F off.' If only I could see him again to tell him how right he was and how much I loved him." His voice wavered, but he kept it together. "When the Haemo project is launched, it will drive the vampire to me. The line is weak, and most won't rebel, but they'll seek shelter, and I'll be there for them. The hunt is nothing compared to love, Caroline. You'll send me more brothers—who knows?—hopefully sisters."

Caroline considered the proposition, not that she'd any choice on the matter. She believed his words. The tear in his eye was real. As long as Haemo was seen through to its fruition, she didn't care who followed this madman.

"And Tillsley?"

"He's mine."

"His death warrant is unavoidable."

"Then you best keep me in the loop, darling. Ciao." Ivansey walked to the doorway and leant against it.

"When I sit on the Coalition, I'll have to order your death," she called to him.

"Once Tillsley has given me what I want, I will return. You'll owe me a little something if you're going to be a meanie and send nastiness in my direction."

She said nothing, praying he'd leave.

Ivansey clicked his tongue in thought. "Perhaps then we can find out what else you're up to. I sense you have something far grander up that devious sleeve of yours. Toodles."

Caroline sat numb. She'd assumed she was going to suffer the same fate Rickson Flatley had. Instead, Ivansey was going to help her. It now dawned on her how he knew of Chambers' research. Garendon's assistant who'd defected had helped source the scientific equipment rewarded to Chambers after attacking the Occursus. Ivansey pieced it all together, and Chambers would believe it was her, his unknown contact from the Coalition, who handed him to Ivansey.

She wasn't anybody's favourite person right now. Chambers was going to be a handful, and so was Sanderson, but not if they worked together...Cogs whirred. Ivansey was right.

She was devious.

39

"FOOKING KEVIN. HE COULD'VE KICKED THE BASTARDS OUT," said Brian.

Arthur fired a karate kick into a wheelie bin and shattered the plastic. "What are we gonna do now, man? We got our beer back, and then, we lost it again. Any other boozer we find will be ruined by the Campire, and Jimmy isn't gonna be on his feet for months."

Sid punched the lamppost he walked past and dented it. He didn't say a word. The lads kept an eye on him. Last time he was this angry, he went on one of his infamous drink-driving runs, knocked out a copper, ran over the perfect human warrior, and killed the most powerful vampire to ever walk the earth before regaining his composure and going for a pint.

"About time a decent vampire bar opened up in this town. I've suffered discrimination for too long."

"Shut up, Rathbone!" Brian shouted. "It ain't a vampire bar; it's a gay bar."

The next lamppost bent in half with the impact of Big Sid's big right hand and crashed down onto a parked Land Rover.

Rathbone, for once, knew when to shut up.

"We'll have to look further afield for another boozer, that's all," said Brian.

"That's my boozer, Brian." They were the first words Sid spoke since they'd left The Phoenix.

"I know it is, but unless you get rid of the Campire, you ain't gonna be drinking good-quality Bolton. And I can't see you two getting on, like."

Another broken lamppost confirmed the point.

"Hey," said Arthur, "Sanderson said if you give him the big right, you can have your benefit money back. You've gotta do it, man. You go in there and lay the smack down. You get your beer, your boozer, and booze money for life."

"It ain't that FOOKING EASY!" Sid turned over every Volkswagen Beetle, Ford Ka, and New Mini he passed. Every car that could've been driven by one of *them lot* took the brunt of his Manrage. In actuality, it would only result in kids having to walk to school in the morning.

The lads walked in silence for a few minutes. A police car pulled up, saw that it was Sid causing the problem, and realised there were more important, safer crimes to deal with, and sped away. Sid was in a bad mood. He'd walked five hundred yards without complaining once or lighting up a single tab. "I want revenge, Brian."

Brian rubbed his hands together, devilishly, as a thought occurred to him. "Don't worry, Sid. I've had an idea."

REECE WAS BACK IN HIS LAB. He had a fresh sample of Arthur's DNA and had taken it through all the necessary enhancements in order to analyse the building blocks that made-up Arthur Peasley. The last sample he'd analysed was contaminated. It had to be. The results didn't make sense. He wouldn't mess up twice.

THREE LADS AND A VAMPIRE were trespassing on the most dangerous land in the Northeast. The SAS wouldn't last a minute here. The lads had snuck onto the Smithson Estate allotments and into Kevin Ackroyd's shed. At least the Bolton Bitter in the shed satisfied all, except Rathbone who refused to drink any because vampires only drank blood and white wine.

But now, the beer was gone and the lads' thoughts turned to...other things. The idea of shagging a doll was alien to all of them, but as the ale started flowing, the plastic ladies exhibited the same wonderful qualities that real women did when alcohol was consumed: they looked better. No one wanted to mention it, in case their fellow drinkers ridiculed them, but every eye in the room was turning more frequently to the harem set up in provocative poses.

"What we gonna do now, like?" asked Sid, eyes fixed on a merkin.

"You ain't shagging one of 'em," said Brian.

"What? You dirty bastard, it never crossed me mind."

"Yeah, reet. Look, it's fooking weird in the first place, and I ain't sticking it in the same plastic hole that some other fooker has."

"Yeah, man. It's a little freaky," agreed Arthur. "Can't we get Rathbone to do it?"

"I ain't shagging a doll," said Rathbone instinctively, before giving the plastic ladies a once over. "Not with you lot watching."

Brian stroked his goatee. "It's the perfect way to get Kev back for giving away our pub. Tell you what, Rathbone, we'll go outside, you do the deed, and you give us a shout when you've done."

"Alreet...but you all owe me a white wine for this."

The lads stood outside in the cold, worried for their safety because of the strange sounds coming from the sheds of the other Allotmenteers. They hoped the greasy, horrible, little bastard would hurry up defiling Kevin's collection of sex dolls quickly.

"He's doing reet with the ladies, these days. Must be since he become a vampire, like," said Sid, considering a switch.

"I guess he did lose his virginity," said Brian. "But, fook me, it were pretty nasty. Now, he's in there shagging plastic dolls. Still, you're reet. He's doing better."

The door opened. "I canna do it," said Rathbone, reappearing from the love shack. Not a vampire of decency, he wore only his shoes and cape.

"What? Rathbone, get back in there and do the fooking job!" Brian took the scene in. "Fook me, where is your dignity?"

"They keep looking at me with their dead eyes. Puts me off."

"Put summat over their head, and get the job done," encouraged Sid, looking everywhere except at the world's smallest vampire penis.

"I played with their tits, like."

"Don't really send a message, does it, Rathbone?" said Brian.

"We have to do something, man," said Arthur. "Shall we burn the shed to the ground, decapitate the dolls, and shit like that?"

"Definitely not. We need Kev to come back up here with more Bolton. There's no way he's gonna stop shagging his dolls, and every male needs a decent amount of ale inside him if he's gonna make love properly."

"Good point," said Arthur.

They needed to make a protest, and luckily, Brian Garforth was the smartest man on the Smithson Estate. Looking out at the little allotment huts with the lights twinkling inside, he knew there were desperate, desperate men inside.

"I got meself an idea, lads."

REECE SHOOK HIS HEAD. The sample yielded the same DNA pattern. The plate was smeared just like last time. Still, he'd take the sample through to the end of the analysis. The last time he'd tried identifying the smear...it had to be wrong. It just had to be. He placed the DNA inside the analyser, His destiny was in its mechanical hands.

"WHY HAVE I GOTTA DO IT?"

"You're a fooking vampire!"

"That's enough of that racist shit. I'll report you!"

"Who to?"

Rathbone put his fists on his hips. "I don't wanna do it, reet?"

"Look, Peter..."

"Oh, yeah? It's fooking 'Peter' now, ain't it? When you fooking want something, it's 'Peter.'"

Brian ignored the accusation. "Look, you're the fastest here by a mile. I'd do it if it was only a thirty-yard dash, but you need to get as many of them allotment weirdoes up here as you can. Plus, if you do get caught, you can regenerate."

"My fooking cape won't. I've got every fooking bodily fluid bar one on this bastard, and I don't want to complete the set."

"Don't be daft, mon. It's foolproof. They're all old codgers, anyroad.

They ain't got a chance of catching you. Look, we'll all get you a bottle of wine if you do it."

Rathbone weighed it up. Every vampire had a price. "Reet, tell us the plan again?"

Minutes later, they were ready. The lads had stripped one of the dolls down to the plastic and strapped her to the back of the vampire, legs open, to entice the Allotmenteers.

"Is that tied on alright?" asked Brian.

Rathbone jumped ten feet in the air before landing back down on his toes. "Aye, that ain't going anywhere."

"Good. All you need to do is leg it through the two main allotment paths. The sight of a woman should bring 'em running. Make sure to knock on a few doors too, they'll fooking hate that. Leg it back through here, dump her inside, and get the fook out of Dodge. We'll be in me Capri over the back car park, engine running. Got it?"

"Aye." Rathbone nodded and swallowed. "I don't feel too well, come to think of it. Dead thirsty, mon."

"You'll be reet. This'll be a breeze. We'll get some booze down us afterwards and you'll feel better."

Rathbone nodded. He really wasn't feeling great. When he'd jumped around earlier, testing the strapped-on sex doll, he hadn't felt as powerful. He'd lost the spring in his step. Still, he'd be quick enough to evade the nearly deads.

"Here goes nothing." Rathbone said, initiating the sortie. He ran like the wind, until the bear trap tactically hidden in the first allotment he entered slowed him down.

"AAARRRRRGGGGGHHHHH!"

He hopped away, but the door of the allotment opened and an enraged, elderly Allotmenteer burst out with a pitchfork in his hand. He was ready to finish anything that had been caught in his booby trap, but something else caught his attention.

Allotmenteers were driven by the most basic instincts, and a naked woman was something alien. The Allotmenteer wanted to kill it, but he also had a strange urge to wiggle his thing that fired funny-tasting water inside of it. Either way, he was in hot pursuit.

Rathbone hopped along the best he could. His screams brought forward more Allotmenteers, all experiencing the same feelings as the first.

"YOU'RE NOT GONNA STEAL MY BEETROOT, YOU TWATCOCK!"

"Oh, bloody hell, not him!" The war cry of the crazy, beetroot-obsessed codger caused Rathbone to lose concentration and fall into one of the allotments. His vampire reactions saved him from horrific burns to his entire body when only one of his hands entered the sulphuric acid moat surrounding the Allotmenteer's turnip patch.

"AAARRRRRRRRGGGHHHHHHHH!"

The door of the hut opened to reveal the crazy, naked old man with the knife just like the one from *Seven* on the end of his erect member.

"How the fook is that thing still up!" cried Rathbone.

The old man was thrusting as he opened the door and thrust with every step he made closer to the vampire in mortal danger.

"AAARRRRRRRRGGGHHHHHHHH!"

"This hasn't gone according to plan, like," said Brian with the understatement of the year.

Brian, Sid, and Arthur sat in the Capri 2.8i, watching the real-life horror show. Rathbone was in trouble. He'd just landed on his sixth booby trap and was crawling, as best he could, from the chasing Allotmenteers. They were slow, but they were persistent. Like the living dead, the nearly deads moved together, but it wasn't the lust for eating brains that drove them. It was the lust for doing something that they weren't quite sure of.

"We've gotta help him, man. He's in a bad way," said Arthur.

"I don't know, he's almost there," said Brian. "And I ain't getting in the way of that crazy, thrusting, old fooker."

"Let's move the car a little closer, at least," said Arthur.

"Fook that. They might scratch me paintwork. Capris don't grow on trees you know. Nah, he'll be reet. Probably."

Rathbone desperately crawled towards Kevin's allotment. He'd lost a lot of blood and was tiring. He wasn't regenerating, and he was so thirsty. It must be blood he needed, but it made him sick thinking about what he did to Maggie's mate. If he could get through the door of Kev's shed, barricade it, and make it out the window, the Allotmenteers would get distracted and he could make it to the getaway car. Them racist pricks were doing nothing to help!

The breathing of the codgers came closer. He could hear the air being cut in twain by the aggressive thrusts of the cock-knife-wielding psycho. Kev's dolls were gonna be put through a rough night.

Through the door of Kev's shed he went, undoing the belt holding the doll on his back. He kicked the door shut to buy him some time and pushed himself up onto a chair and up to the window.

"It's fooking locked!" He pulled at it desperately, but his strength had waned due to his injuries. The window was glazed in sections, so breaking the glass wouldn't help. It was too small for him to crawl through. He struck the wooden frame with all his might, but it wasn't enough.

Desperation set in.

"Fook!"

He desperately hunted for a crowbar or something to jimmy open the wooden frame, but there was nothing; just empty beer barrels, sex dolls, sex toys, and enough lube for a night of passion with an entire bingo hall. The huts on this allotment were built for security. Nothing to a vampire in his prime, but to the greasiest, nastiest, pitiful excuse for a vampire, with third-degree acid burns to one hand, a bear trap stuck to his foot, six broken ribs, a dislocated shoulder, and a lost ear as the result of a C4 detonation, it meant trouble.

"Fook!"

Shadows appeared at the windows, and with them the groaning and the incessant screams of "YOU'RE NOT GONNA STEAL MY BEETROOT, YOU TWATCOCK!" The nearly deads banged on the windows, and although they were too weak to break that way through, the psychological torment was truly terrible.

Rathbone got his body against the door just in time. The Allotmenteers tried to push it open, and only his body weight held them at bay. They weren't strong, but they were relentless, psychotic, and driven by rage, beetroot, and sex dolls.

As suddenly as the banging started, it ceased, as did the moaning and the clawing at the windows. Only then was the faintest of noises heard.

Swish, swish, swish, swish, swish.

The strange sound grew louder and louder and Rathbone looked through the keyhole to investigate.

"AAARRRGHHHHHHHH!"

The cock-wielded knife drove straight through the keyhole and into Rathbone's right eye. The nearly deads hammered on the windows with renewed vigour, for their champion was here, driving his armed penis through the wooden door, again and again. Rathbone's only hope was that his friends would save him.

"FLASH! Ahhhh-AAAAHHH, HE'LL SAVE EVERY ONE OF US!"

The help Rathbone needed wasn't coming.

The lads were heading back for a pint. Brian's Capri banged out the tune and the boys sung along to the classic.

"Do you reckon Rathbone's OK?" asked Sid.

Brian turned down the radio. "No idea, but I weren't gonna fook with that fella with a knife for a cock, were you?"

"Guess not. Ah well, we'll get him a pint when he gets back.

"You canna say fairer than that."

Brian turned the radio up.

"NO ONE BUT THE PURE OF HEART, CAN DRINK TWELVE PINTS OF ALE! WHOOOAA-OOAAAAA"

FINALLY, THE MACHINE STOPPED WHIRRING, and Reece tore the results from the printer. He looked at the spectrum in front of him and the predicted chemical structure for the mysterious band on the DNA sequence. The result was the same as last time.

"You've got to be kidding me!" It couldn't be coincidence, but the molecule embedded in Peasley's DNA was biologically and chemically impossible.

"Humulone? What's humulone doing in a DNA sequence?"

A beep indicated that another instrument had finished its analysis. He ran over and tore the printout of Garforth's DNA.

"Lupulone!...It can't be coincidence."

RATHBONE LAY FACE DOWN in a pool of his own blood and other bodily liquids that were not pleasant and not his. His cape was in a worse state and had soaked up twice its weight in his blood and other bodily fluids that were not pleasant and not his. He'd now collected the set.

He couldn't move. His injuries were catastrophic and, not to mention, really unusual. Middlesbrough A&E would struggle to piece together the evening's events if his body was found. Not that his body would be found. The sun would be up soon and that would be the end. Those bastard "friends" of his had left him for dead. They'd get theirs...Oh, they'd get theirs.

The nearly deads hadn't been merciful. The dolls had taken the brunt, and when the dolls were "used up'" it had been Rathbone who took the surplus of randy codgers. Now, he needed blood, the only thing that could bring him back from death's door. Through the pain, he tried to crawl out of the shed and make his bid for freedom. He would be safe from the Allotmenteers as they were completely spent. If he had the strength, he'd mess with that bastard's beetroots. That old dirty fooker was on heat. He'd get his...Oh, he'd get his.

Something caught Rathbone's eye. From the floor, he could see a barrel of Bolton Bitter, and it was fresh, no spile penetrated the barrel. They must have missed it when they'd searched earlier! He was saved! Well, he was still going to die, but free beer was free beer!

It wouldn't be at its best, but it would still be good. Choosing to stop and drink rather than crawl off in search of blood in order to survive may seem like a daft choice to the Southern man, but a Northern man would pick beer every time.

Rathbone felt his life draining away from him. He pulled himself over to the barrel to taste the best beer in the Northeast one last time. A plastic bung was all that stood in his way. He hoped the beer had settled, but he didn't care, he just wanted Bolton. With his last ounce of strength, he unleashed the liquid, and it gushed forth in a waterfall of joy into his mouth, over his face, and soaked his clothes, ridding him of some of the nastier stains.

REECE, UNCHARACTERISTICALLY, POURED HIMSELF A VODKA.

"Humulone," he said wistfully.

Humulone was an alpha acid, which was obvious to him. What wasn't obvious, and what he'd just discovered from searching journals, was that humulone was a chemical responsible for the bitter taste in ale.

Reece had found lupulone, adhumulone, and isohumulone, all chemicals from the species *Humulus Lupulus:* hops. The presence of these acids in each sample couldn't be coincidence. The chemicals were impregnated into Arthur, Sid, and Brian's DNA in varying levels. It was only Rathbone, the converted vampire, who had none of the chemicals present. Yet, his DNA presented a different phenomenon. There were hundreds of DNA building blocks *missing*.

What had caused Reece the most problems since he'd met Sid and company, resulting in countless embarrassments and a near-broken jaw, was also what had altered their DNA and gave them heavenly gifts.

Beer was the key...and not just any beer. He looked at his results again and shook his head. It was Bolton Bitter that gave them their powers.

The phone rang.

BEER GUSHED DOWN RATHBONE'S THROAT, and he was content to die. The cool, but not cold, ambrosia that is Bolton Best Bitter entered his stomach and the goodness spread to every corner of his immortal body, and with it, strength, power, and healing.

He couldn't drink enough as he felt his large intestine knit back together. Sequentially, his colon, his rectal passage, and his anus shared the rehabilitation of the damage caused by the nearly deads, especially the one with the knife strap-on. He'd get his...Oh, he'd get his.

With the major damage taken care of, the regeneration of his eye, burnt hands, broken ribs, ear, and lacerated foot took moments. Rathbone jumped to his feet and ripped the barrel of life-saving Bolton Bitter from its hiding place and held it above his head, rejoicing in its healing goodness, only stopping the torrent once he choked on some sediment.

He threw the barrel with the strength of the immortal through the side of the shed and strode out into the cold winter night. Sunlight was an hour away, but first, revenge was in order. What could these nearly deads do? He was indestructible!

"Prepare to witness the firepower of this fully armed and operational vampire!"

Rathbone went to war. He'd drunk the best part of twenty litres of Bolton Bitter...and he had a lot of beetroots to piss on.

40

SID, ARTHUR, AND BRIAN SAT ON A PARK BENCH. It was half ten in the morning, and they didn't have a clue where to go drinking. Brian had called in sick for the day, and Arthur was on compassionate leave from his plumbing job.

"We're even with Kev, and now, it's fooking war. I want my pub back." Sid lit up a tab. He was into his emergency supply now, and with his eighty-a-day habit, he only had enough for a couple more weeks. He was lucky he still had a load from when he knocked out Bruce Forsyth.

"Sid, you canna even be in the same room as the fooker," said Brian. "You ain't gonna be able to scrap him 'cos that means you'll have to make physical contact with him."

"I ain't touching him, Brian."

"Then what're ya gonna do?"

"I'm gonna give him a bloody good tellin'."

"What good is that gonna do?"

"I don't give a fook. Tonight, I'm getting my fooking pub back!"

Brian threw his hands in the air. "How you gonna do that then, pal?"

"I'm going door-to-door. If them Jehovah Witnesses can do it, then so can I. I'm gonna round up some support."

"They're reet annoying bastards, Sid, but, in all fairness to 'em, in their hearts, they're trying to save all mankind and shit. You're trying to give a bunch of gays a pasting for drinking in your boozer."

"Exactly." Sid was slowly becoming desensitised to homosexuality, he didn't pass out when the word "gay" was used. "If there's a single place in the whole world that will go marchin' in on a pub, mob-handed, to bring back good, manly drinking—it's fooking Middlesbrough!"

"Leave it, mate. The fact is no one, apart from us, likes The Miner's. If we're gonna get the pub back, we're gonna have to do it ourselves."

"How?"

"We need to get you in training, big fella."

"I ain't doing any exercise, like. I've enough in the tank to knock out any bastard who is drinking my Bolton Bitter!"

"Yeah, baby," said Arthur, "but have you got the bottle to take on the Campire? Could you step up to the plate, man?"

"I...I..." Sid looked defeated already. "He's fooking *horrible*," he said, shaking his head. "I've always been pretty liberal with *them lot,* but he's...he's something else."

"Back at that club in Manchester, Sid, something weird happened. It was as if your auras clashed. You were battling without even touching."

Sid pointed a threatening finger. "He didn't ever fooking touch me, Brian!"

Brian held his hands up. "I know, mate."

Arthur nodded. "He's right, Sid, baby. It was only when the Campire tried it on with me that the deadlock broke."

"So what're ya saying?" asked Sid.

"You need to man-up," said Brian.

"Eh?"

"We need to build your Manergy."

Sid screwed up his face. "What're ya talking about, Brian?"

"It's training time, Sid," Arthur said.

"What have I gotta do?"

"To beat this guy," Brian began, "you need to be open-minded. Your homophobia can't take the mincing, so desensitisation is out. You've got a bad back, and your piles are pretty bad, so salsa dancing is out. What we'll be calling on is good, ol' fashioned, blunt-force trauma. Manpower. Heavy-duty, cast-iron, pile-driving man-time that will rattle that Campire so much, it'll straighten out his ancestors. Every time he sees you down a pint, it's gonna feel like he tried kissing the express train." Brian clamped the big man on the shoulder. "Let's start building some manly bombs."

A silence lingered after the inspirational speech.

"Can we have a couple of beers first?" Sid asked.

"Oh, aye."

SANDERSON WAS TIRED, filthy, and currently the most wanted man on the planet. According to the Coalition, he was the sole reason the Agreement was in danger. He was the reason for the attack on the Haemo plant because he wanted all-out war.

"Bitch!" he bellowed and repeatedly bashed the back of his head against the headrest of the clapped-out Vauxhall Astra he was driving to Middlesbrough. It was the third car he'd stolen since breaking out of the Coalition's headquarters, and he was doing his best to cover his tracks.

He had no idea what Caroline was up to. If only she'd told him what she was doing, he would've helped. Now, it was time to get Tillsley and his friends to safety.

Headlights flashed behind him. Sanderson checked his rear-view mirror, hoping it wasn't a Panda calling for back-up. It wasn't. Only one man could drive such a ridiculous, pretentious car. Reece Chambers.

"I DON'T KNOW ABOUT THIS ONE, BRIAN."

"Sid, a belly flop is the manliest dive a man can do."

"When my daddy was cliff-diving in Acapulco, that was pretty manly," said Arthur.

"I ain't having Sid diving into the River Tees, Arthur. This'll do. A gay man can't belly flop. It's a proven fact."

"Can you please hurry up?" asked a middle-aged gent standing behind Sid on the diving board.

"Look, fook off, or I'll throw you off onto the concrete," threatened Brian.

The boys were ten metres up on the diving board of Middlesbrough's municipal swimming pool. Arthur drew a lot of attention from the ladies in his tight, boxer-short style swimwear, and it was making a lot of the men feel inadequate. In fact, his tackle was causing nearly as much of a stir as the two men standing next to him.

"Are you sure these are increasing my Manergy?" Sid asked Brian.

"Aye, manly men ain't afraid to wear Speedos."

Sid didn't like looking at Brian's ice-white bad boys, the front of which sported a pus-yellow stain, which was likely to be picked up by a Geiger counter. "These are too tight, mon," Sid said, pulling the paisley material out of his crack, unwittingly releasing a foul smell and changing the colour of the gusset.

A young boy standing behind Sid on the board burst into tears at the attack on his senses and took the climb of shame to the bottom. This would result in a month of bullying at school, but greater psychological destruction had been done this day.

"CAN YOU HURRY UP, PLEASE" said the lifeguard through a megaphone.

"FOOK OFF, YA LITTLE TWAT!" yelled Brian across the family-filled pool, adding a two finger salute. "Reet, come on, Sid. Belly flop it is, mon."

Arthur started the ball rolling with an arm stand, back double-somersault tuck that was quickly followed by the swordsman with a running bomb into a family of four. Both lads left the pool and spectated from the edge.

No one could take their eyes from the twenty-five stone hairy monster that stood ten metres above the water. Sid's beer belly ensured maximum velocity.

KABBBBBBBBBBBBBOOOOOOOOOOMMMMM!

Shipwrecking waves slammed into the sides of the pool. Young children flew from the water and elderly spectators were soaked, their blue rinses running.

The hippo resurfaced.

"Feel more manly?" shouted Brian.

Sid weighed up the tsumami's aftermath. "Aye. Aye, I do."

Whatever kids hadn't been ushered out of the pool by their mothers soon ran for the hills when the monster took refuge on dry land minus one set of Speedos that had been ripped asunder by the pure Manergy of his dive.

Manpower was growing.

SANDERSON WAS TEN MILES FROM MIDDLESBROUGH. He'd avoided motorways and major roads, and because of the switching of cars, the journey had taken eight hours instead of four. He was close to reaching Tillsley until Chambers had caught him right at the end. Caroline's work no doubt.

She'd sent them all on a merry dance, including Sanderson. Attacking vampire nightclubs and the Occursus party exerted huge pressure on the Coalition to develop Haemo in case of revolt. And, he thought—they all thought—it was a vampire causing the destruction in order to rally the nation.

He and Chambers were actually working for the same person, yet it was Sanderson who'd get the blame for it all. When the smoke cleared, his name would be remembered for endangering the Agreement. As long as Haemo was launched, he didn't give a shit if he was remembered as a villain.

Sanderson drove farther into the countryside and out of the public eye. He turned down a country lane and got out of the rusty, smelly vehicle. Chambers pulled up on the roadside and got out.

"Nice car."

Sanderson looked Chambers' customised car up and down. "Wish I could say the same."

"I've just heard about your little adventure back at the Coalition," said Chambers, chuckling.

"She told you, huh?"

Chambers sat on the Astra's bonnet and nodded. "The bitch phoned me soon after. Until then, I'd no idea who it was pulling my strings."

"I guess that means she's the reason you attacked the Occursus."

Chambers nodded. "She gave me the information and the resources I required. Then, she set me up. She left me at the mercy of Ivansey."

"She controlled Ivansey too?"

"Oh yes. She phoned me out of the blue, tells me about your little stunt, and then claims that she had nothing to do with Ivansey capturing me. That bastard knew everything about me. I told her to get fucked, so she played her ace: She told me about Haemo."

Sanderson raised his eyebrows. "I'm amazed she told you that."

"The Haemo plant on Teesside was manufacturing an injectable form of the drug, but the purpose of that was to give the vampire a choice. She had Ivansey destroy the plant so the Coalition would panic and support the airborne system that would pacify the vampire population without them even knowing it."

"Why did you help her?"

Chambers shrugged. "A member of the Coalition can make things happen, and I required resources for my research. I couldn't have obtained the equipment anonymously without her."

"And why did she want you dead?"

"According to her, she didn't, but, bottom line—she didn't need me anymore. Haemo is getting closer to being pumped into the air, and my actions already initiated the vampire nation's rebellion. They'll bring it down upon themselves and won't even know it."

Sanderson kicked a stone into the hedgerow. "So why did she call you? She must know you're gunning for whoever it was set you up."

"She isn't stupid. She phoned to tell me all about you. She thinks we're gonna make some sort of double team to smuggle Tillsley to safety. Now I know who she is, I can bargain for more, even if I do have to swallow my pride."

Sanderson shook his head. "After all the bullshit you fed me for being part of the Coalition..."

Chambers jumped off the bonnet, irate. "The difference is that I'm saving mankind. I'm going to stop the bloodshed and put an end to these bastards."

"Maybe if someone had told me about it, I could've helped. Fuck me. I would've joined in a heartbeat."

"Caroline always wanted you to become the scapegoat, but she didn't want to put you through your little adventure of escaping the Coalition and killing all your own agents."

"Fuck you," Sanderson snapped, advancing towards Chambers.

"You may be a good soldier, Sanderson, but you can't control your temper. You would've given the game away."

Sanderson regained himself and turned his back on the vampire hunter.

Chambers said, "She's finished with Ivansey now. How about we finish him off?"

"We?"

"You want in, don't you? Everyone thinks it's you who's been leaking the secrets, so it doesn't really matter if we work together, does it?"

Sanderson couldn't argue with the logic.

"Torch the car. I can get you into The Miner's...if you think you've got what it takes," Chambers chided.

"As soon as this is over, I'm going to pay Caroline a visit."

Chambers smiled. "Me too."

"I DON'T WANNA BUILD A FOOKING CHEST OF DRAWERS, BRIAN."

"Exactly. No one does, but assembling furniture is a man's job."

"This better get me The Miner's Arms back."

"All part of the master plan, mate," said Brian knowingly.

"Why the fook are we out here, anyway?"

"Just in case."

Sid, Brian, and Arthur were in The King Henry's car park, a little pub which didn't serve too-bad ale. Sid was equipped with a Black and Decker Workmate, a flathead screwdriver, a Phillips screwdriver, some instructions for some flat-pack furniture, and a large sledgehammer, although he wasn't sure why he'd need such a big hammer.

"This is stupid. Can't we go have a beer first?"

"We did."

"Can't we go again?"

"Put one drawer together, and we'll have a beer break."

Sid mumbled under his breath and set about building the drawers. Brian had bought the cheapest set the store had, guaranteed to have bits missing, warped wood, and misaligned pre-drilled holes. Sid was red with frustration within seconds of looking at the instructions.

"What prick wrote these?" He was never the most astute of scholars, but Einstein himself couldn't have figured out the instructions, which were for a different piece of furniture that hadn't been invented and written in a language that didn't exist. "Fook it!"

Sid opened up the bag of screws and they flew all over the car park even though he'd tried his best to prevent it.

"Fook!"

"Good. Use your aggressive feelings, Sid. Let the hate flow through you," said Brian, cackling from the sidelines.

Sid tried to snap a drawer unit together but only succeeded in snapping it in half and driving a splinter into his flesh. "Bastards!"

"Your feeble skills are no match for the power of the Pink Side."

Sid ignored him. If he could belly flop from ten metres, he could put a drawer together. He grabbed another piece and tried to calm down. He assembled it on the ground and realised that one side panel was two inches longer than its opposite counterpart. "YOU BASTARD!"

Sid looked at the sledgehammer.

"You want it, don't you?" said Brian. "The hate is swelling in you now. Take the weapon. Use it. Strike the furniture down. Give in to your anger. With each passing moment, you make yourself more of Manrage's servant."

Sid tried to shut out Brian's words. *Must finish the last drawer, must drink beer* went through his brain like a mantra.

He picked up the remaining drawer piece. Everything fit together. Everything was perfect. He worked quickly and efficiently, and within minutes, he was finished, with exception of the handle. He searched through the pack. Nothing. He searched through the pack again. Nothing.

"Young fool..." Brian shook his head. "Only now, at the end, do you understand..."

Sid took the sledgehammer and struck the drawer, shattering it into a million pieces. He threw the Black and Decker Workmate over the roof of the pub.

Brian Garforth cackled. The circle was complete.

41

"WHO KNOWS OF SANDERSON'S BETRAYAL?" asked Bwogi. It was the first Coalition meeting since Pervis's murder and the darkness around the table in the Great Hall seemed more foreboding than usual.

"He hasn't contacted anyone since he spoke to Harry Dean yesterday," said Rempstone, reading from his report.

"Not Dean as well..." despaired Bwogi further.

"I don't believe so," said Caroline. She had this all under control. They were so easy to manipulate.

"They were close friends in the army. What makes you so sure?" asked Bwogi.

"Sanderson was paranoid at the best of times. He didn't trust anyone."

"So why go to Pervis?" Bwogi persisted.

"Pervis was on the edge of a nervous breakdown," said Caroline. "The only reason we didn't put him in the ground was because his job never suffered, and by keeping him safe in the Coalition, we could use his skills. Sanderson thought he could use him. Sanderson was never the brightest of men, but with his military know-how, Pervis would've been a dangerous ally."

"So why kill him?" asked Rempstone.

"Pervis was braver than we gave him credit for. Once Sanderson had revealed his plans, there was no other way out. If I hadn't turned up, maybe Pervis would've escaped with a concussion. It was chance that led me to the office for a meeting with Pervis, and when I arrived, Sanderson was there looking agitated. I suggested we move to my office for a whisky in order to calm him down. He agreed, but once there, he pulled a weapon." Caroline didn't need to put on a show and act disturbed by the situation. Everyone knew her as a hard-nosed bitch. She would've aroused suspicion if she'd pretended to be anything else.

"Pervis saved my life. It was me who Sanderson shot at first. Pervis pushed me to the ground and I suffered a glancing blow. Sanderson punished Pervis for his defiance, and then, luckily for me, the guards were quick to react to the gunfire. He was too strong for them though. We'll struggle to apprehend him." She shook her head. "First Sebastian, now Sanderson. We are crumbling."

"This is the lowest point of our history," mourned Bwogi.

"Tomorrow will be worse, as will the day after. Soon, there'll be war," said Caroline.

"Rempstone," Charles snapped. "How are your forces? What's vampire activity been like over the last couple of days?"

Rempstone's fingers tapped anxiously on the table, and he fidgeted awkwardly in his chair. "We're spread too thinly, Charles. The rate of unsanctioned attacks is rising. Since the Occursus, things have gone from bad to worse."

Augustus added to the doom, "News of Tillsley's involvement in Manchester has spread quickly. The population knows we sent him against Ivansey, and Ivansey has gathered more to him. He doesn't hide. He's still in Middlesbrough. Sanderson was right. He's drawn to Tillsley."

"Then let's deal with it," said Caroline. "Get Harry Dean on the phone. He's the best we've got now."

A junior member of the Coalition stood up and went to a console that silently rose from the floor. She pressed a few buttons. Soon, the ringing of a telephone could be heard.

"Harry?" said Caroline as soon as the phone was answered.

"Yeah, what do you want?" The gruff voice piped through speakers to the Coalition.

"It's Caroline."

"Caroline who?"

"From the Coalition," she replied, not a hint of annoyance in her voice.

"Oh, aye," he said. "How you doing?"

"Where are you, Harry?"

She already knew. He'd taken the arduous, four hundred-mile drive to Middlesbrough after talking to Sanderson and positioned himself a couple of hours west, as not to arouse suspicion. "Lake District," he barked.

"I thought you were at Ardvreck Castle, Dean," said Rempstone curtly.

"Yes, *sir*, I was. Thank you for that particular opportunity, *sir*. Unfortunately, though, we're struggling for resources on the ground and I had to sort out another fucking mess here."

Caroline continued, "Have you heard from Sanderson?"

"Yep, not too long ago."

"What exactly did he say to you, Harry?" asked Charles.

"Crazy son of a bitch reckoned Sebastian, not that I knew who he was till I found him dead, was leaking information. Reckoned he was going to warn you lot."

"I have some confidential, yet disturbing, news for you, Harry," said Caroline. "I-I can hardly believe it myself, but Sanderson was the informant." She hoped the added stutter didn't take it too far.

"No...no way." The disbelief in his voice was clear to the council members.

"He killed Pervis and shot me," she added firmly.

"Is that what you're phoning me for?"

"Yes."

Harry sighed wearily. "He was one of the best damn soldiers I ever knew, but he always had that look in his eyes; one which said they'd seen far too much. I always feared I'd have to put him down."

"You need to gather your agents, Harry. Gather as many as you can and get to Middlesbrough," ordered Caroline. "Raze The Miner's Arms to the ground with Ivansey and Tillsley in it. Those two must die tonight, and when you see Sanderson, only lethal force is an option. He'll never go quietly."

"'The Agreement comes first,' ma'am," Harry recited.

"End this quickly, Harry."

The phone went dead.

"Haemo can't come quick enough," said Bwogi.

Caroline couldn't believe how easy it all was.

REECE AND SANDERSON WERE EN ROUTE TO THE MINER'S ARMS. Both men were ready for the battle ahead. Still, Sanderson was wary of his newfound ally.

"Were you involved in Sebastian's set-up?" asked Sanderson.

Chambers laughed. "Yeah, that was a lot of fun."

"How did you manage it?"

"The kidnapping was simple enough. He was always a cocky, arrogant bastard."

Sanderson tried not to laugh. Talk about the pot calling the kettle black.

"He never thought he'd be the victim of a hunter. Caroline told me everything about his movements. The rest was easy."

"And I thought that was the leak plugged. Ha! She's a dangerous woman. Did she give you the details of my escape?"

"Oh, she doesn't know where you are now."

"How did you find me?"

"You took the route I would've taken."

Sanderson noted the smirk on the vampire hunter's face. They were more similar than Sanderson had originally thought, and it annoyed him greatly.

"As I was saying, Sebastian's capture was easy. The use of an automatic rifle and steel chains is a simple yet thoroughly rewarding experience."

"Amen, brother."

"I have a holding pen. Vitrago couldn't have escaped from the contraption I've constructed." Sanderson noticed Chambers' chest puff up with pride. "I dumped Sebastian in there, and then I had some fun."

"For the pure pleasure?"

"No, a necessity. I had to weaken his body. I needed to injure him so that his feral instincts demanded blood. He had to lose control as soon as he was unleashed on those poor, unsuspecting, Nazi scumbags. The torture was a wonderful bonus."

"How did you kill him? Surely he would've regenerated once he had blood."

"Again, the fun you can have with an assault rifle. Plus, the Nazi bastards from the farmhouse were a tough bunch. I took him and locked in the back of a truck. Told them I had a 'queer' with me and asked if they wanted him. The locks on his chains were remote operated. As soon as they took him in the house, I unleashed him."

Sanderson could see the joy in Chambers' face as he regaled the story. Sanity had left this poor soul a long time ago.

"He sunk his teeth into anything and everything, but a well-placed bullet stopped him feeding before he attacked the next target. Soon, all were dead, and he was in a weakened state on the floor, covered in bullet holes. A couple more ended his sick life."

"I saw the forensics report. There were at least six or seven vampires at the scene. Ivansey was one of them. How?"

"I know my craft. I make sure I keep stocks of vampire DNA."

"How on earth did you get Ivansey's?"

A shadow cast over the hunter's face. "When you find your throat being gripped to the point that your head feels like it is going to pop off, you try to wriggle free no matter how futile the efforts. He attacked me outside The Miner's Arms last year, and my nails collected much of his skin. I made sure I cloned plenty as I saw it coming in useful."

Sanderson shuddered, imagining Chambers cleaning his fingernails, desperately scavenging for minute fragments of skin collected from his father's murderer. The farmhouse was a more disturbing image. "Why the...strange... display?"

A grin cut across Chambers' face. "Strange? Fun more like. Caroline never backed her own agents, just you. You were too busy with Tillsley. Surveillance of Ivansey was left to lesser men. I, however, was busy. I tracked him down during his week in Manchester and discovered the extent of his new and bizarre form. Your men couldn't get close to him. Pathetic." He snorted.

Sanderson said nothing. Chambers was right.

"Caroline needed to pin the leak on somebody and Sebastian was the unlucky one. The display was timed perfectly with Ivansey's 'coming out.' That, plus Ivansey's DNA, set his guilt in stone." Chambers laughed and glanced at Sanderson.

"That it did," Sanderson confirmed, rubbing his forehead.

"I needed a piece of equipment for my research and would've been lost without it. Luckily, Caroline needed a job doing and I had a price. I could hardly call that work, though." He laughed again. "And now it's time to put an end to Ivansey and move one step closer to the master plan."

"The implementation of Haemo?"

Chambers was silent for a second before the sickly grin grew even wider. "Maybe not."

Sanderson was confused. If Chambers didn't want to initiate Haemo, what the hell did he want? Sanderson had let his guard down, but this latest revelation rattled him. Sitting next to Chambers, riding through the streets of Middlesbrough, Sanderson wondered what else was going on inside the head of this delusional psychopath. No human being who could formulate the massacre at the farmhouse was of sound mind.

"So, if you don't want the Haemo project implemented, what do you want?"

"I have been a shadow too long. I hate vampires, Sanderson. I hate them more than you can possibly imagine. I have no friends, no family, just nightmares. I don't deserve that. I deserve to be a hero." Chambers' knuckles whitened as he gripped and twisted the steering wheel in frustration and anger. "That fat, worthless piece of shit Tillsley could be a hero. Why does he deserve such a gift? Garforth can kill them with his putrid semen. Rathbone was turned into a vampire! Do you ever wonder why?"

"Every day," Sanderson said succinctly as he stared out of the window. "I've always wondered what sort of weapon could be made if we understood the power of Sid's fist."

Chambers nodded. "That's what I once thought. That's what Caroline believes I am looking for. I'm getting closer to the answer. Their DNA has been altered, mutated by a biological impossibility...Beer."

Sanderson's gaze snapped from the road to Chambers. "What're you talking about?

"Four building blocks make up DNA, both vampire's and human's: guanine, cytosine, thymine and adenine. These four men are different. So far, I have found lupulone, humulone, adhumulone, and isohumulone in the core DNA matrices of these four men." He spoke quickly, excited to share his findings with another human being. "These are chemicals from the hops responsible for the bitterness of beer. I've just scratched the surface. Bolton Bitter is impregnated into Arthur, Sid, and Brian's DNA. Rathbone, the converted vampire, had none, yet, he has building blocks missing. I believe he needs beer where other vampires need blood."

Chambers ignored the road to see the reaction to his research. Sanderson was unnerved by Chambers' intensity and his certainty in his work. "You're insane."

"No, I'm a scientist."

"A fucking mad one."

"I don't know how, but something's altered their DNA, and I'm sure they weren't born like that. It's too much of a coincidence. If their DNA has been altered, can anyone's?"

They drew ever closer to The Miner's Arms and Sanderson chewed over Chambers' ideas of genetic engineering, which he could only foresee ending in failure, most likely death, but there were more pressing issues.

"No matter what," Chambers said, "we need to survive tonight, first. We're gonna have to take down the Coalition's agents and Ivansey's vampires. I've got the tools. They won't know what hit them."

42

SID TILLSLEY WAS READY. He'd trained for this. He'd prepared. He was cured of his homophobia and that meant if he saw one of *them lot* now, he could punch them in the face without fear. He cracked his knuckles, flicked through a copy of *Tits*, squashed a spider with his bare hands, ate a kebab, downed a pint, pissed on the toilet seat...

And went to get his pub back.

ARTHUR PEASLEY WAS READY. He channelled his hate of the vampire race into his fists. He hadn't seen his child since its birth. He'd lost his woman and his pub. He had to unleash these bottled-up emotions in a way that only a man could: by punching things.

Arthur Peasley left the building.

BRIAN GARFORTH WAS READY. His right hand was currently pumping a weapon of mass destruction that would soon deal death. He was Brian Garforth, and he was a swordsman, but tonight, he was a warrior.

Brian Garforth left for war with a fistful of rubbers.

PETER RATHBONE WAS READY. He looked longingly at the cape in his hands. It was covered in piss, shit, explosion marks, stuff he didn't want to talk about, and more shit and piss. It wouldn't survive a wash. It was time to say farewell to an old friend. He'd been treated like shit since he'd become a vampire. The bastards of Middlesbrough had shown nothing but ignorance towards his race. He dropped the cape into the bin.

"No more."

Tonight, he would drink with his own kind, and he'd drink the nectar that made him strong, Bolton Bitter. He would turn his back on mankind and take his rightful place as a vampire.

And he'd get a new cape on Monday when the shops opened.

SID, ARTHUR, AND BRIAN WALKED THROUGH THE DOOR OF THEIR PUB. This was The Miner's Arms. This was not The First Swallow of Summer. This was where they drunk the best beer in the world. This was where they chewed the fat. This was their pub.

"This ain't our fooking pub!" cried Brian.

The sights: paint job, wood, chrome, art, coasters, matching furniture, a new lager tap.

The sounds: posh sound system playing "mood music."

The smells: lavender.

The touch: feet didn't stick to the floor.

The taste: "BOLTON!"

Sid ran to the bar and ordered three pints of Bolton Bitter. Kev pulled the pints way above the legal limit set by trading standards. Sid watched, wide-eyed, as he gained millilitres of ale, and then poured it down his neck as if his life depended on it. He wiped his top lip and begged for more. Brian and Arthur followed suit.

The lads waited for the price of this magic libation. All this chrome and pine meant a shit pub, and a huge price increase. "It's free, lads," said Kev, sporting a straining pink tuxedo and dicky bow. "Bolton Bitter is free to everyone."

HARRY DEAN DOUBLED THE SPEED LIMIT of the single carriageway, overtaking at every opportunity. Intelligence told him that Tillsley had entered The Miner's and Ivansey was already inside, upstairs.

He had orders to use whatever force necessary, and he was going to need it because there were at least forty vampires in the vicinity.

"Sanderson..." he said forlornly.

All that mattered was upholding the Agreement. Harry faced the situation he'd feared the most. Back-up was on its way, and he hoped to heaven he was sent some good men.

THE CAMPIRE ADMIRED HIMSELF in the mirror of Kevin Ackroyd's bedroom. He'd given Kevin a substantial sum of money for the "pleasure," and also to evict his ghastly spouse. He'd had to redecorate and fumigate before he even considered getting undressed in such a room.

Tonight, he looked immaculate, as he did every night. It had taken him an hour, and the help of Peaches Slackring and three others, just to get into his leather trousers that looked painted on. He wore no shirt to give his darlings the pleasure of admiring his Adonis-like body. The leather jacket, which enveloped his broad, perfect shoulders, had been polished to give almost a mirrored surface, as had his trousers. His moustache was bushier than ever.

Tonight, he would be united with his brothers, and he would finally belong. He would create a new world.

"Show time!"

THE LADS WERE HAMMERED. It hadn't taken long. They sat at a plastic-and-chrome table in the middle of the pub, hammering it down. But, when the lights suddenly dimmed, it reminded them that things weren't quite normal in this pub of theirs.

A spotlight shone down on the door behind the bar leading to Kev's living quarters. The mood music faded out, and The Scissor Sisters took its place. The lads first saw a pair of red high-heel shoes making their way down the stairs. Skin-tight, leopard-skin tights were next, which caught their attention—until the bump in the tights meant that the wearer was packing heat.

Peaches Slackring made his entrance.

43

"NOT THAT FREAKY LITTLE SOD!" said Brian, fingering his Cumapult.

"Good evening, gentlemen," said the squeaky-voiced midget, Peaches Slackring. "We've been expecting you."

"Yeah, but were you expecting this?" said Brian, rising, and drawing his weapon.

Peaches screamed as rubbers hit him square in the face, but—nothing happened, no explosion of ash. "My god, what's *wrong* with you!" he screamed.

"You ain't a vampire?" asked Brian, confused.

"No, you imbecile! I'm only five foot tall, for heaven's sake! *Oh—gak—*! It's like vomit!" He pulled off his feather boa and mopped up the best he could. "It burns!"

Brian began reloading the Cumapult.

"What's that, Brian?" asked the inquisitive Sid.

"You don't wanna know, big fella," said Brian.

"Disgusting!" cried Peaches. "This is worse than the time I was locked in a cage with a horny camel!"

Sid's eyes narrowed at Brian. Something was afoot. Sid himself was doing well, though. The man training had done him proud, and he hadn't passed out when he saw Peaches. He felt ready to deal with anything...

Twenty naked vampires ran down the stairs, past Peaches, and into the pub, dancing to music that drove them into a frenzied, camp rapture. They danced around the three heroes, who quickly stood up, taking back-to-back positions. This was a little more testing for young Sidney.

"Brian...I...I...can't..." Sid was in a scared place.

"You can. Do it for the Bolton," reassured Arthur. "Remember your training!"

"Wait for the Campire, lads," warned Brian. "If we knock him out, the rest will leg it. Be strong, Sid."

Sid shook but held his ground. He thought of *Tits*, his holy book, and it gave him strength.

With a final, gay drumbeat, the music stopped and all the vampires dropped to the floor and bowed their heads. The music changed, and the delicate tones of Bizet's *Carmen* washed over the pub. It was the pub's first dose of culture since Brian hit a student who looked like Harry Potter.

The music had a soothing influence on Sid. He'd never heard such beautiful music before. This all came crashing down when he saw what walked down the stairs.

He could just about cope with twenty wangers swinging through the air, but the Campire making his entrance was something else.

"Hold strong, Sid," urged Brian as the big man shut his eyes. "Once we start punching things, you'll be reet."

Sid didn't say anything. Beads of sweat cascaded from his forehead.

"I'm so glad you could join us, gentlemen," said the Campire, strutting his stuff around the three friends. "I knew you couldn't resist that horrible, brown concoction you crave so desperately." He sneered at the pump. "Kevin, bring these men another drink and a cocktail for me."

"Coming right up, sir!"

At first, Brian hadn't noticed, as the ale had captivated him, but now he clocked Kev's ridiculous, pink tuxedo.

"You look fooking stupid, Kev."

Kev shrugged. "Money in the bank, son. Money in the bank."

Brian looked away in disgust. "Look, you," he said to the Campire. "What the fook...?" he was drowned out by the sound of a cocktail shaking. "Kev! What the fook are you doing?"

"Making a cocktail," replied Kev. "It's a Cosmopolitan, you uneducated little prick."

"I know what it fooking is!" shouted Brian, annoyed that his intelligence had been questioned.

"How do you know that?" asked a suspicious Tillsley, scratching his head in thought.

"What?" Luckily for Brian, the front door opening created a diversion. That diversion was Rathbone, a capeless Rathbone.

"Rathbone, get your arse over here! Where's your cape?" asked Brian.

Rathbone pretended not to notice him and sat himself down at the bar. He'd had enough of being treated like shit by mankind. He had a point to prove and that point was that he liked Bolton Bitter.

"Pint." He demanded off Kev, who reluctantly pulled the ale after garnishing the Cosmopolitan.

Peaches Slackring collected the tray of drinks and took them over to the lads who downed their ales before the Campire received his.

"Another six of them," said Sid, managing to engage Peaches in conversation. Sid wasn't sure what he was but came to the conclusion that he was too short to be one of *them lot*. The only fair way to deal with this little fooker would be to stick him in a suitcase like Roger Moore did to Nick Nack in *The Man with the Golden Gun*.

"Rathbone!" shouted Brian, but he was ignored. "Prick!"

The Campire lounged into a designer beanbag that had been dragged to the centre of the room for him. "So, Sid, you come at last. In this room are twenty brave boys wanting freedom, and it's time you gave it to them. I want to be united with my brothers."

Sid didn't have a clue what he was on about, and the Campire read his thoughts. It wasn't difficult.

"The Tillsley Special is what these men want. They want you to take away their testicles with a swing of your mighty fist. If you do that, then we will convert your pub to the way it was, and the beer will remain free. When I find a brother who wants to join my flock, I'll bring them here for conversion. That's the only thing you have to do. That is the only price."

Sid stood defiantly. The training was working, but nagging doubts forced their way into his mind. There was no way he was touching the skin on another man's sack, but it meant free Bolton. He looked around him, and twenty vampires stood, tackles out. Could he fight them all? If they were clothed, it would be easy, but what if a wanger hit him when he was fighting? Being between a rock and a hard place was a saying Sid didn't want to use right now. It wasn't a choice he wanted to make. So, Brian made it for him.

"Well, you know what I think? I think you should take a dose of your own medicine." Brian pulled the fully stocked Cumapult from behind his back and pulled the trigger.

The Campire ducked, and the condom filled with the foul liquid missed him by a yard. Brian adjusted his aim. A vampire jumped up to protect his master, taking the load full in the face. He raked his nails deep into the flesh of his own cheeks, trying to rid himself of the burning poison. He screamed for a moment and then crumbled into ash.

Arthur jumped into action and landed a spinning, roundhouse kick into the nearest naked vampire, sending him crashing into his neighbour. Brian unleashed a couple more missiles taking down another vampire. "Come on, Sid!"

A mass of writhing, oiled, muscular bodies pushed towards the trio. Brian's weapon was knocked from his hand, and the sheer weight of numbers meant Arthur couldn't use his karate, and a big shot to the kidney took all the wind out of him. Sid stood, impotent, fighting his internal battle: sack versus wanger.

"Sid, for fook's sake! They're going for the Bolton!" Brian lied.

The vampire hunter was back! He killed two vampires with his first punch. The right hook carried enough momentum to take it through the first vampire and into the second. A jab, an uppercut, a headbutt and a right cross later, Sid waded out of the depleted circle of vampires and went to the bar.

"Pint of Bolton, please, Kev."

"ENOUGH!" screamed the Campire. "My brothers! I cannot lose my brothers!"

The remaining vampires spread out. Two held onto Arthur, who sported a black eye and a cut lip, and two held onto Brian who had a broken nose. The vampires left a line of sight between the Campire and Sid, who stood next to Rathbone, ordering his third pint of Bolton.

"Y'all right, Rathbone?"

"Not bad."

"Tillsley!" said the Campire.

Sid ignored him.

"TILLSLEY!" he screamed. That got his attention, because Kev, who knew where the money was, refused to serve him another ale.

"Eh?" said Sid turning round.

"You have killed more of my brothers. But still, I have one more proposition for you. I'm going to give you one more chance, even though you don't deserve it."

The Campire clapped his hands, and out of the toilets came a stretcher on which a man was strapped, completely clothed with the exception of his testicles, which were exposed.

Sid looked quizzically at the old man strapped down with his mouth covered with duct tape. He was unscathed, physically, but not mentally. He looked around wide-eyed in panic.

Realisation dawned on Sid.

"Let him go!" The most important man in Sid's life was in mortal danger.

"Freddy Buggleswaite!" screamed Brian, and received a kick to the stomach, causing him to double up.

"Let him go!" screamed Sid again.

Freddy Buggleswaite—Bolton Brewery's chief brewmaster, award winner, genius, and life-giver—was god to Sid Tillsley.

The Campire laughed a truly villainous laugh, albeit a camp one. He pulled a knife from his coat and placed it under Freddy Buggleswaite's scrotum, whose eyes gleamed with terror at the touch of the cold blade.

"You can't do that. It will ruin everything," Sid pleaded. "He won't be able to brew Bolton!"

"Then give us what we want."

"I...canna!" Sid dropped to his knees.

The Campire made a sudden movement as if he was about to perform the *coup de grâce*.

"NO! You can't take his nuts away! He'll never be able to brew Bolton the same if he's got the woman's hormones!" cried Sid.

"You have a choice, Sid. Time, as well as my patience, is running out. I will end everything in your life if you don't help me. I'll castrate this man, ending your pitiful supply of beer. All you have to do...."

Sid became aware of two vampires approaching from each side. Two scrotums entered his peripheral vision, causing him to cower and shake.

"Sid, you can't let them do it..." pleaded Arthur. "Just help them."

What choice did he have? He had to save the Bolton.

Sid rose with two massive uppercuts.

"YES!" screamed the Campire as the scrotums of the two vampires disappeared. He raised his hands in the air in triumph, much to the relief of Freddy Buggleswaite. However, his celebration lasted only a microsecond, as Sid's uppercuts continued skywards and into the jaws of the freed vampires. Their heads rocked back—and they exploded.

"Fuck you!" screamed the Campire and moved to cut Bolton Bitter off at the source, but a bullet took him reeling to the floor.

Harry Dean stood at the doorway, rifle in hand, smoke rising from the barrel and blowing in the cold winter wind. Coalition agents stood behind, all armed.

Sid ran over to the brewmaster, untied him from the cart, and pulled the duct tape from his mouth.

"Thank you," the man gasped. "W-w-what's going on?"

"Don't worry about that, now, Mr Buggleswaite. We need to get your knackers out of here."

The vampires were caught off guard, but only for a second. They formed a shield around the Campire and prepared for battle. A battle is what they got.

Bullets ripped into the pub and into the vampires.

Arthur and Brian crawled over to where Sid was flat on the deck with the shocked brewmaster. "We need to get him out of here." Sid was functioning again. He was more comfortable with bullets rather than wangers flying around his head.

The vampires were down to ten after Sid and Brian's attack and were taking fire, but they could regenerate. Half of them protected the Campire, and the other half charged the bullets of the twenty agents lined up outside The Miner's.

The lads crawled along the floor by the side of the bar. Arthur led, and then Brian, Buggleswaite, and lastly Sid.

"Lads, go on without me. I need to sort this all out," said Sid.

"Don't do anything stupid!" shouted Brian over the din of gunfire.

"Just keep Mr Buggleswaite safe. Bolton cannot die!"

The three men continued along the floor towards the front door, and Sid met up with Kev, shotgun in hand, hidden behind the bar. "Eh'up, our Kev."

"Sid," acknowledged the barman.

"What's Rathbone doing?"

"He's still at the bar."

They heard a thump, and Rathbone's face appeared at the entrance to the bar. Blood covered his face and the end of his nose was missing from where a bullet had taken it clean off. He said nothing but got back up on his barstool and continued drinking his ale.

"What're you gonna do, Sid?" asked Kev.

"I need to sort this fooking mess out." The hero took a glass from under the bar, placed it on the stand under the Bolton Bitter beer engine, and pulled himself a pint while standing in the middle of a gunfight.

Kevin shook his head.

Brian, Arthur, and Buggleswaite made it outside and crawled to the agents. Harry Dean stopped firing on the vampires and met the three men. "Where's Tillsley?"

"He's behind the bar," said Brian. "Who are you?"

"It doesn't matter." Harry turned to a subordinate. "Barny, take them to the van."

"Hang about, our mate's in there. We ain't fooking going anywhere," said the defiant cumslinger.

"I'll put a fucking bullet in—"

Brian interrupted him, "Yeah, yeah, you must be from the council— what's it called?—the Coalition? Anyroad, is Sanderson on his way?"

Harry looked at Brian quizzically. "You know Sanderson?"

"Aye, good bloke. Sorted us out for beers and has always been good to the big fella."

Harry considered the weasley little man who knew a lot of things he shouldn't. "My orders are to destroy those freaks in there, along with your friend Tillsley. There're no civilians in there. Why don't I order my sergeant to blow the place to kingdom come?" He nodded to an officer who held a grenade launcher.

"Well, firstly," started Brian, "the grenade is gonna do fook all to most of them bastards. They'll scarper as soon as you fire it and take you out in the open. Secondly, that Sanderson was a good bloke and had a lot of faith in our Sid. Thirdly, without Sid throwing his fists, you're fooked."

"Why?"

Brian pointed at The Miner's roof where twenty more vampires stood, waiting to bring death.

44

CHAMBERS AND SANDERSON PULLED ROUND THE CORNER and took in the scene. The streets were empty because of the riot. Vampires swarmed everywhere, and the Coalition's soldiers stood outside the pub, firing in controlled bursts.

"Ivansey must be inside," said Chambers.

"Then let's get to it." Sanderson was hungry for battle. "Come on, what're you waiting for?"

Chambers said nothing. Only when Sanderson turned to face him did he continue. "Caroline never wanted you to escape the Coalition. She's never rated a soldier so highly, but even she thought you'd be killed trying to escape. I'd washed my hands of her. Despite her claims of innocence, she left me for dead at the hands of the vampire who killed my father."

"Then let's do something about it!"

Chambers went on as if Sanderson hadn't spoken, "But then, she offered me something. Something exceptional."

Sanderson's eyes narrowed. He moved slightly so that he could reach his concealed weapon in the quickest time possible.

"Haemo is the work of a genius, but its carrier is something else. A vampire scientist has actually developed a viral carrier to transport it into the body. Can you believe that?"

"What of it?"

"If the carrier can transport a chemical through the vampires autoimmune defence system, then think what it can do to a human's. The effect will be ten, a hundred, a thousand fold, who knows? I may be able to redesign DNA, *my DNA*, to replicate Tillsley's. With Haemo and its carrier, I could turn my fists into weapons."

"And I guess I'm the other end of the bargain, righ—" Sanderson made his move, but never unholstered his gun. Instead, he doubled up, unable to speak, move, or even think. Metal spikes coming out of the car seat had punctured his legs.

"It was six months ago when I first showed someone this car. Tillsley mocked me because there were no weapons on board, so I decided to make some alterations. You have the pleasure of being the first to try them out."

For Sanderson, the agony was too much to bear.

"Electricity is such a simple beast, is it not?"

Sanderson was weak, but he was a fighter. He reached for Chambers throat but was back fisted in the face. There was no chance of fighting back, not in this state, not against this man.

"Caroline will give me Haemo and the carrier. I have their DNA. I don't need those leaches anymore. Ivansey can murder all of them. Say goodbye to your friends."

Chambers turned the car around. There was no coming back from this. Sanderson's senses exploded once more, and finally, darkness came.

"CLOSE COMBAT!" YELLED HARRY DEAN, seeing the new threat of the vampires on the roof.

The agents split into teams of threes. In each group, one man continued his assault on the inside of the pub, suppressing the vampire attack and another drew an electrified baton, while the third pulled out an assault shotgun. The vampires jumped down from the roof and attacked.

"Stick to the plan!" commanded Dean.

"Use Sid. He's your only chance," said Brian calmly.

Sid stood behind the bar, pulling pints and wobbling from alcohol consumption.

"He's pissed," Harry said. "He's not gonna be any good!"

Sid took a seat on the floor behind the bar, a geyser of beer relaying his position.

"Shoot the beer pump."

"What?"

"Shoot the fooking beer pump!" urged Brian.

Harry took dead aim and blew the Bolton Beer engine to smithereens.

"NOOOOOOOOOOOOOOOO!" the wail of Sid, Kevin, and Rathbone was a terrible lament.

Sid and Rathbone attacked.

Sid, one hand on knee, got up from behind the bar, and with only a minor stumble, waded into the vampires.

"Leave the vampire's in the pub!" called Dean, and the agents with assault rifles went to close-quarter fighting.

"Freddy," Brian said to the Bolton brewmaster. "Leg it, mon! Forget what you saw and leg it."

"Thanks for saving me," said Freddy, pale and in shock.

"You can repay me by brewing beer to the same standard you always have."

The old man patted Brian on the shoulder. "Come by for another visit and I'll sort you out for a good piss-up." The old man did a runner.

Brian and Arthur ran in to back up Sid, while Rathbone got stuck in attacking the agents. A shotgun blast to the chest sent him scurrying back behind the bar to where Kev was crying into his pink bow tie.

Harry marvelled at the demolition derby and could see why Sanderson placed his faith in the man from Middlesbrough.

Vampires attacked Sid but none got anywhere near him. His hands were lightning. Within a minute, ten had turned to ash. However, Sid slowed down as did the punches. Vampires drew closer, venturing into striking distance, and suddenly, Sid hit the deck like a sack of spuds.

"SID!" yelled Brian. Arthur defended his fallen chum with karate of an exceptional standard, roundhouse kicks a-plenty. Brian, however, took a different route. He saw his Cumapult lying on the floor and made a dart for it. Rolling, he came up onto one knee with the lethal weapon in his hands. He was a badass once more.

"Hey fun boys!" he cried, and vampires died. The five survivors regrouped in front of the Campire.

"Sid, what happened, man?" asked Arthur.

"A...a...wanger touched my leg, mon. A...wanger."

"Forget that, they've taken the Bolton!"

Sid unleashed a mighty bellow causing the vampires to cower before going in for one final assault. Brian took out the Cumapult's clip. Only one left. He decided it best to save it for the Campire in case Sid couldn't finish the job. But soon, nothing remained but ash and the figure of Sid Tillsley, hands on knees, wheezing. Only the Campire stood strong, proud to the last, picking dust from his moustache while the battle outside the pub continued to rage.

"So, Sidney," said the Campire, "once more, it's just you and I. All those months ago, when we met, who would've thought it would come to this?"

Sid stood up straight. "I don't know who you are, but you took it too far when you threatened the Bolton, lad."

"Quite." The Campire looked Arthur up and down. "You really are an amazing-looking man."

"Fooking stop it!" said Sid and stepped, left foot forward, to land the right. The Campire didn't flinch.

Sid's hand was stayed.

"Do it, Sid!" shouted Arthur and Brian in unison.

Sid gritted his teeth and tried to build up the Manergy. He'd trained for this. His right fist, cocked and ready to fire, shook as the internal struggle between fear, confusion, and stupidity played hell with his delicate mental state.

"He can't," said the Campire smugly. "I told you before, we are poles apart, yin and yang. He cannot kill, and I cannot bring myself to kill him. Other vampires will join my cause. The Agreement has trapped them for hundreds of years, and they long to break from it and to belong. I give them that. I will mourn the loss of my brothers, but there'll be more."

"Sid, hit him!" cried Brian.

Sid stepped forward again, knuckles whitening, but the Campire let out a high-pitched scream stopping Sid in his tracks.

"Chase me, Sid! Chase me!" the Campire squealed as he ran round in a small circle, waving his arms and generally mincing about.

Sid did no such thing, and instead, ran for the safety of the bar.

"You see," the Campire said, facing Brian and Arthur. "He cannot harm me, and look who comes to my aid."

Brian turned to see a wall of semi-naked vampires charging into the pub, diving through the windows and clambering through the doorway. It was up to him to save the day. "Well, if he can't do it, maybe I can." Brian stepped up, pointing the Cumapult in the Campire's face.

Brian wasn't here to play games. Counts of three were for twats and Southerners.

The Campire snarled.

Brian pulled the trigger.

"Is that all you have?" said the Campire, picking the empty rubber from his moustache.

"Ah fook. That was me last one." Brian's shoulders slumped. "I was pumping dry by the end. Me balls were like dried prunes, they were."

The vampires charged into the lads from the 'boro, but the agents attacked them from behind. Sid pulled the malt whisky optic down from the bar and drowned his sorrows. Bolton was medicinal, but this was getting pissed. Kev, seeing the look on Sid's face, didn't dare say anything.

Arthur and Brian dropped onto the floor as the vampires made a shield around their icon. The din was almost impossible to bear as the agents unloaded their weapons into a wall of flesh. Brian crawled away and Arthur followed Brian into the gents.

"Sid isn't gonna be able to fight the Campire, man," shouted Arthur above the noise.

"I know. We didn't have enough time to train him up. I need one more shot from the Cumapult. Just one more."

"You got any spares?"

Brian emptied his pocket. "Just one rubber left, but it's empty."

"I'll guard you in the bogs."

"Let's do it."

Brian Garforth went to wank for victory.

They reached the toilets. "What's all this funky shit, man?" Arthur read the options of the coin-operated contraption that had replaced the old condom machine. "What's that stuff? Force? Ain't that herbal Viagra?"

"It sure is," said Brian. "'Force,'" he read, "'The strongest herbal hardon pill known to man.'"

"Hold on, baby." Arthur landed an accurate side kick into the vending machine, buckling the metal and creating enough room to get his fingers round the back of the panelling. He ripped the panel off with his mighty karate grip.

Brian got stuck into the herbal pills. "How many will I need?"

"I don't know, but the quicker you choke the chicken, the quicker we can put that son of a bitch in the ground."

Brian ate the contents of the dispenser. To any other man, this horrific overdose would've caused severe health problems: facial flushing, difficulty discerning blue from green, headache, dyspepsia, and the risk of heart attack. But, this wasn't any normal man, this was a Northern man. And this Northern man was a swordsman.

"Is it working?" asked Arthur desperately.

"Nah, this fooking shit is for Souther..." Brian was interrupted by a...stirring. Everything hit him at once: his face flushed bright red; a cracking headache split his skull; acute indigestion made its presence known, and the sky through the toilet window, for some reason, looked green.

And then, like a tidal wave, blood flowed.

45

RATHBONE STROKED HIS CHIN when Arthur and Garforth went to the toilet together. This was his chance to get back at Garforth who left him in the hands (and worse) of those bastard Allotmenteers.

Rathbone, being the greasy, horrible, little bastard that he was, managed to avoid detection walking past the agents and the fighting vampires. No one noticed him. No one except the Campire, who recognised the repugnant aura as soon as it was within ten feet of him.

"Ah, the curious one."

"Whatever," dismissed Rathbone. "Look, Sid's mates are in the toilets together, if you're interested."

"Why are you telling me this?"

Rathbone ignored him and went back to the bar to steal some brandy.

The Campire considered whether it was a trap, but he could read Rathbone's thoughts and they were pure evil. The Campire would take pleasure killing the weasel...and he would take exceptional pleasure in Arthur Peasley.

BRIAN SAT ON THE TOILET IN THE MINER'S ARMS' GENTS, his eyes tightly closed while he tried to ignore the gunfire in the background and remember some of his prettier experiences.

"Come on, man! Are you nearly done?" Arthur shouted over door.

"It ain't gonna happen with you fooking talking to me!"

"Hurry up! It doesn't sound good out there. Come on, Brian, you've had enough of them pills to give the Jolly Green Giant the biggest one he ever had!"

"Arthur, thinking of the Jolly Green Giant with a lob-on is not gonna help, for fook's sake!"

The door opened and in minced the Campire. "Hello, Arthur, fancy finding you here?"

Arthur threw some airborne karate punches with an intensity indicative of taking care of business.

"Ooh! I don't mind a little bit of rough." The Campire winked.

BRIAN LOOKED DOWN AT HIS MEMBER. For him, it was enormous. Once afflicted, there was only one thing that could take it away: a fight or a fuck. The fight was here, but so, still, was the throbbing.

He could hear the struggle going on outside the cubicle. He needed to save his friend. He tried desperately to get the beast back in its cage. All the emotions running through his body should've caused his old man to wilt quicker than when he got it out at the clap clinic, but this boner was going nowhere.

"Get off me, you...sick...bastard!"

Hearing Arthur's cries, Brian pulled up his pants, pulled up the trousers of his red wool suit as best he could over his steel member, and doubled over in agony as the trousers pushed it into his body.

"SID," SAID RATHBONE, brandy bottle in hand, much to the disdain of Kevin, who would've said something if his pub hadn't already been shot to pieces. "Arthur and Brian are in the bogs."

Sid, who was dangerously drunk, slurred, "Sshoo, I'm happy here—*hic!*—alone with this whishhky." He looked longingly at the broken beer engine and took a massive swig from the bottle.

"The vampires said that Kev keeps a spare barrel of Bolton in the bogs."

Even though it made no sense at all, Sid saw it as a chance. He was drunk and an idiot. He got to his feet, banging off the bar, the optic wall, and the bar again. Finally, he staggered into the lounge area, and after a big stumble into a couple of vampires, whom he killed for their rudeness, he headed for the toilets.

THE CAMPIRE HAD ARTHUR AGAINST THE WALL, his hands scooted around the beautiful man's toned, ripped body like an octopus with previous convictions for molestation who was enjoying reoffending. Arthur used his karate as best he could to swat the hands of the Campire, but the Campire was too quick for Arthur when put under this sort of pressure. The Campire was just toying with him. He could kill him any time he wanted.

"Get the fook off me, man!"

"You'd prefer me to play rough, would you?"

The Campire drove his head into Arthur's nose, adding to his black eye and cut lip. Arthur's head smashed into the wall tiles behind him. The combined effect brought a blackness, which he fought with all his will.

The Campire threw him to the toilet floor and laughed. "Where are you little man?" he called to Brian. "Are you too scared to help your friend? Come out when you're ready, and death will be waiting."

BRIAN WAS IN SEVERE PAIN and did his best to stand up, but his red woollen trousers were ripped asunder, and his paisley pants protruded through with the red glow of his affliction. "Shite!"

Brian may have been a womaniser, a terrible father, a burden on society, a thief, a crook, and a right wanker, but he was a good friend. He slammed open the door of the toilet in order to rescue his mate.

ARTHUR LAY ON THE FLOOR, still groggy from the headbutt and the fall, with the Campire straddled on top of him. Arthur could feel the Campire's moustache tickling his cheeks.

The Campire whispered into his ear. "I don't care how beautiful you are, I want you dead. I want everyone in this town dead."

Arthur had to fight. He mustered all his strength and reached around to grab the Campire in a headlock. He pulled the Campire's head to his chest, and heard a loud ripping sound.

What the fuck was that? he thought.

SID STAGGERED TO THE DOOR, stumbling and mumbling, "Have to get...Bolton. Need...a fooking pint—*hic*—like."

HARRY DEAN RELOADED for what felt like the hundredth time of the day. He'd lost half his agents, but they were fighting so bravely. The shotgun and electric batons were working well, and only a dozen vampires remained.

Suddenly, the vampires stopped fighting. "Hold fire!" he yelled. His men needed the break. The Campire was gone. The agents followed the eyes of the vampires that looked past Sid and into the gents' toilets.

WHAT SHOULD BRIAN DO? His friend was being smothered by the Campire whose disabling, tight, leather trousers had split. Brian was confronted with the sight of a plucked, bleached, vampire ringpiece.

"Help, Brian! Get...get...this fucking thing off me!"

Brian was scared. His boner hadn't receded a millimetre, and, if anything, it was still growing, causing him to feel lightheaded. He had to save his friend, but his boner stuck out—not surprisingly—like a massive erection, and the Campire thing would have his wicked way with it. He couldn't beat the vampire with physical power, and Sid was too scared to fight. How could he save his friend?

"The Force...Brian...use the Force...," came the weak voice of Arthur.

Brian looked once more at the Campire's exposed ringpiece...and knew what he had to do.

Brian thought of England...

BRIAN SWAM through the cool currents of the sea and the water soothed his body. The distant call of a gull echoed softly against the towering cliffs next to him. It was so tranquil, floating on the North Sea with his childhood sweetheart.

She swam to shore and beckoned him. The beach was deserted, and on this mid-summer's evening, they lay next to each other on the sand and made sweet, beautiful love under the stars. He reached the moment. The exquisite moment...

SID OPENED THE TOILET DOOR.

"OOOOOOHHHHHHH YA BASTARDS!" cried Brian.

HARRY DEAN, HIS AGENTS, THE VAMPIRES, AND SID, for a brief second, witnessed the look of utter contentment on the Campire's face, and the look of guilty relief on Brian Garforth's. An explosion of dust ended the vision of forbidden passion. The dust settled, and all that was left was an unconscious Arthur, and Brian, on his knees, pants round his ankles with a small pile of ash sat on the end of his waning member.

"Dirty bastard!" shouted Rathbone.

That broke the trance everyone was under. The vampires, on seeing the death of their icon, ran for their lives. The agents, exhausted and mostly injured, didn't give chase as they were spent...like Brian was.

Brian looked at Sid. Sid looked at Brian. Even though Brian had saved the day, he realised trouble was afoot.

Sid threw up and passed out.

46

HARRY SPENT TIME WITH HIS AGENTS. They were soldiers, good and true, and that's why he picked them. The medical squad took away the glorious dead. It would take a long time for the survivors to get over the sights and sounds of the day. All of them had put their lives on the line, and he would never forget it. He'd given the barman a wedge of cash, and he was now providing the boys with refreshments.

Harry himself stayed away from the bar. There were some battles he didn't need to fight right now.

What a crazy day. He'd seen Tillsley in full flight, and the rumours were true; he was a one-man army against the vampire. He'd killed twenty with his bare hands. Arthur was a hell of a fighter too, brave as a lion, and he looked so familiar. Then, there was that greasy, little, horrible bastard who had somehow been turned into a vampire. And last, but not least, Brian. What a day he'd had.

Sanderson had kept all this quiet, but Harry suspected he'd tried to drop a clue with his last words to him: "Tillsley is special. He needs his friends around him." He'd wanted to keep it from the Coalition, but that wasn't going to happen after the entire squad saw Brian and Ivansey's...*encounter*...in the gents'.

Orders were to finish off Tillsley, which wouldn't be difficult as he was still unconscious on the floor. He hadn't moved since he witnessed Ivansey's...unusual demise. Harry was to kill Tillsley's friends too.

"Is everyone ready to leave?" Harry asked his agents. He looked for all the nods. "Make your way to the vehicles. Peterson?"

"Yep," said the youngster, his arm in a sling from where Sanderson grazed him, a giant bruise coloured his jaw.

"Stay here with me. You'll help me clean up." The other agents knew what he meant and filed out, helping the wounded. "We'll debrief back at the Coalition," he called after them.

Once the agents were gone, Harry conversed with Peterson who told him about his last encounter with Sanderson and his escape from Coalition headquarters.

"You really think Sanderson was set up?" asked Harry.

"It's no secret that I look up to him, sir, but the best thing he could have done was kill me. He let me live. He told me he was set up. I believe him."

"What a mess," said Harry, draining a glass of water, wishing it was something stronger. "We've got orders to kill Sid, his friends, and any witnesses. What do you think?"

"Sanderson wanted to protect them for a reason, sir. You saw what these men can do. The way things are going, we may need them. War is on its way. Ivansey was a totem for those vampires. Sid can be a totem for mankind."

Harry looked over to where the big man lay in a pool of his own vomit.

"I've never disobeyed an order in my life, kid, and do you know what, before all this shit came down, nor had Sanderson. Sid looks like he can bring change to anyone."

"Yes, sir."

Harry made his decision. "These men have to disappear. This has to be seamless, Peterson. We're dead if not."

"Arrrrrrrrrrgggghhffffookin 'ell!" Sid rejoined the land of the living.

Ten minutes later, the three lads were all sitting in silence, all a few feet away from each other, staring at the floor, while Harry took them through everything.

The three lads all needed death certificates. Brian and Arthur had to quit their jobs, which didn't seem to bother them. Anything that linked them to their names had to die. They'd be wiped off the written face of Teesside, forever.

Sid was quiet, although he looked terribly hungover. His friends kept looking over at him, with the utmost concern on their faces. "Who was the other civvy that was tied to the table?" asked Harry.

"Who?" said Brian, putting on a bad job of acting innocent.

"There was a man tied up who Sid saved."

"He's just an old fella who drinks here from time-to-time. Our Sid don't like seeing the elderly picked on. We're the only family he's got, so don't worry."

Harry took a second and considered the situation before letting it go. "OK."

Brian breathed a visible sigh of relief.

"What about Rathbone? Where's he?"

"He legged it with the vampires."

"We can say he died with the other vampires. Has he got a job?"

"Don't be daft," said Brian. "Besides, I can't imagine there being many records of the twat."

"Family?"

"None that speak to him."

"You'll have to tell him he's officially dead, just like you are, Brian. Can you do that?"

"Aye, if I have to talk to him, like."

"Good." Harry turned to the bar. "Last is you, Kevin. I noticed that you have chosen a different name for the pub. Have you registered it?"

"'Course not," he said, offended.

"You need to. The name 'The Miner's Arms' must be stricken from the records, and you'll need to sign the pub over to your wife as we're going to need a death certificate for you too, I'm afraid."

Kevin crossed his arms defensively. "I won't fooking sign over to her."

"There's an easier way," said Harry cocking and pointing his gun at the landlord's fat belly.

Kevin dropped his head."Very well."

"What about them?" asked Peterson, pointing to the group of lads at the corner of the bar watching Tarrant on the TV.

"Where'd they come from?" asked Harry, surprised.

"The lads are always here," said Kevin. "You need not bother about them."

Harry paused for a second, reflecting internally, before coming to a decision and nodding. "We'll be in touch. You're best not to talk of this to everyone. If it gets back to the Coalition, you'll be dead and so will we." The lads didn't look like they were going to talk to anyone ever again.

"Come on, Peterson."

The two agents left The First Swallow of Summer.

BRIAN WAITED UNTIL THE AGENTS WERE WELL AWAY. The lack of conversation in the pub tortured him.

"Sid...I—"

"I saw, Brian!" cried Sid. "I *saw!*" He got up, covered his eyes, and ran out of the pub.

"Oh, no." Brian despaired.

Arthur put a hand on his shoulder. "You did what you had to do, man. You saved my life."

Brian looked vacantly into the distance. "He'll never forgive me."

HARRY STOOD IN FRONT OF THE COALITION. He'd never been inside the Great Hall, and he instantly disliked it. He didn't know half the people here and he didn't want to. Four chairs were empty, and he hoped he wasn't asked to fill one of them.

"Congratulations, Harry," said Caroline, clapping heartily, smiling brightly, just like the rest of the arseholes.

"Thank you, Caroline. I have filed recommendations for accolades and bonuses to be awarded to the servicemen that partook in the mission. They fought fiercely and against the odds," he said sincerely.

"What of the vampires you didn't manage to kill?" asked Charles.

Harry knew Charles. He knew he was the kind of prick who'd prefer to talk about the tiny failures rather than the huge successes. "They fled with the death of Ivansey."

"Quite an unusual death, don't you think?" asked Caroline.

"Yes, ma'am."

"I would have hoped you'd have brought Garforth in for examination," said Charles.

"Orders were orders, sir," he said regimentally.

Rempstone shook his head. "You've never been one to think on your feet, have you, Dean?"

"*Sir*, I'm paid to follow orders. I'm paid to uphold the Agreement, and if you look at my service record, you'll find that no one has ever done it better, *sir*." Harry ensured maximum sarcasm for the word but kept cool. Best not to arouse suspicion by acting different.

"Good work, Dean," repeated Caroline, leaving no doubt that it was her opinion that mattered. "Tillsley and Ivansey are gone and that's thanks to you."

"Thank you, ma'am. But, ma'am, if I may?" he ventured.

"Say your piece, Dean. You have more than earned it."

"Sanderson may have betrayed the Coalition, but there was never a break in his vigilant efforts to keep vampire activity from spilling onto the streets. We need more resources, ma'am. Things are getting worse and we're struggling to cope."

"Rempstone?" she said.

"We're doing the best we can with the budget we have."

Harry fought the urge not to spit on the floor. "Forgive me, ma'am, but we could do a better job with more money. I'm sure you'd prefer the Agreement to hold, rather than our share price." Harry enjoyed the snarl Rempstone sent in his direction.

"Absolutely." Caroline nodded. "We need men like you in the field, Dean. Have a word with one of the clerks and name the resources you require. Thank you."

"Thank you, ma'am." Harry turned on his heel and left the room. He heaved a sigh of relief, thankful to be outside and thankful they'd believed him. He knew they did because he was still alive. Now, it was time to get back to keeping the country in one piece. He hoped he wouldn't regret the decisions he'd made.

AS SOON AS HARRY LEFT THE ROOM, THE MEETING CONTINUED.

"He's a good man," said Caroline.

"Yes," said Bwogi. "He's rid us of two problems and we stand whole again."

"Whole?" mocked Charles. "The attacks are increasing, and the fact that we haven't seen Borg Hemsman for a while worries me. He's planning something. Every day we weaken. Every day we come closer to collapse."

"And Haemo?" asked Caroline. She looked over at Garendon, who was, as usual, busy scribbling away on a piece of paper. "Garendon, how's the Haemo project?"

"What? Oh! Sorry. Yes, I have successfully combined Haemo with a carrier."

"You've done it?" she said incredulously.

"Oh, yes. It was easier than I thought, to be honest."

"When will it be ready?"

"Scale up is the tricky thing, you see. We're working around the clock, but I believe we could cover the major cities in three months, and then look at a more widespread production."

"We are saved," said Bwogi, raising his hands to the heavens.

Augustus snarled. "We are doomed."

47

SANDERSON SLOWLY CAME TO, not knowing where he was except that it was dark, and he was chilled to the bone. He lay on his back with the uncomfortable feeling of wetness soaking through his jacket. The soft ground gave under his movements. This wasn't going to end well.

"Smile for the camera," said Chambers, holding up a smartphone. "I want the Haemo and the carrier, ASAP."

"It shall be yours." Caroline's voice came through the phone's speaker. "Say goodbye to Sanderson for me. It's a shame. He was a good man."

"You can have the pleasure of watching him die."

Sanderson could see the outline of the gun and knew he was done. Tricked and stabbed in the back. It was the only way they'd get him. His last act took all his strength. Just in time, he managed to raise his middle finger before his brains scattered across the ground.

BRIAN SAT ON THE PARK BENCH OUTSIDE THE PEACOCK PUB. They served Bolton that wasn't kept too badly, and it would suffice for him and Arthur until The First Swallow of Summer was back up and running. It shouldn't take long. Kev would polyfill the bullet holes and install a new beer engine for the Bolton. Sure, they were all officially dead, but this was Middlesbrough, and no one here would talk to any Southern council bastards, anyway.

It was good to see Freddy Buggleswaite again, chief brewer of the finest beer in all the land. Brian was glad he'd escaped unscathed and hoped the whole situation wouldn't affect the taste of his beer.

Brian checked the time: a minute to nine. Yesterday, Arthur had gone to see the big man in order to give him Brian's written message, as planned:

> *Sid,*
> *We need to talk. Things aren't what they seem. I saved Arthur's life and, mate, I saved your life. We need to talk this through. Meet you outside The Peacock, 9pm on Friday night. Their Bolton is top notch.*
>
> *Brian.*

Arthur reported that Sid hadn't said much, but he'd at least read the letter. It was time to build bridges. It was going to be a long process.

CAROLINE SAT IN HER OFFICE and poured herself a brandy. With the exception of a few hiccups, everything had gone to plan. No, *better* than planned. Not in her wildest dreams did she ever expect the full, viral Haemo plants to be developed and launched so soon.

Chambers was turning into a useful ally. She'd toyed with which of the two she'd keep, Sanderson or Chambers, and she was glad of her decision. Chambers had samples of Haemo now, and he could do with it what he wished, but she needed some more bargaining chips if she was going to use him in the future.

She toasted the death of Michael Vitrago, something she'd done many times since Sparle had killed him. If only she could have seen it. If only it had been a slower, more agonising end to the bastard's sick life.

She was closing in on her goal.

REECE MARVELLED AT THE SCIENCE taking place under his microscope. Haemo was a miracle. It released the energy from its bonds direct into a vampire's blood stream so fast it was undetectable: Intermolecular fuel. If he could recreate a version that would work in humans, he could become more powerful than he possibly imagined.

He continued to research the four lads' DNA, still astonished it was their beloved Bolton Bitter that had mutated their genetic code. It made no sense at all, but that was their common link.

It was time to work on the viral carrier. If he was going to mutate his genes to replicate those of the Middlesbrough scumbags, he had to understand it completely. He would become the ultimate hunter. He would gain vengeance on all who had wronged him. The vampires were all going to die by his hand. Every last fucking one of them.

BORG HEMSMAN LOOKED OUT from top of Middlesbrough's famous Transporter Bridge.

His hand rested on a child's shoulder. The wind struggled to move the boy's thick, black, perfect hair that he'd inherited from his father, Arthur Peasley.

"You're going to be part of a new age," said Borg proudly. "I don't know how powerful you'll become, but you will avenge the death of your mother, and you will free the vampire from captivity. You will destroy the Agreement, my boy." Borg's eyes shone bright now his purpose was clear.

"You're not like any other. You should still be a baby. I will take care of you no matter what. You will be a king; that, I promise. We will avenge your mother, your beautiful mother, by destroying her nemesis. Your father Arthur Peasley killed her, but don't worry. Soon, revenge will be yours."

The child didn't say a word. Instead, he picked a cheeseburger out of his pocket and devoured it.

SID HELD THE BUNCH OF POSIES IN HIS HAND. He was off to meet a lady. This was the first date with the lass he'd met on the 'net a week back. He'd made the effort by putting on deodorant and by remaining sober enough to drive almost legally.

He'd received the note from Brian. A session on the ale would do him good, but that couldn't happen now. He'd lost his best mate. His best mate was one of *them lot.*

This was a new beginning for Sid. It was time to settle down with a good woman, and he was meeting one at Gino's Italian restaurant. He hoped it would go better than the last date he had there.

Sid was early for a change. He was meeting her inside at nine-fifteen and it was only just turning nine. He turned down the road leading to Gino's and there, sat on a bench, was Brian. He forgot the note had said to meet at The Peacock located two doors farther down.

"Fook."

Brian caught a glimpse of Sid and stood up. "Sid! Come on, mate. Let's talk it over a pint."

"I've got a date!" he cried. "With a woman!" he added.

Brian slumped onto the bench. "But, Sid..."

"Sorry, Brian. I'm a fanny man."

EPILOGUE:
A FEW RUBBERS MORE

PEACHES SLACKRING had escaped the massacre at The First Swallow of Summer without a scratch. It'd taken a few days to get rid of the smell of the weasel's disgusting essence that had covered his hair. The thought repulsed him, but it hadn't stopped him partaking in similar activities over the weekend.

Gay bars were the only place he was safe. He had nightmares of Sid Tillsley turning up and crushing him like an ant. Tillsley destroyed the vampires as if they didn't possess such wonderful biceps and pecs, but Tillsley couldn't cope with the beauty of Peaches' former master. He dabbed a tear from his eye. It was the way that he would've wanted to go.

Peaches walked through the streets of Middlesbrough when he suddenly realised he was being followed. He sped up, trying to look inconspicuous despite his stilettos. There was a long way to go before he reached his maisonette, and these streets were not safe for such a delicate flower. He turned down an alleyway to take a short cut.

"Tillsley!"

The giant stepped forward from the shadows. Peaches squinted. What was the big man carrying? Realisation drained the colour from beneath his made-up and powdered face. "Oh no...not that! Anything but that! I beg you!"

"Get in the fooking suitcase, Nick Nack."

First there was *The Great Right Hope*, the tale of the ultimate vampire hunter, Sid Tillsley, punching a massive vampire monster...in the face!

Then there was *A Fistful of Rubbers*, where Sid's best mate Brian Garforth buggered a vampire...to death!

And now...
the final book in The Sid Tillsley Chronicles (2nd Edition)

ACRACKNOPHOBIA

When Sid Tillsley, the most prolific and lethal vampire hunter in the world cancels his subscription to *Tits* magazine, Middlesbrough locals know that something isn't right. And that's an understatement...

The vampire nation is ready to launch an assault on society. The Coalition, a council of vampires and humans whose purpose is to hide the existence of the creatures of the night, are almost powerless to stop them. Their one hope is a molecule: Haemo, a drug that suppresses the vampire's need to feed. If Haemo doesn't work and the vampires take to the streets, life will never be the same again, and a new, barbaric, violent age will devour mankind.

Unfortunately, Sid cannot be called upon, for Sid has landed himself a legitimate job, is paying taxes, has stopped smoking and drinking, and hasn't had a kebab in over a month!

But why? How? What could possibly change a Northern man so set in his ways? Vampires could never be so cruel.

Such devilry, such wickedness can only be the work of...womenfolk!

THE GREAT RIGHT HOPE

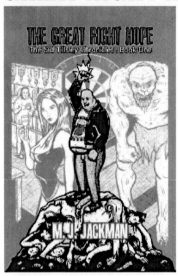

Book One of The Sid Tillsley Chronicles (2nd Edition)

Even the best vampires need a good smack...

Sid Tillsley, forty-six, is an alcoholic benefit fraudster from Middlesbrough. He's sexist, homophobic, overweight, extremely lazy, and a dogger. However, there is *one* thing setting him apart from the rest of his fellow Northerners.

Sid Tillsley can kill vampires with a single punch.

In Northeast England, a monster has arisen, and one that doesn't subscribe to *Tits* magazine. A vampire beast is stalking the Yorkshire moors, mutilating and destroying everything in its path. The vampire elders fear the Firmamentum has cast its shadow on the world once more—a phenomenon that occurs every few millennia when a human and a vampire are born, ultimately powerful, and destined to oppose each other.

The Coalition, a council of vampires and humans whose purpose is to hide the existence of the creatures of the night, believe Sid to be the Bellator, the chosen one destined to fight the vampire beast. But, Sid is more concerned about drinking down the pub with his mates, and maybe, just maybe, ending his two year drought with the ladies. Besides, Sid has more important things to worry about. The Benefit Office is on to him, and, if they see him scrapping immortal vampire monsters from Hell, they'll take away his disability benefits.

A FISTFUL OF RUBBERS

Book Two of The Sid Tillsley Chronicles (2nd Edition)

Sid Tillsley, forty-six, is an alcoholic from Middlesbrough. He's sexist, homophobic, overweight, extremely lazy, and a dogger. However, there are now *two* things setting him apart from the rest of his fellow Northerners. Sid Tillsley can kill vampires with a single punch.

AND, he's no longer claiming benefits.

In the eyes of everyone apart from the taxman, Sid Tillsley is officially a vampire hunter. The old hunter, Reece Chambers, is using Sid to strike fear into the heart of the vampire nation, and Sid is doing so with gusto—for he gets a packet of fags for every vampire he knocks out.

But all is not rosy in Sid's world...

The Coalition, a council of vampires and humans whose purpose is to hide the existence of the creatures of the night, have shut down his local pub in a horrific act of cruelty, separating Sid and his mates from their beloved Bolton Bitter. Sid doesn't realise that he has a fight coming, one that will test him to his very limits. There's something else lurking in the shadows, or rather, the closet. A Northern man will punch anything in the face, but what terrifies him, what saturates him with carnal fear, is a direct attack on his sexuality...and the Campire draws near.

About the Author

"M J Jackman is one of the most talented, exciting, and hilarious writers to explode onto the fiction scene in the twenty-first century," was what Jackman hoped to read in the papers after the release of The Sid Tillsley Chronicles. He hoped his mastery of the written word and his elegant wit would bring celebrity status, which, in turn, would bring fast women, hard drugs and liquor, and then slower, more understanding women.

To date, he has successfully installed a decking area into his garden.

You can follow Jackman's antics on Twitter (@Mark_Jackman) and Sid's antic's on Facebook (search Sid Tillsley Chronicles)

Oh, and he's gone back to university to be a "mature student." And, no, he hasn't gone back to learn how to write (arsewipe!).

He gets an NUS discount.

Even his own characters would hate him.

Lightning Source UK Ltd.
Milton Keynes UK
UKOW02f1149200916

283404UK00001B/57/P